Virtue Epistemology and the Analysis of Knowledge

Also available from Bloomsbury:

Free Will and Epistemology, by Robert Lockie
Intellectual Agency and Virtue Epistemology: A Montessori Perspective, by
Patrick R. Frierson
Intellectual Humility, by Ian M. Church and Peter L. Samuelson
Knowledge, Number and Reality, edited by Nils Kürbis, Bahram Assadian
and Jonathan Nassim
The History of Understanding in Analytic Philosophy, edited by
Adam Tamas Tuboly

Virtue Epistemology and the Analysis of Knowledge

Toward a Non-reductive Model

Ian M. Church

BLOOMSBURY ACADEMIC
LONDON • NEW YORK • OXFORD • NEW DELHI • SYDNEY

BLOOMSBURY ACADEMIC
Bloomsbury Publishing Plc
50 Bedford Square, London, WC1B 3DP, UK
1385 Broadway, New York, NY 10018, USA
29 Earlsfort Terrace, Dublin 2, Ireland

BLOOMSBURY, BLOOMSBURY ACADEMIC and the Diana logo are trademarks of Bloomsbury Publishing Plc

First published in Great Britain 2023
This paperback edition published 2024

Copyright © Ian M. Church, 2023

Ian M. Church has asserted his right under the Copyright, Designs and Patents Act, 1988, to be identified as Author of this work.

For legal purposes the Acknowledgments on p. ix constitute an extension of this copyright page.

Cover image: filo/Getty Images

All rights reserved. No part of this publication may be reproduced or transmitted in any form or by any means, electronic or mechanical, including photocopying, recording, or any information storage or retrieval system, without prior permission in writing from the publishers.

Bloomsbury Publishing Plc does not have any control over, or responsibility for, any third-party websites referred to or in this book. All internet addresses given in this book were correct at the time of going to press. The author and publisher regret any inconvenience caused if addresses have changed or sites have ceased to exist, but can accept no responsibility for any such changes.

A catalogue record for this book is available from the British Library.

A catalog record for this book is available from the Library of Congress.

ISBN: HB: 978-1-3502-5838-9
PB: 978-1-3502-5842-6
ePDF: 978-1-3502-5839-6
eBook: 978-1-3502-5840-2

Typeset by Deanta Global Publishing Services, Chennai, India

To find out more about our authors and books visit www.bloomsbury.com and sign up for our newsletters.

For my wife, Corrie. Without her love, encouragement, and friendship, this book would not have been possible.

Contents

List of Illustrations	viii
Acknowledgments	ix
Introduction	1

Part I Diagnosing the Problem

1	Luck and Gettier Problems	19
2	Objections	41

Part II Applying the Diagnosis

3	Agent-reliabilism	73
4	Agent-responsibilism	99
5	Proper Functionalism	115

Part III Toward Non-reductive Virtue Epistemology

6	Prolegomena to Non-reductive Virtue Epistemology	147
7	Knowledge as Virtue	169
8	New Horizons	192

Notes	209
Bibliography	231
Index	241

Illustrations

Figures

1.1	Space of relevant possible worlds	27
1.2	Bivariant degrees of luck	29
2.1	Map of the proposed diagnosis of the Gettier Problem	42
2.2	Weinberg, Nichols, and Stich Gettier results	61

Tables

1.1	Distribution of Events Across Possible Worlds	28
6.1	Possible Relationships between Knowledge and Epistemic Virtue	154

Acknowledgments

Work on this monograph goes back many years, with some ideas being developed as I worked on my doctoral thesis. As such, my doctoral supervisor, Patrick Greenough, deserves some special gratitude. Patrick tirelessly and cheerfully saw my research through turbulent and transitional times. His wisdom, guidance, encouragement, and friendship were invaluable to my research and my development as a scholar.

Substantial portions of the research in this book have been presented at other institutions, and I am exceedingly grateful for all of the feedback I received. I'm grateful for the faculty and students at the University of St Andrews, Ball State University, the City University of New York, Rutgers University, Taylor University, the University of Edinburgh, Stirling University, Fuller Seminary, Saint Louis University, the University of Notre Dame, and Hillsdale College. In particular, I would like to thank Alan Millar, Michael Levin, Philip Ebert, Katherine Hawley, Alvin Plantinga, Duncan Pritchard, Ernest Sosa, James Spiegel, Justin Barrett, Chris Tucker, Robert Hartman, and John Greco.

As I finished this book, I was able to teach a seminar at Hillsdale College entitled "Intellectual Virtues and Society," which was instrumental in shaping some of the ideas that went into Chapters 7 and 8. I'm enormously grateful for the students in that class, for all their perceptive feedback. In particular, I'd like to thank Sarah D'Spain, Chandler Hart, Conor Mulligan, Long Nguyen, Oliver Aho, Polyxeni Drath, Jake Studebaker, Alex Schnell, Elizabeth Bianchi, Jesse David, and Zach Pylypuik. I am also extremely grateful for my colleagues at Hillsdale who either directly provided feedback on some of the ideas found in this book or otherwise supported me in the work of writing it. In particular, I'd like to thank Tom Burke and Blake McAllister. I am also grateful to Paul Rezkalla, who worked for me as a postdoctoral researcher as I finished this book, for providing helpful feedback on some of the material in the last chapter of this book.

I am also enormously grateful to the John Templeton Foundation, who funded various projects that allowed me to continue working on this material over the years. To be sure, while this work was done in part with the support of the Foundation, all the views in this book are my own and don't necessarily reflect the views of the Foundation.

In writing this book, I have drawn, with permission, from some of my previously published work. Portions of article "Getting 'Lucky' with Gettier" (2013), *The European Journal of Philosophy*, volume 21, issue 1, were used in Chapter 1. Portions of my chapter in *The Routledge Handbook of the Psychology and Philosophy of Luck* (2019), edited by Ian Church and Robert Hartman, entitled "The Gettier Problem," were used in Chapters 1 and 2. For part of Chapter 3, "Virtue Epistemology and the Gettier Dilemma" (2021), *Metaphilosophy*, volume 52, issue 5, as well as "Manifest Failure Failure: The Gettier Problem Revived" (2013), volume 41. For part of Chapter 5, "50 Years of Gettier: A New Direction in Religious Epistemology?" (2015), *Journal of Analytic Theology*, volume 3.

Finally, I would like to thank my wife, Corrie, to whom this book is dedicated. Throughout the writing of this book, she worked tirelessly as a graphic designer, an artist, a homemaker, and the mother of our four boys, Aed, Asher, Ari, and Arran (collectively, "The A Team"!). She has been a tremendous friend and companion, and this book would not have been possible without her love, support, and patience.

Introduction

Epistemology is on the move. On the one hand, there is a growing dissatisfaction with the project of explicating knowledge in terms of a reductive analysis, in terms of necessary and jointly sufficient conditions. Ever since 1963 when Edmund Gettier challenged the sufficiency of the standard analysis of knowledge with a series of counterexamples, all attempts to defend it have been shown either to lead to further Gettier-style counterexamples or to produce an analysis of knowledge that is unfeasible.[1] On the other, there is the increasing popularity of virtue-theoretic approaches to epistemology. Tracking our intuitions across a range of cases, virtue epistemology offers new and exciting solutions to a variety of problems afflicting other accounts of knowledge. *The goal of this book is to endorse both of these trends and the move away from the reductive analysis model while affirming virtue-theoretic epistemology.*

Unfortunately, however, within the contemporary literature, these trends are largely at odds. Prominent renditions of virtue epistemology assume the reductive analysis model and have largely resisted movement toward non-reductive virtue-theoretic accounts.[2] In this book, I do three things. First, I elucidate and defend a diagnosis of the dominant reason for abandoning the reductive model, namely, the Gettier Problem. Second, I apply this diagnosis to the three most prominent versions of contemporary virtue epistemology—virtue reliabilism, virtue responsibilism, and proper functionalism—arguing that virtue epistemology simply offers no new cures. Third and finally, I explicate some ways in which we might pursue non-reductive virtue epistemology, and I conclude by proposing a particular non-reductive approach to virtue epistemology—a non-reductive proper functionalism.

Before getting started, we need to do some brief stage setting. In this chapter, I first elucidate and outline in very broad strokes the two trends in contemporary epistemology that motivate this book's thesis: *the growing pessimism regarding the analysis of knowledge* and *the ascendancy of virtue epistemology*. In Section 1, I chart the growing dissatisfaction with the reductive analysis model of knowledge. In Section 2, I explicate the contours of the virtue-theoretic epistemologies that dominate the current epistemic landscape. In Section 3, I conclude by summarizing in detail the rest of the book, chapter by chapter.

Section 1: Current Trends in Epistemology, Part 1: A Growing Dissatisfaction

Before we consider the post-Gettier fallout that has led so many epistemologists to be pessimistic regarding the analysis of knowledge, we should be clear regarding just what it means to pursue a reductive analysis of knowledge. Consider Matthias Steup's explanation:

> The objective of the analysis of knowledge is to state the conditions that are individually necessary and jointly sufficient for propositional knowledge: knowledge that such-and-such is the case. . . . The concept to be analyzed—the analysandum—is commonly expressed using the schema "S knows that p," where "S" refers to the knowing subject, and "p" to the proposition that is known. A proposed analysis consists of a statement of the following form: S knows that p if and only if __. The blank is to be replaced by the analysans: a list of conditions that are individually necessary and jointly sufficient. To test whether a proposed analysis is correct, we must ask (a) whether every possible case in which the conditions listed in the analysans are met is a case in which S knows that p, and (b) whether every possible case in which S knows that p is a case in which each of these conditions is met. When we ask (a), we wish to find out whether the proposed analysans is sufficient for S's knowing that p; when we ask (b), we wish to determine whether each of the conditions listed in the analysans is necessary. (Steup 2006, 1)

The reductive analysis of knowledge, in sum, is the project of explicating knowledge in terms of a list of necessary and jointly sufficient conditions. While this is certainly right, more needs to be said. After all, *being Tully* is both necessary and sufficient for *being Cicero*, but that does not mean that *being Tully* is a reductive analysis of *being Cicero*. The reductive analysis of knowledge not only entails the pursuit of necessary and jointly sufficient conditions; it entails the pursuit of necessary and jointly sufficient conditions that are purported to be conceptually prior to knowledge. The reductive analysis of knowledge project is the project of *building up to knowledge*, so to speak, from various necessary conditions that are taken to be conceptually prior to knowledge—conditions such as truth and belief. Just as terms like "bachelor" and "vixen" yield reductive analyses in the more primitive terms of unmarried men and female foxes respectively, "knowledge," it is assumed, will yield a reductive analysis in the purportedly more primitive terms of truth, belief, and *whatever else makes true belief knowledge* (call it warrant).

Epistemologists have always wanted to know what knowledge was, and in at least the past sixty years, this inquiry has taken the shape of a reductive analysis of its necessary and jointly sufficient conditions. We may at the outset wonder whether such an approach is fundamentally misguided; after all, why should we think knowledge yields a reductive analysis in the first place?[3] Why would we think "knowledge" is like "bachelor" or "vixen"? In any case, while I will in this book eventually suggest that such an approach to propositional knowledge is fundamentally misguided, all we need to appreciate now is that this approach is precisely what has dominated contemporary epistemology.

Enter Gettier. It's a story that is well known—a story that is retold in almost every epistemology course. Since the time of Plato, so the story goes, we were all raised on our mothers' knees learning that knowledge consisted of justification, truth, and belief; since time immemorial, *justified true belief* has been taken to be the necessary and jointly sufficient conditions for knowledge.[4] But then, with the publication of Edmund Gettier's 1963 paper "Is Justified True Belief Knowledge?" everything changed. Consider the following classic counterexample:

> **Classic Case**: Smith and Jones are applying for the same job. Smith has very strong evidence for thinking that Jones will get the job (e.g., the employer tells Smith that he will hire Jones, etc.), and for thinking that Jones has 10 coins in his pocket (e.g., Jones emptied his pockets in front of Smith and then clearly, slowly, in good lighting, and perhaps even counting out loud, placed 10 coins in his pocket). As such, Smith forms a belief in the general proposition that "the man who gets the job has 10 coins in his pocket." As it turns out, however, Smith gets the job and he also happens to have 10 coins in his pocket. (paraphrased from Gettier 1963, 122)

In this case, Smith seemingly has a justified true belief that "the man who gets the job has 10 coins in his pocket," but, as almost everyone agrees, surely Smith's belief is not knowledge. As such, *justified true belief* is simply not sufficient for knowledge.[5]

As such, epistemologists quickly tried to find ways to save or repair the *justified true belief* analysis—typically by trying either to strengthen the justification condition or to add more conditions (e.g., *justified true belief* plus some fourth condition). What ensued was a confusing and cacophonous array of justification (e.g., justification as evidence, justification as reliability, internalist justification, and externalist justification) and additional conditions on knowledge (e.g., safety conditions, sensitivity conditions, and defeasibility conditions). All of this sought to understand knowledge via reductive analysis, all of which assumed a *warranted true belief* analysis of knowledge (where "warrant" stands for "whatever turns true belief into knowledge"). Unfortunately, none of these proposals (in any combination) achieved any lasting success against Gettier counterexamples—either falling into further Gettier-style counterexamples or leading to unpalatable conclusions (such as radical skepticism).[6] Providing a feasible reductive analysis of knowledge, it seems, is a Sisyphean endeavor.

Some commentators have put the state of contemporary post-Gettier epistemology rather mildly:

> Gettier sparked a period of pronounced epistemological energy and innovation—all with a single two-and-a-half page article. There is no consensus, however, that any one of the attempts to solve the Gettier challenge has succeeded in fully defining what it is to have knowledge of a truth or fact. So, the force of that challenge continues to be felt in various ways, and to various extents, within epistemology. (Hetherington 2005, 1)

Others, however, have been perhaps a bit more pessimistic (and, by my lights, perhaps a bit more accurate):

> Since Gettier refuted the traditional analysis of knows as has a justified true belief in 1963, a succession of increasingly complex analyses have been overturned by increasingly complex counterexamples. . . . The pursuit of analyses is a degenerating research programme. (Williamson 2000, 30–1)

> Since [the Gettier Problem] is demonstrably unsolvable, it follows not only that the tripartite [*warranted true belief*] account is logically inadequate as it is, but also that it is irretrievably so in principle. [The Gettier Problem] is not a mere anomaly, requiring the rectification of an otherwise stable and acceptable account of propositional knowledge. It is proof that the core of the approach needs to be abandoned. (Floridi 2004, 76)

In any case, the situation seems dim. Knowledge has not yet yielded a viable reductive analysis, and there is no indication that it will any time soon. As such, many philosophers have grown pessimistic regarding such a project. Indeed, many philosophers have been tempted either to give up on knowledge altogether or to start looking for an alternative model from which to do epistemology.

Of course, it is the contention of this book that this latter option, looking for an alternative model from which to do epistemology, is generally the right move. Giving up on knowledge altogether seems a bit harsh, especially if other, viable options are available. And, given the growing pessimism regarding the reductive analysis project, there seems to be sufficient ground for exploring such alternatives in earnest. For the lovers of virtue-theoretic epistemology, however, there are some major hurdles. The prominent iterations of virtue epistemology in the contemporary literature assume the reductive model, and, what is more, some of them even openly purport to have solved the Gettier Problem, to have provided viable reductive analyses of knowledge that do not yield Gettier counterexamples. As such, anyone who is duly pessimistic regarding the reductive analysis project, yet an advocate of virtue-theoretic epistemology, simply must address the prominent reductive iterations of virtue epistemology if a move toward non-reductive virtue epistemology is to be sufficiently warranted.

Section 2: Current Trends in Epistemology, Part 2: Virtue Epistemology

Despite the growing trend to abandon the reductive analysis of knowledge in favor of alternative epistemic models, reductive virtue-theoretic epistemologies have for over thirty years become increasingly popular and commonplace.[7] The move away from the reductive model has not yet come to bear on virtue epistemology. In this section, I briefly explicate the basic tenets of virtue epistemology—the other major trend within epistemology that motivates the thesis of this book.[8]

What is virtue epistemology? To be sure, as it has surged in popularity over the past thirty years, virtue epistemology has developed into a multitude of positions; nevertheless, every variant of virtue epistemology holds to two basic resolutions: (1) that epistemology is a normative discipline and (2) that "intellectual agents and communities are the primary source of epistemic value and the primary focus of epistemic evaluation" (Greco and Turri 2011, para. 1). The former amounts to (a) a rejection of Quine's proposal in "Epistemology Naturalized" (1969) that epistemologists should give up on attempts to discern what is reasonable to believe in favor of projects within cognitive psychology and (b) a call for epistemologists to "focus their efforts on understanding epistemic norms, value and evaluation" (Greco and Turri 2011, sec. 1).[9] And to better understand the second resolution think of virtue *ethics'* niche within moral philosophy. For the two titans of moral philosophy, Kantian deontology and utilitarianism, the starting place for moral evaluation is *action*. For Kantians and for utilitarians, the question to ask when doing ethics is "What should I do?" (Kantians roughly answering "act in accord with what you can will to be a universal maxim"; utilitarians roughly answering "act in accord with what brings about the greatest happiness for the greatest number.") For virtue ethicists, however, the starting place for moral evaluation, where the rubber meets the road, so to speak, is the *agent*—his or her character—and subsequently the virtue ethicist asks a different question, "How should I live?"[10] To put it roughly, then, instead of focusing on the beliefs of agents (whether or not they are justified, safe, etc.), virtue epistemologists predominantly focus on the agent himself or herself—on whether he or she has the right sort of epistemic character, the right sort of cognitive faculties, whether he or she is epistemically virtuous or not. To be sure, other theories of knowledge will give some account of epistemic virtues—good memory, intellectual courage, etc.—but usually in terms of knowledge; the radical claim that virtue epistemology makes, however, is that knowledge is defined in terms of virtue.[11]

Virtue epistemology, so defined, has developed by and large into two distinct schools: agent-reliabilism and responsibilism or neo-Aristotelianism.[12] The primary difference between the schools is their application of "virtue" terminology. Agent-reliabilism, being modeled along reliabilist lines, applies virtue terminology mechanically—in the same way we might talk about a virtuous knife. In other words, just as we might call a knife virtuous if it does what it is supposed to do (cut things, be sharp, etc.), agent-reliabilism calls various cognitive faculties such as memory and perception virtuous insofar as they are reliably functioning the way they are supposed to. That is, agent-reliabilism focuses on the reliable functioning (virtuous functioning) of a given agent's cognitive faculties. Neo-Aristotelianism, on the other hand, applies virtue terminology in a way we are perhaps more familiar with—in terms of specific character traits such as open-mindedness, intellectual courage, and intellectual perseverance.

But why is it so important to have agents as the primary object of epistemic assessment? What motivates such a move? To answer this question, let's consider what motived the development of agent-reliabilism virtue epistemology, the most popular version of virtue epistemology.[13] Agent-reliabilism virtue epistemologies, like the ones we will be considering, developed out of a dissatisfaction with process reliabilism—the view that, to put it roughly, S knows a true proposition *p* if and only if *p* was formed by a reliable process. Naturally enough, there are some serious concerns for such a view (i.e., the "generality problem"); however, the agent-reliabilists' primary concern was that knowledge ascriptions based on reliable processes do not always appropriately involve a given agent—that process reliabilism seems to allow agents to "possess knowledge even though the reliability in question in no way reflects a cognitive achievement on their part" (Pritchard 2005, 187). One way this occurs is when a given reliable process does not appropriately relate to facts. For example, consider the following case by John Greco:

> **René and the Gambler's Fallacy:** René thinks he can beat the roulette tables with a system he has devised. Reasoning according to the Gambler's Fallacy, he believes that numbers which have not come up for long strings are more likely to come up next. However, unlike Descartes' demon victim, our René has a demon helper. Acting as a kind of epistemic guardian, the demon arranges reality so as to make the belief come out as true. Given the ever present interventions of the helpful demon, René's belief forming process is highly reliable. But this is because the world is made to conform to René's beliefs, rather than because René's beliefs conform to the world. (Greco 1999, 286)[14]

Though René's beliefs happen to be based on a reliable process, it is completely accidental; it is certainly no thanks to any effort of René's. Even though René's beliefs are formed by a reliable process—the helper demon—intuitively he does not have knowledge.

Another way that knowledge ascriptions based on reliable processes do not always appropriately involve a given agent is in the case of reliable cognitive malfunctions. Consider a case originally developed by Alvin Plantinga in which our protagonist has a brain lesion that causes him to believe he has a brain lesion:

> **Brain Lesion:** Suppose . . . that S suffers from this sort of disorder and accordingly believes that he suffers from a brain lesion. Add that he has no evidence at all for this belief: no symptoms of which he is aware, no testimony on the part of physicians or other expert witnesses, nothing. (Add, if you like, that he has much evidence against it, but then add also that the malfunction induced by the lesion makes it impossible for him to take appropriate account of this evidence.) Then the relevant [process] will certainly be reliable but the resulting belief—that he has a brain lesion—will have little by way of warrant for S. (Plantinga 1993a, 199)[15]

Again, though S's belief that he has a brain lesion is formed via a reliable process, we would not ascribe knowledge to it since it is only formed out of a glitch in S's cognitive equipment. It is simply accidental that the brain lesion causes S to form the said belief, and as such S had nothing to do with its formation. Though there may be some worries as to what constitutes a given person's cognitive equipment (Why is S's brain lesion not a part of his cognitive equipment?

What if he had the lesion since birth?), we nevertheless have strong intuitions that beliefs formed as a direct result of a cognitive malfunction cannot be knowledge.[16] S's belief that he has a brain lesion cannot be knowledge simply because, though formed via reliable process, the agent, S, was not appropriately involved in its formation.

It is the agent-reliabilists' focus on the epistemically virtuous agent (i.e., the agent with mechanically sound cognitive equipment) that is the cornerstone of their epistemology. It is their particular focus on the properly functioning human knower (and his/her cognitive competencies) that is meant to distinguish their accounts from all others. The agent-reliabilists' notions of proper function, cognitive competency, and intellectual achievement are, in contrast with other theories of warrant, meant to connect a given agent rightly to the facts (cf. René and the Gambler's Fallacy) and, of course, rightly preclude knowledge from cases of malfunction (cf. Brain Lesion). According to the agent-reliabilists, other theories of warrant fail due to their inability to track warrant ascription in accord with the proper functioning of the relevant cognitive faculties behind a given belief's genesis. It is this special focus on the epistemic agent and his or her properly functioning cognitive competencies that agent-reliabilism virtue epistemologists see as "the rock on which [competing] accounts of warrant founder" (Plantinga 1993b, 4).

Having briefly explicated the basic tenets of virtue-theoretic epistemology, it is worth noting that none of them demand a reductive analysis of knowledge. There is nothing about virtue epistemology *qua* virtue epistemology that requires an analysis of knowledge in terms of necessary and jointly sufficient (and conceptually primitive) conditions. As such, it seems as though the *only* reason virtue epistemology developed along reductive lines is that such were the suppositions of its time. Be that as it may, given the sheer prominence of reductive virtue epistemologies, anyone interested in exploring the possibility of *non-reductive* virtue epistemology, in keeping with the trends explicated in Section 1, simply must address the reductive approaches to virtue epistemology already in the literature and further motivate their abandonment.

And that is the goal of this book: to explicate and defend a diagnosis of the main reason for abandoning *any* reductive account of knowledge, the Gettier Problem; to apply this diagnosis to prominent versions of reductive virtue epistemology, elucidating their shortcomings in light of their commitments to the reductive analysis project; to explore by way of prolegomena the possibility of non-reductive virtue epistemology; and finally to propose a specific account of non-reductive virtue epistemology.

Section 3: Book Outline

Having elucidated the two current trends in contemporary epistemology that motivate the goal of exploring non-reductive virtue epistemology, we are ready to consider in more detail how this project will be undertaken. As I have noted, this book can be divided into three parts: (i) the diagnosis of the problem afflicting reductive analyses, (ii) the application of the diagnosis to prominent renditions of reductive virtue epistemology, and (iii) the exploration of viable alternatives to the reductive model. These parts will be subdivided into seven chapters. Part I consists of Chapters 1 and 2, Part II consists of Chapters 3, 4, and 5, and Part III consists of Chapters 6, 7, and 8. My goal in this final section of the chapter is to explicate and summarize these seven chapters briefly, giving the reader a broad idea of what to expect throughout this book.

Chapter 1: "Luck and Gettier Problems." The main reason for the growing dissatisfaction with the reductive analysis project is no doubt the Gettier Problem. The inability to define knowledge in terms of necessary and jointly sufficient conditions that are not susceptible to Gettier counterexamples is perhaps the greatest difficulty facing reductive accounts. So, to diagnose what is wrong with the reductive analysis project, we need to diagnose the Gettier Problem; we need to understand when and why Gettier counterexamples occur. That's the goal of this first chapter.

According to Linda Zagzebski's 1994 diagnosis of Gettier problems, if whatever we take to bridge the gap between true belief and knowledge (call it warrant) bears some violable relationship to truth, then it will be possible for that belief to be so warranted and true for reasons unrelated to the warrant (Zagzebski 1994, 65). That is to say, so long as we reasonably assume that warrant is neither divorced from truth nor inseparable from it (such options being epistemically unpalatable), Gettier cases are "inescapable" (Zagzebski 1994, 65).

As eloquent and intuitive as Zagzebski's diagnosis of Gettier problems may be, the prominent advocates of virtue epistemology have apparently not taken it altogether seriously. If Zagzebski is right, this has very dim consequences for any palatable reductive analysis of knowledge; however, virtue epistemologists continue to work from such a model. Though there is a common trend in contemporary epistemology to abandon the standard analysis of knowledge in favor of alternative models, this trend has not yet extended to those working within virtue epistemology.

In Chapter 1, I lend credence to Zagzebski's diagnosis (and the movement away from the standard analysis) by analyzing the nature of luck. It is widely accepted that the lesson to be learned from Gettier problems is that knowledge is incompatible with luck or at least a certain species thereof.[17] As such, understanding the nature of luck is central to understanding the Gettier Problem.[18] Thanks by and large to Duncan Pritchard's seminal work, *Epistemic Luck* (2005), a great deal of literature has been developed recently concerning the nature of luck and anti-luck epistemology. The literature, however, has yet to explore the intuitive idea that luck comes in degrees.[19] I propose that once luck is recognized to admit degrees, even the slightest non zero degree of luck (of the relevant sort) precludes knowledge. Connecting this to Zagzebski's thesis, I propose that a given theory of warrant must guarantee truth in order to avoid Gettier counterexamples (or subsequently deny that warrant bears any relationship whatsoever to the truth), simply because a sufficient reductive analysis of knowledge (whether a virtue epistemology or not) cannot allow for knowledge that is even marginally lucky.

I justify this proposal by treating Pritchard's work as archetypal. Motivated by the intuition that luck suits degrees, I do two things in Chapter 1: (i) I argue for a consistent extension of Pritchard's modal account of luck (hereafter MAL—perhaps the most seminal theory of luck in the epistemic literature) that suits degrees of luck; and (ii) I argue that such an extension highlights the inability of Pritchard's safety theory (the linchpin of his anti-luck epistemology) to feasibly avoid Gettier counterexamples. Though we will only focus on Pritchard's account of luck and corresponding anti-luck epistemology in this chapter, prima facie parallel arguments can be made for divergent accounts as well. And this is precisely what we will see when we consider the prominent virtue epistemologies of Chapters 3, 4, and 5. If the only way to avoid Gettier problems is to prohibit beliefs that are even marginally lucky from being knowledge, as I hope to demonstrate using Pritchard's account, then the diagnosis for the reductive analysis project is truly bleak indeed.

Chapter 2: "Objections." Now, as I see it, there are four families of objections someone might level against such a diagnosis of the Gettier Problem. First, someone may level the objection that assuming an inviolable relationship between warrant and truth does not lead to radical skepticism. Likewise, someone may level the objection that assuming a close (though not inviolable) relationship between warrant and truth does not always lead to further Gettier counterexamples. Third, someone might level the objection that assuming that warrant bears no relationship to truth is not, in fact, counterintuitive. Fourth and finally, someone may level a meta-objection that calls into question the epistemic import of Gettier-style counterexamples altogether. While in the middle part of this book (i.e., in Part II) we will see the proposed connection between radical skepticism and the inviolable warrant/truth relation vindicated in all the relevant instances,[20] it is nevertheless important that we guard against the latter three types of objections, especially insofar as these sorts of objections are manifest in the contemporary literature. And that is precisely what I do in Chapter 2.

First, we consider Daniel Howard-Snyder, Frances Howard-Snyder, and Neil Feit's paper, "Infallibilism and Gettier's Legacy" (2003), which directly objects to our conclusion in Chapter 1 that a close but not inviolable relationship between warrant and truth will always lead to Gettier counterexamples; I argue that their proposed solution to the Gettier Problem is, ironically, only successful insofar as it conforms to the proposed diagnosis. Second, we consider recent work by Stephen Hetherington (particularly from his book *Good Knowledge, Bad Knowledge*, 2001), which proposes an analysis of knowledge that assumes a divorced relationship between warrant and truth; I argue that Hetherington's epistemology is counterintuitive and that it need not be advocated in light of viable alternatives. Third and finally, we consider landmark papers by Brian Weatherson (2003) and Jonathan M. Weinberg, Shaun Nichols, and Stephen Stich (2001), which call into question the epistemic import of Gettier counterexamples; I argue that such criticisms either lead to intractable forms of skepticism or can otherwise be defused.

With our grim diagnosis of the Gettier Problem in hand (Chapter 1) and defended (Chapter 2), we can now turn our attention to prominent accounts of virtue epistemology in the contemporary literature and better see why their attempts to solve the Gettier Problem are unsuccessful.

Chapter 3: "Agent-reliabilism." The most prominent version of agent-reliabilism virtue epistemology in the contemporary literature—indeed, perhaps the most prominent version of any virtue epistemology in the literature—sees knowledge as a kind of *success from ability*, where (roughly) a belief is knowledge if it is *true because formed by a cognitive competence*. In this chapter we will explore this brand of virtue epistemology and how it fares against the diagnosis of the Gettier Problem developed in Chapter 1.

Starting with the seminal work of Ernest Sosa in *A Virtue Epistemology* (2007), *Reflective Knowledge* (2009), and *Knowing Full Well* (2011), we will, in Section 1, introduce the broad contours of the view. In Section 2, we will explore how *success from ability* or *true because competent* accounts of knowledge have been challenged in the literature, particularly in regard to the Gettier Problem. I argue that the Gettier Problem facing analyses of knowledge has not been properly appreciated by virtue epistemologist or even virtue epistemology's most vocal critics—that the situation facing reductive accounts of knowledge is far more insidious and dire than most virtue epistemologists seem to acknowledge. In Sections 3 and 4, we will consider how some related agent-reliabilist accounts have attempted to viably defuse the Gettier Problem. In Section 3, we will consider John Greco's recent defense of the *knowledge as success from ability* hypothesis in "A (Different) Virtue Epistemology" (2012). We will see (i) just how the critiques elucidated in §2 have (mis)shaped the dialectic between virtue epistemology and what is required in solving Gettier counterexamples and (ii) how this has led to virtue epistemologists like Greco underestimating the widespread insidiousness of Gettier counterexamples. Finally, in Section 4, we will consider John Turri's virtue epistemology in "Manifest Failure: The Gettier Problem Solved" (2011), where Turri—building off of the work of Sosa—baldly claims to have solved the Gettier Problem. I argue that any success against Gettier counterexamples afforded by Turri's notion of manifestation is merely fleeting, that strengthened counterexamples can be easily produced. Tellingly, in every case—from Sosa to Greco, to Turri—we will see a recurring theme: the prominent versions of agent-reliabilist virtue epistemology cannot solve the Gettier Problem. Indeed, we will see that they fail to solve the Problem precisely along the lines predicted in Chapter 1.

Chapter 4: "Agent-Responsibilism." Agent-responsibilism (or neo-Aristotelian) virtue epistemology stands as another dominant view in the contemporary literature that aims to provide a viable reductive account of knowledge. And the seminal agent-responsibilist account of knowledge is, no doubt, Linda Zagzebski's theory of knowledge as it is explicated in *Virtues of the Mind* (1996) and "What Is Knowledge?" (1999). According to Michael Levin, Linda Zagzebski's agent-reliabilist virtue epistemology is "the only version of virtue epistemology" that "tackles the [Gettier Problem] head on" (2004, 397). Indeed, according to Levin, if Zagzebski's version of virtue epistemology fails to provide a viable analysis, then "the prospects for . . . other versions are not good" (2004, 397).

In this chapter, we will look at Zagzebski's seminal, agent-responsibilist virtue epistemology and consider whether or not it does indeed provide a viable analysis of knowledge when it comes to Gettier counterexamples. In trying to provide such an analysis, Zagzebski knows she has to somehow balance between both horns of her own dilemma—the dilemma facing all analyses of knowledge we explicated in Chapter 1 and the dilemma between facing Gettier counterexamples or risk falling into radical skepticism. In Section 1, we will consider Michael

Levin's 2004 critique of Zagzebski's analysis and explore whether striking such a balance ultimately leaves Zagzebski's analysis fundamentally incomplete. Then, in Section 2, I will argue that the revelation that luck suits degrees (cf. Chapter 1) radically limits the ability of Zagzebski's account of knowledge—whether it is fundamentally incomplete or not—ever to viably surmount the Gettier counterexample.

Chapter 5: "Proper Functionalism." Alvin Plantinga's account of knowledge is one of the most iconic epistemologies of the twentieth century—offering an analysis of knowledge in terms of properly functioning cognitive faculties—a view that developed throughout his monumental warrant trilogy: *Warrant: The Current Debate* (1993), *Warrant and Proper Function* (1993), and *Warranted Christian Belief* (2000). While a species of agent-reliabilist virtue epistemology, Plantinga's proper functionalism is markedly different from the agent-reliabilism of Sosa, Greco, and Turri, and it draws from and intersects with concepts and debates in philosophy of religion and theology and has become a touchstone for a distinct breed of virtue epistemology. Taking Plantinga's account as archetypal, I argue (again) that we have systematic reasons to believe that no reductive proper functionalism can viably surmount the Gettier Problem—that the future of virtue epistemology is not with *reductive* proper functionalism.

I work toward this goal in two sections, following the chronological development of Plantinga's virtue-theoretic analysis of knowledge. In Section 1, we will elucidate and critique Plantinga's analysis of knowledge as it is found in *Warrant and Proper Function* (1993). In Section 2, I elucidate and critique the proposed modifications to Plantinga's original account found, first, in "Respondeo" (1996) and "Warrant and Accidentally True Belief" (1997) and, then, in *Warranted Christian Belief* (2000). In both sections, we will find our proposed diagnosis of Gettier problems vindicated, with each iteration and proposal failing precisely along the lines our diagnosis predicted.

By the end of this chapter, we will have seen all of the prominent attempts to provide a viable virtue-theoretic reductive analysis of knowledge fail and fail precisely as we predicted. If the Gettier Problem is really unsolvable, as I've suggested, how should virtue epistemology move forward? What might non-reductive virtue epistemology look like? We'll address these questions in the final three chapters.

Chapter 6: "Prolegomena to Non-reductive Virtue Epistemology." While I advocate the trend to abandon the reductive analysis of knowledge in favor of alternative epistemic models by criticizing dominant forms of virtue epistemology, it is nevertheless my conviction that accounting for virtue within epistemology is ultimately meritorious—that there are significant advantages to pursuing virtue-theoretic epistemology even if we must renounce the analyzability of knowledge. Having (i) championed contemporary virtue epistemology as one of the most sophisticated and popular species of reductive analysis to date and (ii) argued that, given the proposed diagnosis of the Gettier Problem, we have very good reason to doubt that any reductive analysis (virtue-theoretic or otherwise) can feasibly surmount Gettier counterexamples (as demonstrated in the work of Plantinga, Sosa, Zagzebski, and others), I nevertheless want to explore in this chapter the possibility of adapting virtue-theoretic epistemology to suit an alternative epistemic model. In Chapter 6, I elucidate and outline the seminal alternative epistemic model to date, namely, the non-reductive model of knowledge developed by Timothy Williamson in *Knowledge and Its Limits* (2000). Then, I explore how virtue might be incorporated within a non-reductive model, generally. Finally, I reconsider the possibility of non-reductive virtue epistemology in light of Williamson's specific non-reductive epistemology and the respective virtue-theoretic concepts developed in the previous chapters.

Chapter 7: "Knowledge as Virtue." Having considered by way of prolegomena the possibilities for incorporating virtue within a non-reductive model of knowledge, in this chapter I argue for a specific version of non-reductive virtue epistemology, a non-reductive proper functionalism, that identifies *knowledge as virtue*. This proposal, to put it roughly, identifies knowledge as necessary and sufficient for epistemic virtue (understood in terms of proper functionalism) and identifies epistemic virtue as necessary and sufficient for knowledge, and yet it treats both concepts as conceptually primitive (such that neither is analyzed in terms of the other). In the first section of this chapter, we'll reconsider the seminal accounts of epistemic virtue within the contemporary literature—agent-responsibilism, agent-reliabilism (of the Sosa and Greco variety), and proper functionalism[21]—and I'll make a case for proper functionalism. In Section 2, I will put forward some arguments in favor of the *knowledge as virtue* model for non-reductive virtue epistemology, which will leave us a non-reductive proper functionalism where epistemic virtue is co-primitive with knowledge. Finally, in Section 3, I will give a first approximation of this non-reductive proper functionalism and then explore how it might address several perennial challenges within epistemology, including the Gettier Problem, Fake Barn problems, the value of knowledge, and more.

Chapter 8: "New Horizons." As the epistemological literature continues to evolve, what challenges and opportunities might this new account of non-reductive virtue epistemology face? In the final chapter of this book, we briefly consider two such horizons, and I try to give some reasons for thinking that the non-reductive proper functionalism developed in the previous chapter will be particularly well situated to face them.

First, we'll consider an emerging challenge for contemporary epistemology from the flourishing literature of experimental philosophy—the project of taking the tools and resources of psychology, cognitive science, sociology, anthropology, etc. (i.e., the human sciences) and bringing them to bear on seminal questions within philosophy, toward genuine philosophical ends. I'll argue that experimental philosophy has highlighted a question that a lot of work currently done within contemporary epistemology has to contend with: Why should we think that the methods we employ within contemporary epistemology (and philosophy more broadly)—being often driven by intuitions—are veritic or grounded in reality? I call the challenge of providing a viable answer to that question *the grounding problem*.

The second "new horizon" comes from the recent "social turn" within epistemology. While questions regarding disagreement and testimony (issues that are sometimes categorized under the heading of *interpersonal social epistemology*) are addressed in other chapters (particularly Chapters 3 and 7), in this section, I want to briefly point to another facet of social epistemology, namely, *group knowledge* and *group belief*, topics that fall under the banner of what Alvin Goldman categorizes as *collective social epistemology* (2020, 12).

In this section, I'll argue that virtue epistemology will face a unique challenge when it comes to *collective social epistemology*. How might virtue epistemology be extended to account for group belief and group knowledge? Some virtue epistemologists have, to be sure, started going in this direction (see Kallestrup 2016); however, I'll argue that if virtue epistemology is going to viably take this leg of the social turn, it will face challenges from emerging literature in the field of anthropology. I'll argue that contemporary research within anthropology has highlighted examples of group belief and group knowledge that (i) any viable account of group belief or group knowledge needs to account for and (ii) are difficult to square with a lot of research within contemporary analytic epistemology. I'll call this *the anthropological challenge*.

For both of these new horizons—for both *the grounding problem* and *the anthropological challenge*—I'll argue that the non-reductive proper functionalism developed in Chapter 7 is particularly well positioned to face them in future research, especially in contrast to other dominant accounts of epistemic virtue in the literature.

Part I

Diagnosing the Problem

1

Luck and Gettier Problems

No doubt, the main reason for the growing dissatisfaction with the reductive analysis project is the Gettier Problem. The inability to define knowledge in terms of necessary and jointly sufficient (and conceptually more primitive) conditions that are not susceptible to Gettier counterexamples is perhaps the greatest problem with reductive accounts. So, to diagnose what is wrong with the reductive analysis project, we need to diagnose the Gettier Problem; we need to understand when and why Gettier counterexamples occur. This is precisely what we will be doing in this chapter.

According to Linda Zagzebski's 1994 diagnosis of Gettier problems, if whatever we take to bridge the gap between true belief and knowledge (call it warrant) bears some violable relationship to truth, then it will be possible for that belief to be so warranted and true for reasons unrelated to the warrant (Zagzebski 1994, 65).[1] Consider it this way. There are three relationships warrant can bear to truth within any given reductive analysis:

An Inviolable Relation: Warrant necessarily entails truth. (Zagzebski 1994, 69–70)[2]

Close (but not Inviolable) Relation: Warrant generally tracks truth, but not necessarily so.[3]

Divorced Relation: Warrant bears no relation to truth whatsoever.[4]

Zagzebski's diagnosis, then, is simply that so long as a given reductive analysis assumes a close relation, Gettier counterexamples will be unavoidable.[5] That is to say, so long as we reasonably assume that warrant is neither divorced from truth nor inseparable from it (such options being epistemically unpalatable), Gettier cases are "inescapable" (Zagzebski 1994, 65).

As eloquent and intuitive as Zagzebski's diagnosis of Gettier problems may be, many of the prominent advocates of virtue epistemology have apparently not taken it altogether seriously. If Zagzebski is right, this has very dim consequences for any palatable reductive analysis of knowledge; however, virtue epistemologists continue to work from such a model. Though there is a common trend in contemporary epistemology to abandon the standard analysis of knowledge in favor of alternative models, this trend has not yet fully extended to those working within virtue epistemology.

In this chapter, I add credence to Zagzebski's diagnosis (and the movement away from the standard analysis) by considering the nature of luck. It is widely accepted that the lesson to be learned from Gettier problems is that knowledge is incompatible with luck or at least a certain species thereof.[6] As such, understanding the nature of luck is central to understanding the Gettier Problem.[7] Thanks by and large to Duncan Pritchard's seminal work, *Epistemic Luck* (2005), a great deal of literature has been developed recently concerning the nature of luck and anti-luck epistemology. Aside from my article, "Getting 'Lucky' with Gettier" (2013), the literature has been surprisingly silent when it comes to the intuitive idea that luck comes in degrees.[8] I propose that once luck is recognized to admit degrees, even the slightest nonzero degree of luck (of the relevant sort) precludes knowledge. Connecting this to Zagzebski's thesis, I propose that a given theory of warrant must guarantee truth in order to avoid Gettier counterexamples (or subsequently deny that warrant bears any relationship whatsoever to the truth), simply because a sufficient reductive analysis of knowledge (whether a virtue epistemology or not) cannot allow for knowledge that is even marginally lucky.

I justify this proposal by treating Pritchard's work as archetypal. Motivated by the intuition that luck suits degrees, I do two things in this chapter: first, I argue for a consistent extension of Pritchard's modal account of luck (hereafter MAL—perhaps the most seminal theory of luck in the epistemological literature) that suits degrees of luck; second, I argue that such an extension highlights the inability of Pritchard's safety theory (the linchpin of his anti-luck epistemology) to feasibly avoid Gettier counterexamples. Though we will only focus on Pritchard's account of luck and corresponding anti-luck epistemology, prima facie parallel arguments can be made for divergent accounts as well. And this is precisely what we will see when we consider the prominent virtue epistemologies of Chapters 3, 4, and 5. If the only way to avoid Gettier problems is to prohibit beliefs that are even marginally lucky from being considered knowledge, as I hope to demonstrate using Pritchard's account, then the diagnosis for the reductive analysis project is truly bleak indeed.

Section 1: Degrees of Luck

In *Epistemic Luck*, Duncan Pritchard notes that in the contemporary literature luck is often conflated with accidents, chance, or a lack of control; however, whatever luck is, Pritchard notes that such conceptions of luck do not sufficiently characterize it. For example, if S is purposely playing the lottery, it may be lucky if S wins, but it would be strange to call such a lottery win an *accident* (Pritchard 2005, 126). The problem with conflating luck with *chance*, according to Pritchard, is that most of us would say that in order for a given event to be lucky it must affect an agent; with chance, however, no agent needs to be involved. It may be a matter of *chance* that a landslide did or did not occur on such and such a mountain, but most of us would not call such an event a matter of luck if no one was affected (Pritchard 2005, 126). Pritchard notes that conflating luck with an absence of control is perhaps the most common characterization of luck. This is due to an influential paper by Thomas Nagel in which he so defines a particular species of moral luck (Pritchard 2005, 127).[9] Such a characterization, however, has been recognized to be at best a necessary condition on (moral) luck; it is, after all, out of our *control* that the sun rose this morning, but few of us would describe its rising as lucky (Pritchard 2005, 127).[10] What is more, typifying luck as a lack of control is doubly problematic when it comes to *epistemic* luck, given that many epistemologists would adhere to doxastic involuntarism for a whole host of perceptual beliefs (Pritchard 2005, 127). It seems reasonable to think that I have no control over whether or not I believe that "I am now being appeared to redly" when I am so appeared to, but few would identify such a belief as lucky. In light of this, Pritchard notes that though it may seem to be intuitive to characterize luck in terms of accidents, chance, or a lack of control, "there is no straightforward way available of accounting for luck in these terms" (Pritchard 2005, 127).

Pritchard puts forward MAL as a theory of luck that appropriately tracks our intuitions across the relevant cases. According to Pritchard's 2005 account, it consists of two conditions:

> L1: If an event is lucky, then it is an event that occurs in the actual world but which does not occur in a wide class of the nearest possible worlds where the relevant initial conditions for that event are the same as in the actual world. (Pritchard 2005, 128)

> L2: If an event is lucky, then it is an event that is significant to the agent concerned (or would be significant, were the agent to be availed of the relevant facts). (Pritchard 2005, 132)[11]

MAL seems to accurately identify paradigm cases such as lottery wins as lucky (contra an *accident* conception of luck), and it also seems to prevent sunrises, being appeared to redly, and isolated (insignificant to an appropriate agent) landslides from being deemed lucky as well (contra *chance* and *lack of control* conceptions of luck). To be sure, Pritchard notes that there is an inherent vagueness to MAL, though we do seem to have a good intuitive grasp as to how L1 and L2 are meant to function. Pritchard is willing to let us be guided by our intuitions, and, given our current purposes, so am I.

* * *

Aside: In "Pritchard's Epistemic Luck" (2006) and "What Luck Is Not" (2008), Jennifer Lackey raises an objection to MAL through a counterexample she calls Buried Treasure:

> **Buried Treasure:** Sophie, knowing that she had very little time left to live, wanted to bury on the island she inhabited a chest filled with all of her earthly treasures. As she walked around trying to determine the best site for proper burial, her central criteria were, first, that a suitable location must be on the northwest corner of the island, where she had spent many of her fondest moments in life, and secondly, that it had to be a spot where rose bushes could flourish, since these were her favorite flowers. As it happened, there was only one particular patch of land on the northwest corner of the island where the soil was rich enough for roses to thrive. Sophie, being excellent at detecting such soil, immediately located this patch of land and buried her treasure, along with seeds for future roses to bloom, in the one and only spot that fulfilled her two criteria. One month later, Vincent, a distant neighbour of Sophie's, was driving in the northwest corner of the island, which was also his most beloved place to visit, and was looking for a place to plant a rose bush in memory of his mother who had died ten years earlier, since these were her favourite flowers. Being excellent at detecting the proper soil for rose bushes to thrive in, he immediately located the same patch of land as Sophie had found one month earlier. As he began digging a hole for the bush, he was astonished to discover a buried treasure in the ground. (Lackey 2006, 285)[12]

The fact that Vincent found the buried treasure intuitively seems lucky even though it does not appear to meet L1. According to Lackey, Vincent finds the treasure both in the actual world and in a wide range of nearby possible worlds. If one is not convinced of this being the case, Lackey notes that it can be modified to make this more apparent without doing damage to our initial intuition (e.g., the topography of the island is invariant; the only flower that

Sophie and Vincent's mother have ever liked is roses; Sophie has always had this specific detailed plan to bury her possessions once she was informed of her illness; etc.) (Lackey 2006, 286). To be sure, Buried Treasure does not seem to be an isolated case. According to Lackey, to make additional cases all someone has to do, roughly, is pick a paradigmatic instance of luck and then "construct a case involving such an event in which both its central aspects are counterfactually robust, though there is no deliberate or otherwise relevant connection between them," then modifying the case as need be so that the lucky event is bound to happen in all (or most) nearby possible worlds.

Though Lackey takes Buried Treasure to be a clear counterexample to MAL, it seems to me that it rests on a dubious conception of how possible worlds are ordered. Lackey assumes (according to my reading of her) that the closeness of possible worlds should be determined by whether, downstream of some relevant initial conditions, a given event was bound or determined to happen. But why should we think a thing like that? Pritchard does not defend a method for judging the closeness of worlds and neither does Lackey, so until we have independent reason to think the closeness of possible worlds should be judged how Lackey assumes, it is not clear that Buried Treasure even offers a counterexample to MAL let alone a reason to think that MAL is "fundamentally misguided."

To be sure, it is not just that the defender of MAL has no reason to accept Lackey's assumption concerning how possible worlds are ordered; it is that the defender of MAL has very good reason to reject it. Assuming that the closeness of a world is indeed discerned by whether, downstream of some relevant initial conditions, a given event was bound or determined to happen not only leads to hairy cases such as Buried Treasure; it undermines some of MAL's principal goals. For example, one of Pritchard's chief objectives in proposing MAL is to understand the luck involved in Gettier counterexamples better; however, once Lackey's assumption has been made, it looks like someone could make a luckless Gettier case. For example, if we were to expand on a classic Gettier case such that the relevant events were bound to happen (Smith was just bound to lie to Jones about owning a Ford, etc.), it would no longer exhibit luck according to Lackey's reading of MAL. This is a bizarre conclusion to say the least; after all, it is almost universally agreed that the lesson to be learned from Gettier cases is that knowledge is incompatible with (at least a species of) luck. So insofar as the defender of MAL would want to say that classic cases exhibit luck even if the relevant events were predetermined somehow, I think we have not only a blatant reason for thinking that the defender of MAL should reject Lackey's assumption but, what is more, that Lackey's assumption simply was never a part of MAL even at its conception.

The reason we think Vincent is lucky to find the treasure is not based on the event's causal indeterminacy but simply on the fact that planting roses does not usually yield treasure; planting roses is not apt for finding treasure. Instead of determining modality in MAL in terms of causality we should, I think, determine modality in terms of something like aptness. Consider Buried Treasure once again. We could indeed evaluate modality in terms of the causal-context provided in Buried Treasure, which does seem to yield the result that Vincent's specific instance of rose planting that yielded treasure would indeed occur in most close possible worlds. As such, given that we take Vincent's finding the buried treasure to be lucky, this seems to be contra MAL. However, we can instead evaluate modality in terms of the likelihood or aptness of any given rose-planting event yielding treasure, in which case the fact that Vincent found treasure by planting roses is an event that would occur in relatively few close possible worlds (in accord with MAL). In other words, take X_n to be the set of all rose-planting events, of which X_1, Vincent's specific rose-planting event, is one of them. Even if X_1 was predetermined to happen via some story of causal relations, we can still judge X_1 as an event that would occur in few close possible worlds in light of X_n. We take rose planting to be an inapt method for finding buried treasure (no one, barring special cases, would plant roses in hopes of making such a find), and so, insofar as this plays a large role in our luck ascriptions in Buried Treasure, we have reason to determine the modality of X_1 in terms of X_n and not how Lackey is assuming. Of course, Lackey might reply with a case like Buried Treasure Addendum:

> **Buried Treasure Addendum:** The people in Vincent and Sophia's world have a subconscious desire to bury their treasure in locations that have such and such a smell; these locations just so happen to correspond to places with soil suitable for planting roses perfectly. After generations and generations of people with this subconscious desire, almost every place in the world suitable for planting roses has treasure buried there. Planting roses, then, is an activity that is very apt for finding treasure, though, we should add, no one is aware of this—no one has discovered the correspondence between rose-soil and treasure. What is more, all of this is in addition to the circumstances outlined in Buried Treasure (e.g., Vincent and Sophia live on an island with only one place suitable for roses (which, we shall assume, was one of the very few such places without treasure already when it came time for Sophia to bury hers), both Sophia and Vincent's mother have always liked only roses, Sophia and Vincent had planned on taking their respective actions long in advance, etc.).

If we think Vincent is lucky in Buried Treasure Addendum, we have a counterexample to the reading of MAL in which we judge modality in terms of aptness; however, I think we can comfortably deny that Vincent is lucky here. Finding the buried treasure may seem lucky to Vincent, which it surely would, but this does not mean it was a truly lucky event. Becoming violently ill may seem terribly unlucky to the first person who ate a Jack-O'-Lantern mushroom (also known as Omphalotus olearius; a mushroom that tastes and smells edible and indeed delicious), but that doesn't mean that it is; as a matter of fact, when you eat Jack-O'-Lantern mushrooms you get sick. Hence, quintessentially lucky events (which Lackey takes finding buried treasure to be) may not necessarily be lucky.

* * *

MAL is a theory of luck; it tells us when a given event is lucky. As such, it is simply not meant to tell us how lucky a given event is; it is not meant to tell us how luck admits degrees. Nevertheless, given that it is indeed very intuitive that luck comes in degrees, we have an interest in exploring a suitable extension of MAL that will do just this.[13] To be sure, the most philosophically interesting part of Pritchard's *modal* account of luck is, unsurprisingly, its modal condition. As such, in developing an extension of MAL to account for luck coming in degrees, my focus will be Pritchard's modal condition, L1—generally leaving Pritchard's significance condition, L2, as an assumed necessary condition for luck.

But how should degrees of luck be modeled? At first blush, one may think degrees should be modeled according to the number of nearest possible worlds in which the event in question occurs, perhaps extending L1 like this:

> **L1-I**: An event will be lucky according to the degree to which it is an event that occurs in the actual world but does not occur in a wide class of nearest possible worlds where the relevant initial conditions for that event are the same as in the actual world.

That is to say, an event, E, will be lucky to degree D, where D varies directly with the proportion of nearby possible worlds where the relevant initial conditions for E are satisfied and E does not occur. L1-I rightly predicts, for example, that winning a lottery where you had 1 out of 1,000,000 chances is luckier than winning a lottery where you had 1 out of 1,000 chances simply because there will be (so it seems) proportionally fewer close possible worlds in which you win in the former case than in the latter. Changing the game, L1-I similarly predicts that winning a round of roulette by betting on black is less lucky than winning a round of roulette by betting on black 28 simply because there will be (so it seems) proportionally fewer close possible worlds in which you win in the latter than in the former. As such, L1-I appears to ascribe luckiness in such paradigmatic cases rightly; however, on further reflection, L1-I no longer seems sufficient. Consider the following case:

> **Haven:** Haven is an exceedingly safe place. Haven is so safe that it is incredibly unlikely that anyone visiting will be shot. Visitor comes to Haven and is able to leave without being shot.

For the sake of argument, let us say that Haven is so safe that when Visitor visits there are no nearby possible worlds in which he is shot; though, perhaps, there *are* distant worlds where Visitor is so harmed in Haven. Nevertheless, according to L1-I, Visitor's not being shot exhibits *zero* degrees of luck; after all, in none of the nearest possible worlds is Visitor shot when he comes to Haven. But this does not seem correct—surely even distant possible worlds affect an event's luckiness. For example, say that Visitor came to a *perfectly* safe place—call it Heaven—a place where he remains unshot in all possible worlds both near and far. Seemingly, Visitor's not being shot in Haven is luckier than his not being shot in Heaven, yet L1-I does not account for this.[14]

As such, we should look to all possible worlds with the relevant initial conditions and not just the set of nearest ones—perhaps extending L1 like this:

> **L1-II**: An event will be lucky according to the degree to which it is an event that occurs in the actual world but does not occur in other possible worlds where the relevant initial conditions for that event are the same as in the actual world.

That is to say, an event, E, will be lucky to degree D, where D varies directly with the proportion of other possible worlds (*both near and far*) where the relevant initial conditions for E are satisfied and E does not occur. L1-II not only appropriately handles lottery/roulette cases, but it also rightly predicts that remaining unshot in Heaven is less lucky than remaining unshot in Haven. However, an additional clarification needs to be made. Though we should consider all of the relevant possible worlds in modeling degrees of luck, surely closer possible worlds should be weighted more heavily. For example, consider the following case:

> **Ill-Fated Kangaroos:** If a kangaroo loses its tail, it will presumably not be able to walk in nearly all close possible worlds—though in distant possible worlds, let's assume, kangaroos know how to use crutches and can in fact walk without tails. If a kangaroo loses an ear, presumably it will continue to be able to walk in

nearly all close possible worlds—though in distant possible worlds, let's assume, ears play a more central role in a kangaroo's ability to walk. Kangaroo-Jim loses his tail and is still able to walk. Kangaroo-Bill loses an ear and is still able to walk.[15]

Everything else being equal, an event that occurs in close possible worlds (Kangaroo-Bill being able to walk without an ear) is surely less lucky than an event that occurs only in more distant worlds (Kangaroo-Jim being able to walk without a tail)—the former occurring more readily than the latter.

As a final first approximation, the extension of L1 that seems to model degrees of luck rightly looks something like this:

> **L1-III:** An event will be lucky according to the degree to which it is an event that occurs in the actual world but does not occur in other possible worlds (where the relevant initial conditions for that event are the same as in the actual world) such that closer worlds are weighted more than distant worlds.

Consider the following diagram, where A signifies the actual world, P1-3 signify the sets of relevant possible worlds, and the dash-circle signifies the set of "the nearest possible worlds":

In Figure 1.1, P1, P2, and P3 are arranged according to their similarity to A, where closer proximity to A signifies a greater similarity to A. Let us say that E1, E2, E3, E4, and E5 are events that occur in A and which have, let us suppose, the

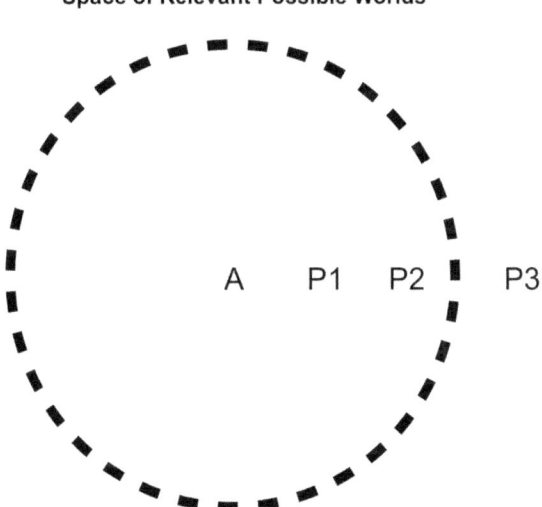

Figure 1.1 Space of relevant possible worlds.

Table 1.1 Distribution of Events Across Possible Worlds

Events	Possible Worlds
E1	A, P1, P2, P3
E2	A, P1, P2
E3	A, P1
E4	A, P2
E5	A

same relevant initial conditions. Additionally, assume that these are conditions that P1, P2, and P3 meet. In addition to occurring in A, E1 occurs in P1, P2, and P3. In addition to occurring in A, E2 occurs in P1 and P2. In addition to occurring in A, E3 occurs in P1. In addition to occurring in A, E4 occurs in P2. Finally, E5 occurs only in A (see Table 1.1). For our consideration, let us also say that P1, P2, and P3 account for all possible worlds where the relevant initial conditions are the same. Ordering these events from highest to lowest degree of luck (from luckiest to least lucky), they are: E5, E4, E3, E2, E1. Understandably, E5 is the luckiest event because it occurs in the actual world but in no other relevant possible world. E4 is the second luckiest event because, though it occurs in P2, it does not occur in the closest possible worlds P1—as such, it would have been easier for E4 not to have occurred than E3, which does occur in the closest possible worlds. E2 is the second to least lucky as it occurs in all but the most distant P3 worlds. E1, of course, is the least lucky as it occurs in all possible worlds.

* * *

Aside: Though unnecessary for the abovementioned argumentation, it is worth noting that one could also see luck as varying in L2, in accord with how significant the given event is to the protagonist in question. Seemingly, finding $5 on the street is lucky, but perhaps finding $100 is much luckier, even if both events occur in the same proportions of relevant possible worlds. As such, we could modify L2 accordingly:

> L2-I: An event is lucky according to the degree to which it is an event that is significant to the agent concerned (or would be significant, were the agent to be availed of the relevant facts).

Finally, given that the relationship between L1-III and L2-I is dynamic, luckiness can be graphed accordingly (where luck increases with shading) (Figure 1.2).

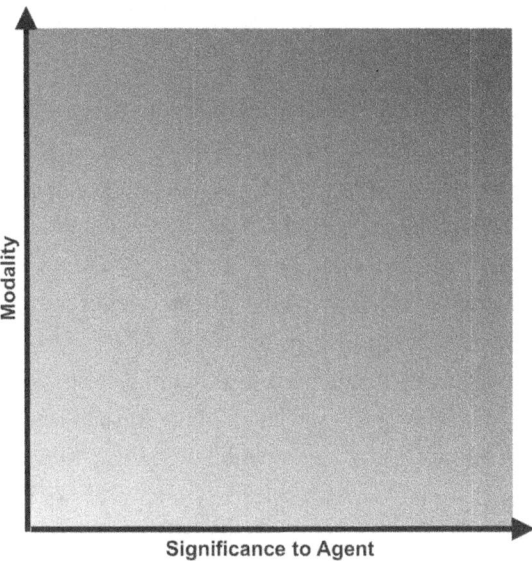

Figure 1.2 Bivariant degrees of luck.

Our intuitions may be vague on the parameters of what counts as lucky in such an analysis, but such vagueness seems to be a part of how we use the term. So the fact that this revised analysis captures this should, I think, go to its credit. What is more, it is worth noting that such an all-permeating conception of luck (after all, by this analysis most events no matter how modally probable or only remotely significant to an agent will be deemed to have traces of luck) matches Zagzebski's diagnosis of the Gettier Problem, which saw luck as irreparably saturating the human condition.[16]

* * *

Although more could easily be said, I think we can take L1-III as a more or less healthy extension for MAL (hereafter MAL-III) that accounts for our intuition that luck admits degrees. Not only does MAL-III tell us why some events are luckier than others in paradigmatic cases such as lottery wins, but it also helps us assess minute degrees of luckiness. However, given that luck is the central and fundamental component of Gettier cases, how we think of luck, be it in terms of MAL alone or in terms of MAL with a degree's extension, will affect how we attempt to surmount Gettier problems. In the next section, we will consider Pritchard's safety theory in light of the MAL-III extension and test how successful it is at precluding a specific Gettier case.

Section 2: Pritchard's Anti-luck Epistemology

In developing his safety theory, Pritchard is trying to establish an analysis of knowledge that avoids Gettier counterexamples. It is almost universally agreed that the lesson to be learned from Gettier cases is that knowledge is incompatible with luck—that luck is the central and fundamental component of all Gettier cases.[17] Naturally enough, therefore, how Pritchard conceives of luck in general (MAL) will play a critical role both in how he conceives of the problem raised by Gettier cases and how it might be surmounted via safety.

Gettier cases, according to Pritchard, are caused by a specific species of luck (Pritchard 2005, 145–8). As such, the lesson to be learned from Gettier cases is not so much that knowledge is incompatible with luck *simpliciter* but, rather, that knowledge is incompatible with this particular *species* of it. By these lights, any successful analysis of knowledge, therefore, must (at the very least) track knowledge ascriptions in accord with this species' absence.

Pritchard calls this species of luck that is behind Gettier cases "Veritic Epistemic Luck." According to Pritchard, a given agent's belief exhibits Veritic Epistemic Luck when the following description is met:

> **Veritic Epistemic Luck**: It is a matter of luck that the agent's belief is true. (Pritchard 2005, 146)

In other words, in light of MAL, a given agent's true belief exemplifies Veritic Epistemic Luck when: (1) in a wide class of nearest possible worlds the belief is false, and (2) the belief's truth or falsity is significant to the agent. To be sure, Veritic Epistemic Luck is *not* meant to refer to cases where it is a matter of luck that *the propositional content* of an agent's belief is true. Surely, such luck *is* compatible with knowledge; surely, for example, we can have knowledge of who won the lottery, where lightning struck, what number rolling a die produced, etc. Given that Veritic Epistemic Luck is meant to be the species of luck behind Gettier cases and subsequently incompatible with knowledge, Veritic Epistemic Luck must refer to something else. Pritchard goes on to elucidate what Veritic Epistemic Luck demands, namely, that

> the agent's belief is true in the actual world, but that in a wide class of nearby possible worlds in which the relevant initial conditions are the same as the actual world—and this will mean, in the basic case that the agent at the very least *forms the same belief in the same way* as in the actual world—the belief is false. (Pritchard 2005, 146; emphasis mine)

So in order for something to be an instance of Veritic Epistemic Luck, not only does it have to be a matter of luck that the agent's belief is true, but it has to be lucky given the way it was formed. By Veritic Epistemic Luck, Pritchard means something like "It is a matter of luck, *given the way the belief is formed*, that the belief is true."

There are, to be sure, two subspecies of veritic epistemic luck, *environmental luck* and *intervening luck*, and only the latter is considered to be relevant to Gettier counterexamples. A classic example of environmental luck is found in the Fake Barn case:

> FAKE BARNS: Henry is driving in the country with his son. For the boy's edification Henry identifies various objects on the landscape as they come into view. "That's a cow," says Henry, "That's a tractor," "That's a silo," "That's a barn," etc. Henry has no doubt about the identity of these objects; in particular, he has no doubt that the last-mentioned object is a barn, which indeed it is. Each of the identified objects has features characteristic of its type. Moreover, each object is fully in view, Henry has excellent eyesight, and he has enough time to look at them reasonably carefully, since there is little traffic to distract him. . . . Suppose we are told that, unknown to Henry, the district he has just entered is full of papier-mâché facsimiles of barns. These facsimiles look from the road exactly like barns, but are really just façades, without back walls or interiors, quite incapable of being used as barns. They are so cleverly constructed that travelers invariably mistake them for barns. Having just entered this district, Henry has not encountered any facsimiles; the object he sees is a genuine barn. But if the barn on that site were a facsimile, Henry would mistake it for a barn. (Goldman 1976, 772–3)[18]

In such a case, it's a matter of luck, given the way the belief was formed, that Henry's belief is true—satisfying my gloss of Pritchard's definition of veritic luck. And even though Henry saw a real barn and formed a true belief based off of that perception, he fails to know, because his reasons for thinking "that's a barn" are not sufficient in such an environment—where, by hypothesis, he is unable to distinguish real barns from fake barns. Given the environment, his reasons for thinking that "that's a barn" could have very easily led to a false belief, if he just so happened to be looking at one of the facsimiles.[19]

Gettier cases are different. Recall the Classic Case from the beginning of this chapter. In such a case, it's a matter of luck, given the way the belief was formed, that Smith's belief is true—satisfying the definition of veritic luck—because his reasons for thinking that "the man who gets the job has 10 coins in his pocket" do not rightly capture why the belief is true. *The protagonist in Gettier cases is the victim of double luck*.[20] Due to some bad luck, Smith's reason for believing that "the man who gets the job has 10 coins in his pocket," in the Classic Case, is significantly undermined: Smith heard from the employer that Jones is going to be hired and saw that Jones has ten coins in his pocket, leading to the belief in question; however, Jones doesn't get the job, undermining Smith's belief. Thanks to some countervailing good luck, however, Smith's belief turns out to be true *for other reasons*: unbeknownst to Smith, he gets the job, and he also has ten coins in his pocket. The reasons for Smith's belief are not insufficient due to an unfavorable environment (as in cases like Fake Barns). Smith's reasons for his belief are insufficient because they are significantly undermined as a result of bad luck and would have led to a false belief if it hadn't been for the countervailing or intervening luck making Smith's belief true for significantly different reasons. This subspecies of veritic luck, which Pritchard calls *intervening luck*, is the luck involved in Gettier cases. A belief exhibits intervening luck, then, when it is a matter of luck, given the way the belief is formed, the belief is true, to the extent that what makes the belief true is not captured by the belief's warrant (due to the "double luck" at play).

By these lights, to avoid Gettier cases and Fake Barn-style cases entirely one needs to have an epistemology that does not attribute knowledge to beliefs that exhibit intervening epistemic luck—luck that, given the way the belief was formed, the belief is true for reasons not captured by the warrant. So, given MAL and Pritchard's analysis of Gettier problems, he fashions his safety theory to do just this.

> **Pritchard's Safety Theory**: For all agents . . . if an agent knows a contingent proposition ψ, then, in nearly all (if not all) nearby possible worlds in which she forms her belief about ψ in the same way as she forms her belief in the actual world, that agent only believes that ψ when ψ is true. (Pritchard 2005, 163)

Once given MAL, such that something is lucky if it meets L1 and L2, and Pritchard's understanding of what species of luck is behind Gettier problems, Pritchard's safety theory is a natural solution. It is specially designed to prevent any belief from being deemed knowledge that is only luckily (as described in MAL) connected to the reasons behind its genesis.[21] Such a belief could be so believed by an agent in nearly all (if not all) nearby possible worlds in which it is formed in the same way (e.g., for the same reasons) as in the actual world and yet be false. When a belief exhibits Veritic Epistemic Luck, Pritchard's safety theory will not be met; thus, according to Pritchard's analysis, such a belief will not be knowledge. Recall the classic Gettier case (e.g. Classic Case) where Smith and

Jones apply for the same job (found in the Introduction). Smith's belief may very well be justified and true, but because it would not still be true in many nearby possible worlds in which Smith forms the belief in the same way (worlds where, for example, Smith has more or less than ten coins in his pocket), it is not safe and therefore not an instance of knowledge. Also recall Alvin Goldman's Fake Barns case: Henry's belief may very well be justified and true, but because it would not still be true in many nearby possible worlds in which Henry forms the belief in the same way (e.g., worlds where he is actually looking at a barn façade), it is not safe and therefore, so it goes, not an instance of knowledge.

According to *Epistemic Luck* (2005), in order for belief to be knowledge it must be true and safe as per Pritchard's safety theory. Such an analysis of knowledge, once given MAL and Pritchard's diagnostics of Gettier cases, is meant to be Gettier-proof. To be sure, we may be inclined to agree that once this much has been accepted, Pritchard has indeed established a version of the standard analysis that is immune to Gettier cases; however, as we shall soon see, adopting MAL-III calls this into question—having serious ramifications for the success of Pritchard's analysis at avoiding Gettier counterexamples.

Pritchard, relating Veritic Epistemic Luck back to his general conception of luck (MAL), says that it arises when a given "agent's belief is true in the actual world, but . . . in *a wide class of nearby possible worlds* in which the relevant initial conditions are the same as in the actual world . . . the belief is false" (Pritchard 2005, 146; emphasis mine). However, given that luck comes in degrees, Veritic Epistemic Luck is far more insidious than that. Veritic Epistemic Luck crops up not only if the belief in question is false in "a wide class of nearby possible worlds" but, rather, to at least some degree, if the belief in question is false in any (or nearly any) possible world whatsoever! According to MAL-III, Veritic Epistemic Luck comes in degrees. I may be very gullible and believe some dastardly fellows who, for fun, tell me there is buried treasure in my backyard, such that when my belief turns out to be true (there indeed happens to be treasure in my backyard, unbeknownst to my fellows) it exhibits a large degree of Veritic Epistemic Luck. There are any number of possible worlds, given my gullibility, where I believe whatever dastardly fellows tell me and it is false. On the other hand, I may be very cold and skeptical and (eventually) believe the testimony of legitimate experts of lost treasure, who tell me that there is treasure in my backyard based on such and such legitimate data (maps, pirate diaries, descriptions of the treasure's location, etc.) such that my belief, which happens to be true for complex reasons unrelated to the expert's data analysis, is only marginally exhibiting Veritic Epistemic Luck. As we might imagine, there are relatively very few possible worlds in which I form a calculated belief based on the honest testimony of experts in which it happens to be false.

Crucially, as we saw from the Haven/Heaven case, distant possible worlds seem to affect how lucky a given event is. The question then becomes whether or not minute degrees of Veritic Epistemic Luck are of any epistemic consequence.[22] A safety theorist like Pritchard may very well agree that luck comes in degrees but deny that anyone fails to know a given belief when that belief is believed in the same way and yet false in *distant* possible worlds. Consider a case originally developed by Linda Zagzebski in "The Inescapability of Gettier Problems" (1994):

> **Dr. Jones and the Virus:** Smith is ill and exhibits a unique set of symptoms, S. Given these symptoms, Dr. Jones forms the belief that "Smith has Virus X," which she deduces from the true proposition that "Virus X is the only known virus to exhibit S." What is more, Dr. Jones does a blood test which verifies that Smith's body contains antibodies for Virus X, further justifying Jones's belief. Based on the evidence, it is extremely plausible that Smith has Virus X. As it happens, however, Smith's symptoms are in fact due to an unknown virus, Virus Y, which exhibits identical symptoms to Virus X; Smith exhibits antibodies for Virus X only because of an idiosyncratic feature of Smith's biochemistry which causes his immune system to maintain high levels of antibodies long past a given infection. Nevertheless, Dr. Jones's belief turns out to be true divorced from Smith's symptoms or his blood work, because Smith was infected with Virus X just before meeting with Dr. Jones—the infection being so recent that bloodwork cannot detect it and it is causing no symptoms. (paraphrased from Zagzebski 1994, 71)

Dr. Jones is completely non-culpable in her belief formation—no false belief plays a causal or evidential role in her justification (Zagzebski 1994, 71). Indeed, many theorists would suppose that the evidence in question is adequate for knowledge. Seemingly, no false beliefs are in the immediate neighborhood, and Dr. Jones would believe that Smith has Virus X in a wide range of counterfactual situations (Zagzebski 1994, 71). Whether or not Dr. Jones's belief meets Pritchard's safety theory, and whether or not Pritchard's anti-luck epistemology is indeed Gettier-proof, will depend on whether or not in all (or nearly all) nearby possible worlds Dr. Jones would believe that "Smith has Virus X" only when it is true.

Pritchard's safety theory is caught between a rock and a hard place. Given the set of nearby possible worlds where Smith did not happen to *just recently* become infected with Virus X, perhaps Pritchard's safety condition is not met—in many nearby worlds in which Dr. Jones's belief is formed in the same way (on the same basis), the belief would be false. However, the case can be strengthened; we can make it such that there are fewer close possible worlds where Dr. Jones forms a false belief, as it were. Suppose we stipulated that, unbeknownst to anyone at the time, Virus X was running rampant just outside the hospital and that it is in fact incredibly unlikely that Smith would *not* have caught the virus when he did. So revised, it is less certain that Dr. Jones's belief fails Pritchard's condition—conceivably in very few (if any) nearby possible worlds would Dr. Jones's belief not be true. In other words, it looks like the luck at play in Dr. Jones and the Virus, so revised, would lead to a false belief in few (if any) nearby possible worlds.[23] Even though the Veritic Epistemic Luck involved in Dr. Jones's belief in the strengthened case is of a relatively minute degree, it is still enough to preclude knowledge. To be clear, Pritchard could strengthen his safety condition and say that the truth of Dr. Jones's belief is still (somehow) too unlikely—that the possible worlds in which Dr. Jones's belief is false though formed in the same way (worlds where Virus X is *not* running rampant outside the hospital, for example) are still too prevalent for safety to be satisfied. However, as we play this game (i.e., I keep strengthening the case, and Pritchard keeps strengthening his safety condition), we get to a point where the only possible worlds in which Dr. Jones's belief is false are very distant, and insofar as Dr. Jones's belief can still be "Gettierized" (i.e., made true for reasons divorced from the way the belief in question was formed), we find ourselves in a dilemma: *either Pritchard's safety condition is eventually strengthened such that no belief counts as knowledge unless it would be true in all (or nearly all) possible worlds in which the belief is formed in the same way, drastically limiting what we know, or Pritchard's safety condition is going to fall victim to Gettier cases such as Dr. Jones and the Virus, thus making his analysis of knowledge insufficient.*

To be fair, Pritchard has revised his safety condition since *Epistemic Luck* (2005); unfortunately, however, such revisions run into the same dilemma. For example, consider the rendition of safety Pritchard endorses in "Anti-Luck Epistemology" (2007):

> **Pritchard's 2007 Safety Theory:** S's belief is safe *iff* in most near-by possible worlds in which S continues to form her belief about the target proposition in the same way as in the actual world, and in all very close near-by possible worlds in which S continues to form her belief about the target proposition in the same way as in the actual world, the belief continues to be true. (Pritchard 2007, 292)

Whatever advantages this iteration of safety may have over the one Pritchard develops in *Epistemic Luck* (2005), what is important to see for our purposes is simply that Pritchard's 2007 Safety Theory is still *only* concerned with close possible worlds. As such, it will not be able to prevent Gettier counterexamples like the strengthened Dr. Jones and the Virus case—counterexamples where the belief in question is "Gettierized" though true in all the relevant close possible worlds. Just like its predecessor, the only way Pritchard's 2007 Safety Theory can fully avoid Gettier problems is if it is so strengthened that it precludes knowledge for any belief that exhibits even the slightest degree of Veritic Epistemic Luck—a move that would radically limit what we know.[24]

Pritchard's modal account of luck is the seminal account to date, and I think it is more or less correct. What is more, I think Pritchard is exactly right to point to Veritic Epistemic Luck as the culprit behind Gettier cases. However, by not appreciating degrees of luck, the anti-luck epistemology he subsequently develops misses its mark. In this chapter, I argued for a consistent extension of MAL that accounted for our intuition that luck suits degrees. Once extended, however, we saw how Pritchard's analysis of knowledge seems to fall apart in a dilemma—either his safety theory will be too strong to be palatable or too weak to preclude Gettier cases like Dr. Jones and the Virus.[25]

What is more, there is no reason to think that the effects of accounting for degrees of luck are localized to Pritchard's analysis; seemingly parallel arguments could be made with divergent accounts of luck or divergent analyses of knowledge. What counterexamples such as the strengthened Dr. Jones and the Virus case show is that Gettier problems can arise out of even a minute degree of luck. As such, any anti-luck condition in a given theory of warrant that permits even the slightest degree of luck will be susceptible to Gettier counterexamples.

This is, to be sure, all in keeping with Zagzebski's diagnosis: if whatever is taken to bridge the gap between true belief and knowledge (call it warrant) does not guarantee the truth of the belief, then it will be possible to create a Gettier case. It will be possible for a belief to be so warranted and only luckily true for reasons unrelated to the warrant (Zagzebski 1994, 65). Given degrees of luck, that seems exactly right. If even the slightest degree of Veritic Epistemic Luck precludes knowledge, then the warrant of any Gettier-proof version of the reductive analysis (be it a virtue epistemology or not) must guarantee the truth of the belief in question. As Timothy Williamson noted in his book *Knowledge and Its Limits* (2000), "Since Gettier refuted the traditional analysis of *knows* as *has justified true belief* in 1963, a succession of increasingly complex analyses have been overturned by increasingly complex counterexamples," which, given that luck is indeed as permeating as I am suggesting, is just what one might expect (Williamson 2000, 30). Such a conclusion, perhaps, is simply further testament to the growing trend in the contemporary literature to abandon the standard analysis altogether and pursue alternative models from which to do epistemology.

One more point: The starting place that almost everyone seems to agree on is that if it is possible to have a warranted, false belief, then it is possible for such a belief to be so warranted and true for reasons not captured by the warrant. (We will consider an objection to this view in the next chapter.) In other words, if we assume that warrant is fallible, then Gettier problems will be unavoidable.[26] So, if we're going to try to avoid Gettier counterexamples, whatever bridges the gap between true belief and knowledge must be infallible.[27]

But what is perhaps less appreciated in the literature is just how strong this claim is. If a given account of warrant doesn't make it impossible for a belief to be so warranted and false, then that account of warrant cannot avoid Gettier counterexamples. For example, if a given account of warrant rules out the possibility of a warranted false belief in all *close* possible worlds—which is already a strong account of warrant—it can still be vulnerable to Gettier counterexamples, since it hasn't ruled out the possibility of a warranted false belief in *distant* possible worlds. A distant possible world could obtain, and the belief could be so warranted and true for other reasons. In other words, the belief could still be Gettiered.[28] Continuing with the modal example, any truly infallible account of warrant aimed at avoiding Gettier counterexamples must preclude the possibility of a warranted false belief *in all possible worlds*. That said, if a given belief is warranted and if it is impossible for it to be so warranted and false, then there is a real worry that we might never have a warranted beliefs, and so never have knowledge. It looks like radical skepticism might be looming on the immediate horizon.

A possible worry: Some theories of warrant—for example, causal theories and achievement theories—seem to necessitate truth but without leading to radical skepticism. For example, consider the following account of knowledge: *S knows p iff S's belief that p is caused by the fact that p*. Here, it looks like truth is built *into* the account of knowledge such that it's not possible to have a warranted false belief, yet it is not obvious that it leads to skeptical conclusions. As such, the abovementioned diagnosis of the Gettier Problem seems incorrect; an account of warrant can entail truth without leading to skepticism.

A response: While such an account might *appear* to be infallibilistic about warrant, it's easy to see that such an account of knowledge is actually fallibilistic upon closer inspection. First of all, note that it's easy to generate a Gettier case against it. Consider the following:

SPRING: While visiting a local children's museum, S looks across a room to see what looks like a spring in a large box and forms the belief "There's a spring in that box!." What S sees, however, is mere hologram of a spring generated by a series of mirrors within the box, which reflect the actual spring, which (luckily) is elsewhere within the box. (Given the current setup, the hologram of the spring couldn't be there if the actual spring wasn't elsewhere in the box.)

S's belief that "There's a spring in that box" is caused by the fact that there is indeed a spring elsewhere in the box (being reflected by the mirrors). The aforementioned definition of knowledge seems to be satisfied, though the belief is Gettiered. Seeing the way in which such an account can be Gettiered helps us see that it employs a fallibilistic account of warrant. Critically for the proposed diagnosis of the Gettier Problem, we need to know the following: if *S knows p iff S's belief that p is caused by the fact that p*, then what bridges the gap between the true belief and the knowledge? In other words, what is functioning as *warrant* in such an account of knowledge? Answer: It's the sort of causal relationship that stands between *p* and the corresponding belief. And what cases like SPRING show is that it's possible to be in *the very same sort of relationship* without having a true belief. The hologram of the spring—the very same causal source—could have, with a different configuration of mirrors, just as easily caused a false belief (if, for example, the actual spring wasn't in the box but was being reflected from somewhere else, perhaps the floorboards). Being false, such a belief is clearly not knowledge; however, the *warrant* seems to remain intact. As such, the theories of warrant, in such cases, are fallibilistic; and, as expected, they lead to Gettier counterexamples. (This will be argued further in Chapters 3, 4, and 5.)

But what is more, the only way such an account could truly avoid Gettier counterexamples is if it was impossible for a given causal relationship to lead to anything other than a true belief. If we assumed that *S knows p iff S's belief that p is caused by the fact that p*, and we assumed that any given cause had to guarantee the truth of *p* (the same sort of cause couldn't have produced a false belief), then Gettier problems can indeed be avoided. But now it looks like skepticism is looming on the horizon. Very few (if any) of our beliefs have causes that couldn't have possibly led to a false belief. And as such, it seems like such an account of knowledge, as predicted, is extremely difficult to satisfy. *So, the Gettier Problem leaves us with a dilemma: either assume a fallibilistic account of warrant and face Gettier counterexamples or assume an infallibilistic account of warrant and risk radical, intractable skepticism. And insofar as neither leg of this dilemma is attractive, the Gettier Problem seems unsolvable.*

Let's put this a bit more formally. Let's start, again, with the widely agreed upon claim that fallibilist accounts of warrant will always face Gettier counterexamples:

1) If it is possible for a warranted belief to be false ($\Diamond$(Wb • ¬b)), then it is possible for a belief to be so warranted and true for reasons not captured by the warrant.

Add to this, the strong intuition that Gettier cases are incompatible with knowledge, which effectively forces us to deny 1's consequent.

2) Knowledge precludes the possibility of warranted belief that is true for reasons not captured by the warrant (i.e., Gettier cases are not instances of knowledge).

And by denying 1's consequent, we have to also deny its antecedent via *modus tollens*, which is the denial of fallibilism:

3) It is not possible for a warranted belief to be false.

   ($\neg$($\Diamond$(Wb • ¬b))).

And that is logically equivalent to the following:

4) It's necessarily the case that: if a belief is warranted, then it is true ($\Box$(Wb→b)).

Starting with the modest assumption that fallibilistic accounts of warrant will always be vulnerable to Gettier counterexamples (1) and the intuition that Gettier cases are incompatible with knowledge (2), we're straightforwardly led to infallibilism (4). But if warrant sufficient for knowledge *necessarily* entails the truth of the given belief, then it is not clear that an infallibilistic account of warrant could ever be met, leaving infallibilism under the threat of radical skepticism.

In sum, then: the Gettier Problem is the problem of developing a reductive analysis of knowledge that viably precludes the intervening luck at work in Gettier counterexamples. And once we appreciate that luck comes in degrees, we're able to better see just how difficult such a task is.

At the start of this chapter, we set out to consider why the Gettier Problem has proven to be so very problematic, seemingly evading a viable solution for over fifty years. Now, perhaps, we're in a better position to see why the Problem is so very problematic. Any viable reductive analysis of knowledge faces a dilemma between being vulnerable to Gettier counterexamples or risk collapsing into radical skepticism. In keeping with Zagzebski's (1994) diagnosis, the only way to avoid intervening luck, it seems, is to assume an infallible theory of warrant, to require a given theory of warrant to guarantee the truth of the belief in question, ruling out the possibility of the belief being true for reasons not captured by the warrant. Ruling out the possibility of intervening luck, however, seems to require a theory of warrant that guarantees the truth of the belief in question; and given that we rarely possess enough warrant to guarantee the truth of our beliefs, then we're left with the worry that we might not ever have enough warrant for knowledge, leaving us with skepticism.

We will see this dilemma, *between Gettier and skepticism*, play out again and again in Chapters 3–5 as we consider various attempts by virtue epistemologists to offer a viable reductive analysis of knowledge, to solve the Gettier Problem. Afterwards, we'll be poised to explore some non-reductive options that virtue epistemologists might pursue. Before we get to any of that, however, we need to defend abovementioned diagnosis of the Gettier Problem against some prominent objections.

2

Objections

Let us quickly take stock. Taking the standard analysis of knowledge to be *warranted true belief* (where "warrant" is whatever we take to bridge the gap between true belief and knowledge), the diagnosis advocated in the previous chapter suggested that so long as warrant is closely but not inviolably related to truth, Gettier counterexamples will be unavoidable. In other words, so long as we reasonably assume that warrant is neither divorced from truth nor inseparable from it (such options being epistemically unpalatable), Gettier cases are "inescapable" (Zagzebski 1994, 65). Consider Figure 2.1.

As we discussed in the previous chapter, warrant can bear one of three relationships to truth: an inviolable relationship, a close relationship, or a divorced relationship. The problem, however, is that none of these relationships seems viable. As we will discover, presupposing an inviolable relationship between warrant and truth readily seems to lead to radical skepticism (it does at least in every analysis of warrant we will consider). Given the prevalence of luck, presupposing a close (but not inviolable) relationship between warrant and truth always seems to lead to further Gettier counterexamples. Finally, presupposing that warrant bears no relationship to truth seems completely counterintuitive.

There are four objections someone might level against such a diagnosis of the Gettier Problem. First, someone may level the objection that assuming an inviolable relationship between warrant and truth does not lead to radical skepticism. Likewise, someone may level the objection that assuming a close (though not inviolable) relationship between warrant and truth does not always lead to further Gettier counterexamples. Third, someone might level the objection that assuming that warrant bears no relationship to truth is not, in fact, counterintuitive. Fourth and finally, someone may level a meta-objection that calls into question the epistemic import of Gettier-style counterexamples altogether. While in the next part of this book we will see the proposed

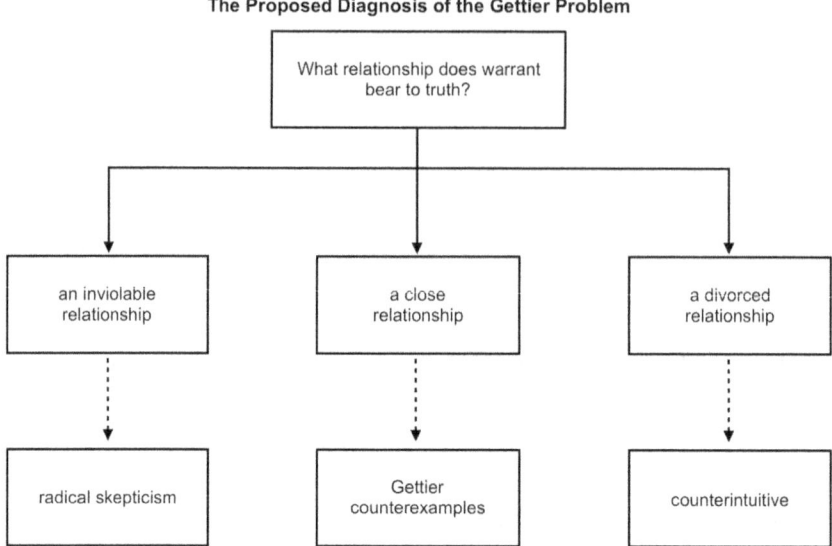

Figure 2.1 Map of the proposed diagnosis of the Gettier Problem.

connection between radical skepticism and the inviolable warrant/truth relation vindicated in all the relevant instances, it is nevertheless important that we guard against the latter three types of objections, especially insofar as these sorts of objections are manifest in the contemporary literature.

And that is precisely what I do in this chapter. In the first section, we consider Daniel Howard-Snyder, Frances Howard-Snyder, and Neil Feit's paper, "Infallibilism and Gettier's Legacy" (2003), which directly objects to our conclusion in the previous chapter that a close but not inviolable relationship between warrant and truth will always lead to Gettier counterexamples; I argue that their proposed solution to the Gettier Problem is, ironically, only successful insofar as it conforms to the proposed diagnosis. In the second section, we consider seminal work by Stephen Hetherington (particularly from his book *Good Knowledge, Bad Knowledge* 2001), which proposes an analysis of knowledge that assumes a divorced relationship between warrant and truth; I argue that Hetherington's epistemology is counterintuitive and that it need not be advocated in light of viable alternatives. Finally, in Section 3, we consider landmark papers by Brian Weatherson (2003) and Jonathan M. Weinberg, Shaun Nichols, and Stephen Stich (2001), which call into question the epistemic import of Gettier counterexamples; I argue that such criticisms either lead to intractable forms of skepticism or can otherwise be defused.

Section 1: The Howard-Snyder/Feit Objection

In their paper, "Infallibilism and Gettier's Legacy" (2003), Daniel Howard-Snyder, Frances Howard-Snyder, and Neil Feit consider what they call three nonpartisan arguments against fallibilism (i.e., arguments that are not committed to a specific account of warrant and that are against the view that a belief can be at once warranted and false) and contend that each is lacking. Most importantly for our purposes, however, they contend that an argument for infallibilism based on the sort of diagnosis of the Gettier Problem proposed in the previous chapter is simply flawed. Contra what was said in Chapter 1, Howard-Snyder et al. argue that the Gettier Problem can indeed be solved fallibilistically, while assuming that warrant bears a close but not inviolable relationship to truth. In this section, we will consider this argument and Howard-Snyder et al.'s opposition to it, and I will argue that in light of our analysis of luck provided in the previous chapter, Howard-Snyder et al.'s opposition falls flat—ironically failing precisely along the lines predicted by the proposed diagnosis of Gettier problems.[1]

A typical response to the Gettier Problem is to try to make the relationship between warrant and truth so close that it is simply impossible for a warranted belief to be Gettiered (made true for reasons not predicted by the warrant)—a response that has repeatedly led epistemologists to try to endorse some form of infallibilism. The functional argument at work here, according to Howard-Snyder et al., goes something like this:

1. If a belief can be at once warranted and false, then the Gettier Problem cannot be solved.
2. The Gettier Problem can be solved.[2]
3. So, a belief cannot be at once warranted and false. (D. Howard-Snyder, F. Howard-Snyder, and Feit 2003, 135)

The first premise, the key premise, is precisely what the proposed diagnosis of Gettier Problem would predict, and this is precisely what Howard-Snyder et al. hope to challenge. So, if we are to defend the second branch of the trilemma portrayed in Figure 2.1, response to Howard-Snyder et al. seems appropriate.

The infallibilist response to the Gettier Problem is, to be sure, an increasingly popular one; as Howard-Snyder et al. sweepingly point out:

> Scott Sturgeon—purporting to express "the standard post-Gettier model of propositional knowledge"—recently wrote that the Gettier Problem can be avoided only by saying that S knows that *p* if and only if S believes *p* and S's

belief is fully justified, where S's belief is *fully* justified only if it is true.³ Early on, defeasibility theorists decided that if their accounts did not have the consequence that warrant entails truth, they would be subject to Gettier cases, and so they fortified them accordingly. Causal theorists are likewise motivated by Gettier to endorse infallibilism. Recall the first words of the locus classicus of the genus: "Since Edmund L. Gettier reminded us recently of a certain important inadequacy of the traditional analysis of 'S knows that *p*,' several attempts have been made to correct that analysis. In this paper I [Alvin Goldman] shall offer still another analysis . . . , one which will avert Gettier's problem."⁴ Reflecting on certain cases, Goldman concluded that one is warranted in believing *p* only if the fact that *p* is causally connected in an appropriate way with the one's believe *p*. Of course, the fact that *p* cannot be thus connected to one's believing *p* unless it is a fact that *p*, and so *p* is true; so his causal theory implies that warrant entails truth, a consequence endorsed in order to "circumvent Gettier's counterexamples."⁵ As a process reliabilist, Goldman conceives of the reliability of a process in terms of how it operates in actual and relevant alternative situations. Those alternatives which are relevant are conceived in such a way that warrant entails truth. Why? To avoid Gettier cases, he says.⁶ Robert Nozick added condition (iii) [his sensitivity condition] to his "truth-tracking" theory—S knows that *p* only if S wouldn't believe that *p* if *p* weren't true—precisely because he wishes to "exclude cases of the sort first described by Edmund Gettier."⁷ Fred Dretske argued that one has a warranted belief that *p* only if one has a "conclusive reason" for *p*, a reason that "eliminates" the conjunction of that reason and the denial of *p* as a possible state of affairs. What motivated him to lay down this condition? "[T]he conviction (supported by Gettier-like examples) that knowledge if it embodies an evidential relation at all, must embody a strong enough one to eliminate the possibility of mistake."⁸ Even Roderick Chisholm—who explicitly wished to avoid infallibilism in his response to the Gettier Problem—in the end conceded that "what is known must be evident but not defectively evident," where a proposition is not defectively evident only if the propositions on which it is based do *not* make evident a proposition that is *false*.⁹ (D. Howard-Snyder, F. Howard-Snyder, and Feit 2003, 306, 307)

What is more, it is worth noting that the prominent virtue epistemologists under consideration in this book are no different; as we will see in the next couple of chapters, both Alvin Plantinga and Ernest Sosa have, in recent work, fallen into accord with an infallibilist response to the Gettier Problem. Be that as it may, the point is clear: epistemologists from across the board have, in accord with the proposed diagnosis, chosen to try to provide a feasible analysis of knowledge through inviolably connecting warrant with truth, through infallibilism. It is the perceived exigency of such a move that Howard-Snyder et al. wish to challenge by proposing a fallibilism-friendly solution to the Gettier Problem.

Before they give us their solution, Howard-Snyder et al. first have us reconsider one of the original Gettier case where Smith and Jones apply for the same job (found in the Introduction). We could, of course, try to defuse such a case by saying "we cannot have warranted beliefs based on inferences from false beliefs," but as Howard-Snyder et al. point out, "cases that lack this feature are a dime a dozen"; further counterexamples (e.g., Fake Barns-type cases) can be easily produced (D. Howard-Snyder, F. Howard-Snyder, and Feit 2003, 307–8). That said, if we are to find a fallibilism-friendly solution, we must look elsewhere.

According to Howard-Snyder et al., "the distinctive feature of standard Gettier cases like these is that the reason Smith believes p or the processes involved in his believing p are not properly related to those facts that render p true" (D. Howard-Snyder, F. Howard-Snyder, and Feit 2003, 308). After all, being told by a reliable source that Jones is going to get the job and counting the coins in his pocket, in the end, had nothing to do with the truth of the relevant belief. "It's a matter of sheer serendipity that [Smith's] belief that p is true given his reasons for believing p or the processes involved in his believing p" (D. Howard-Snyder, F. Howard-Snyder, and Feit 2003, 308).

Now, where we take this "distinctive feature" of Gettier cases to be indicative of the proposed diagnosis of Chapter 1 (after all, if a given theory of warrant does not entail truth, of course it will be possible for a given belief to be "Gettiered"—to be true for reasons divorced from the warrant), Howard-Snyder et al. take it as directly translatable into a (fallibilism-friendly) anti-Gettier condition on knowledge. Their first proposal:

> S's belief that p is warranted only if S's belief that p is not accidentally true for S.
> (D. Howard-Snyder, F. Howard-Snyder, and Feit 2003, 308)

What does it mean for a belief to be "accidentally true for S"? According to Howard-Snyder et al., "accidentally true for S" is shorthand for "such that what makes p true is not properly related to the reasons for, or processes involved in, S's believing p" (D. Howard-Snyder, F. Howard-Snyder, and Feit 2003, 308). What does it mean for the truth of a given belief to be "properly related" to the relevant reasons or processes involved in S's believing it? Howard-Snyder et al. don't say. Regardless, such a condition certainly seems to eliminate Gettier cases (especially since it seems to translate directly into "S's belief that p is warranted only if S's belief is not 'Gettiered'"), and it seems to do so without committing to infallibilism; according to this condition, it will be possible for a warranted belief to be false since being false "trivially satisfies this condition" (D. Howard-Snyder, F. Howard-Snyder, and Feit 2003, 309).

As Howard-Snyder et al. point out, however, such a condition is arguably not adequate on at least two scores. First, we want a given anti-Gettier condition on warrant to tell us something about the nature of warrant. As they explain:

> Our first candidate fails on this score. The condition it lays down is equivalent to the following disjunctive condition: S's belief that p is warranted only if S's belief that p is false *or* nonaccidentally true for S. It divides the cases into true and false beliefs. What it says about warranted true beliefs is helpful in understanding the nature of warrant: they must be *nonaccidentally* true. But what it says about false beliefs is completely unhelpful. Any old completely unjustified and unreliably formed belief could meet this condition on warrant, so long as it was false. So this condition tells us nothing about the nature of warrant in the case of false belief. (D. Howard-Snyder, F. Howard-Snyder, and Feit 2003, 309)

So, given that Howard-Snyder et al. *want* a condition on warrant that tells us *something* "about the nature of warrant in the case of false belief[s]," we should look elsewhere. The second worry is that their initial proposal seems to imply that being false is an epistemic step in the right direction, since being false trivially satisfies their condition; and insofar as we should avoid avoidable implausibilities, Howard-Snyder et al. again acquiesce that we should look elsewhere (D. Howard-Snyder, F. Howard-Snyder, and Feit 2003, 309).

Thankfully for Howard-Snyder et al.'s account, such worries are easily avoided. The preferable fallibilism-friendly condition on warrant that they endorse is:

> S's belief that p is warranted only if S's belief that p would not be accidentally true for S, if it were true. (D. Howard-Snyder, F. Howard-Snyder, and Feit 2003, 309)

"[T]he distinctive feature of standard Gettier cases," according to Howard-Snyder et al., remember, "is that the reason [S] believes p or the processes involved in his believing p are not properly related to those facts that render p true." As such, what Howard-Snyder et al. have done is straightforwardly convert their diagnosis of Gettier counterexamples into an anti-Gettier condition on warrant; interpreting this latter condition as simply demanding that "S's belief that p" will only be warranted if "the following subjunctive conditional is true: if S's belief that p were true, then it would also be true that what makes p true is properly related to the reasons for, or the processes involved in, S believing p" (D. Howard-Snyder, F. Howard-Snyder, and Feit 2003, 309). And (although we are still not told what it means for the truth that p to be "properly related" to S's believing that p) given (a) that this latter condition avoids the worries afflicting the former condition, and (b) that there is no reason to think this latter condition precludes the possibility of a warranted false belief, Howard-Snyder et al. have seemingly provided us with a fallibilism-friendly way to circumvent the Gettier Problem, without, so they would hold, sacrificing feasibility.

Now, as Howard-Snyder et al. point out, there are several different worries we may have for such a condition on warrant. According to Scott Sturgeon, the difficulty with finding a solution to the Gettier Problem is the difficulty of finding "the minimal link" between warrant and truth without succumbing to Gettier counterexample (Sturgeon 1993, 157). As such, we may worry that Howard-Snyder et al.'s condition does not provide such a *minimal* link.[10] Alternatively, we may, with Linda Zagzebski, simply worry that Howard-Snyder et al.'s condition is "vague, negative, lacks practical import, . . . has little to recommend it theoretically," and "like the definition *justified true belief that is not a Gettier case* . . . ad hoc" (Zagzebski 1999, 103).[11] But so as to avoid devolving into debates regarding vagueness and just how we should understand "minimal" terminology, I want to largely put such worries aside. Instead, I want to focus on a more fundamental problem—the problem that Howard-Snyder et al.'s proposed condition on warrant simply doesn't work; the problem that, in accord with the diagnosis of Gettier counterexamples offered in Chapter 1, Howard-Snyder et al.'s proposed condition will lead either to radical skepticism or further Gettier counterexamples.

Before we do that, however, I do want to consider Zagzebski's objection that Howard-Snyder et al.'s condition on warrant is ad hoc, because regardless of whether or not it falls on the dilemma outlined in the previous chapter, Howard-Snyder et al.'s condition should nevertheless be rejected as ad hockery. In response to Zagzebski's accusation, Howard-Snyder et al. say the following:

> We disagree that our condition is like "justified true belief *that avoids Gettier cases*." Our condition does not express a string of unrelated features with a proper name in it; ours leads to some understanding. More plausibly, perhaps Zagzebski's point is that *no* condition on warrant should be such that its "sole advantage is to answer counterexamples"; it must be "plausible even if no one had ever thought of Gettier cases."[12] But, is adhocery of this sort really a defect? Even if it is, it's not clear that our condition is ad hoc. Why suppose that if no one had thought of Gettier cases, no one would have thought our condition was plausible? (D. Howard-Snyder, F. Howard-Snyder, and Feit 2003, 316)

There are a couple of things worth noting in response. If the Gettier Problem is, as Howard-Snyder et al. seem to claim, the problem of the reasons for a given belief not being "properly related" to what makes the said belief true, then Howard-Snyder et al.'s condition on warrant explicitly and straightforwardly amounts to "S's belief is warranted so long as it avoids Gettier cases." It is certainly no more informative. From the very beginning everyone knew that Gettier problems show that something is wrong with the fit between warrant and truth, so having a general condition that prohibits knowledge of beliefs with "a bad fit" is un-illuminating and patent ad hockery. Telling us that Gettier cases involve "accidentally true beliefs" does not help in the least; we already knew *that*. As such, it is quite clear that no one would have thought of their condition without thinking about Gettier cases, because their condition is a straightforward denial of Gettier cases. Seemingly, someone could not come up with the condition for warrant ¬c without also coming up with c.

Even if Howard-Snyder et al.'s proposed condition on warrant *is* somehow feasible and not ad hoc, I now want to argue that, based on two plausible readings of their condition, it runs into precisely the sort of dilemma predicted by our diagnosis of the Gettier Problem offered in the previous chapter—ironically lending credence to the view that infallibilism is indeed part of Gettier's legacy. I want to argue, in accord with our proposed diagnosis, that no matter how we understand Howard-Snyder et al.'s condition it will seemingly either run into Gettier counterexamples or lead to radical skepticism through infallibilism.

The first plausible reading of Howard-Snyder et al.'s proposed condition of warrant is one where it prohibits luckily true beliefs. I think it is fairly clear that Howard-Snyder et al. could easily be conflating "X is lucky" with "X is accidental" such that when they prohibit accidentally true beliefs (or beliefs whose reasons are not properly related to the belief's truth), they are really prohibiting something like luckily true beliefs.[13] What is more, given their extrapolation of their account (the "properly related" business), it also seems fairly clear that when they prohibit accidentally true beliefs they are really prohibiting something very much like veritically lucky true beliefs of the previous chapter. In other words, it seems like Howard-Snyder et al. could easily be read as prohibiting beliefs that, given the way they were formed, are only luckily true. Now, if this is right, the problems they run into are straightforward. As we noted in the previous chapter, luck comes in degrees, and as we argued, even a minute degree of luck is of significant epistemic import. And given (1) that almost every belief we hold is at least minutely (veritically) lucky and (2) that Gettier counterexamples can be created out of even a minute degree of luck (consider the strengthened version of Dr. Jones and the Virus), then Howard-Snyder et al.'s only hope for avoiding Gettier counterexamples is to make their condition prohibit even marginally lucky beliefs; in so doing, however, they would likely be committing themselves to radical skepticism—seemingly, very few of even our most secure beliefs are completely luck-less. Given that an all-out ban on lucky beliefs would effectively make it impossible for a belief to be warranted and false, ironically, it seems as though the only way Howard-Snyder et al.'s condition, so understood, can *really* avoid Gettier counterexamples is if it commits to infallibilism.

But perhaps that's not the way to read Howard-Snyder et al.'s condition after all, plausible though such an interpretation may be. Perhaps instead, when they prohibit accidentally true beliefs (i.e., beliefs whose reasons do not properly relate to the truth), they are prohibiting beliefs that are somehow true for the wrong reasons (whatever precisely that means)—beliefs that are true for reasons that *your* reasons, evidence, or cognitive processes would not have predicted. Surely this is precisely what is at issue in Gettier counterexamples (and seemingly Howard-Snyder et al. have no qualms with *directly* importing whatever they see as defining Gettier counterexamples into a condition on warrant), so perhaps *this* is the way to read their proposed condition on warrant. Sadly, however, they are going to run into similar troubles as the previous reading. Surely being "true for the right reasons" or being "true for reasons my evidence would predict" is a matter of degree. And seemingly, the vast majority of our beliefs are, to at least some minute extent, going to be true for reasons we could not have predicted. For example, my secure belief that, as I am writing this, I am a "visiting scholar" at Rutgers University is surely knowledge, but it is probably true, at least in part, for reasons my evidence does not account for—reasons like, such and such a form was filled out (which I had nothing to do with) making my tenure at Rutgers official, etc. So surely Howard-Snyder et al. would not want to establish an all-out prohibition on beliefs that are not *entirely* true for the right reasons, reasons predicted by my evidence, because such a prohibition would seemingly push us toward radical skepticism—denying knowledge to most of even our most epistemically secure and everyday beliefs. But unless Howard-Snyder et al. make such a prohibition, it looks as though Gettier counterexamples are going to be inevitable; degrees of luck, as it were, will seemingly map onto degrees of "being true for the right reasons." Consider the following example:

> **The Horticulturalist:** David is an expert horticulturalist, able to competently distinguish between the some 20,000 different species of orchid. David is presented with an orchid and asked to identify its species. Using his amazing skill

he can clearly tell that this particular orchid is either going to be an X-species or a Y-species (which look quite similar), and upon even further expert analysis he comes to the conclusion that it is an X-species of orchid, which it is. However, Kevin, David's nemesis and an expert horticulturalist in his own right, decided the night before to, using his skill as a horticulturalist, make the X-species of orchid look like a Y-species of orchid. Thankfully, however, Alvin, David's other expert horticulturalist nemesis (who is conveniently not on speaking terms with Kevin), decided to try to trick David in the same way—arriving shortly after Kevin left, perceiving that the orchid was a Y-species, and cleverly making it look, once again, like an X-species. As such, while David's belief that the given orchid is an X-species of orchid is largely for the right reasons (he was, after all, able to narrow down the possibilities from over 20,000 to just two), he does not ultimately *know* that it is an X-species of orchid since he was effectively Gettiered by the combined efforts of Kevin and Alvin.

Howard-Snyder et al. could always object that the relevant belief of protagonists like David is not true enough for the right reasons, but strengthened cases can always be produced. As such, given the right-reasons reading, it once again looks as though the only way for Howard-Snyder et al.'s proposed condition on warrant to completely avoid Gettier counterexamples is if it prohibits any belief from being knowledge that is true for any reason not predicted by the given agent's evidence, reasons, or cognitive processes. As such, if Howard-Snyder et al.'s condition is to avoid Gettier counterexamples, it will, in accord with our diagnosis, seemingly lead us to radical skepticism. And insofar as it is not possible for a warranted belief to be false while satisfying "true for the *completely* right reasons" reading of their condition, it looks again as though, ironically, the only way for their condition to surmount the Gettier Problem is to acquiesce to infallibilism.

In Chapter 1, I proposed a diagnosis of the Gettier Problem, which leveled a trilemma against any version of the standard analysis of knowledge (roughly, *warranted true belief*) in accord with the three ways warrant might relate to truth. It was proposed that if we assume that warrant is close but not inviolably connected with truth (i.e., if we assume fallibilism), Gettier counterexamples will be unavoidable. Recent work by Daniel Howard-Snyder, Frances Howard-Snyder, and Neil Feit called this conclusion into question—arguably offering a fallibilist-friendly solution to the Gettier Problem. Thankfully for our proposed diagnosis, however, this solution was found lacking—being ad hoc and (based on two plausible readings) unable to surmount the Gettier Problem without requiring infallibilism (and leading to radical skepticism), which is precisely what Chapter 1's diagnosis would predict. As such, this leg of the trilemma still stands.

Section 2: The Hetherington Objection

Even if we are right that the only way to avoid Gettier counterexamples is to assume either an inviolable (i.e., infallibilistic) relationship between truth and warrant, or no relationship at all, someone may nevertheless deny that such strategies are deeply problematic. While we will see in subsequent chapters that infallibilism is indeed infeasible (leading to radical skepticism in all of the relevant cases), our goal in this subsection is to defend the proposed diagnosis of the Gettier Problem against those who might try to defuse Gettier counterexamples by denying warrant any relationship to truth (i.e., by denying that the luck involved in Gettier cases necessarily precludes knowledge). While it is indeed almost universally accepted that warrant should bear at least *some* relation to truth, we should, for the sake of due diligence, address dissent.

For over a decade, Stephen Hetherington has been perhaps the most eminent and vocal advocate of just such a view—the view that knowledge does not require warrant to bear any relationship to truth. Starting with his landmark book *Good Knowledge, Bad Knowledge* (2001), we will, in this subsection, consider Hetherington's understanding of knowledge and his response to Gettier problems—subsequently arguing that Hetherington's epistemology is simply not viable, especially in light of other proposals now on offer.[14]

Like so many great philosophical projects before it, Hetherington begins *Good Knowledge, Bad Knowledge* with a wholesale rejection of a long-standing and nearly platitudinous assumption in hopes of revitalizing various stale and/or tricky debates. The long-standing assumption that Hetherington wants to call into question is what he calls Epistemic Absolutism:

> **Epistemic Absolutism:** Knowledge is absolute, in the sense that it is impossible for a person to have *better*, or to have *worse*, knowledge of a fact. (Hetherington 2001, 3)

According to Hetherington, most epistemologists assume that knowledge is something that you simply have or lack, that knowledge is something that does not, as he puts it, admit degrees. And while Hetherington grants that there is an absolute point where a given belief will either start or stop being knowledge (i.e., it is not as if Hetherington thinks that all beliefs are some degree of knowledge), he nevertheless thinks that knowledge is the sort of thing that can, once had, become either better or worse.

To be clear, consider the following example:

Flood: One day, at t_1, Bill's uncle, who is known to lie frequently, tells him that there has been a massive flood in Indiana, where Bill is originally from. At t_2, Bill checks the various newspapers and finds that there has indeed been a massive flood in Indiana. Later that day, at t_3, Bill calls various trustworthy friends in Indiana to make sure they are safe and hears their accounts of the flooding.

According to Hetherington, most epistemologists would give Flood the following analysis: while Bill's uncle's testimony may provide some warrant for believing that there has been a flood in Indiana, given the uncle's propensity to lying, Bill does not know that there has been a massive flood in Indiana at t_1; at t_2, after reading the newspapers, Bill is seemingly now warranted enough to know that there has been a massive flood in Indiana; finally, at t_3, Bill now knows, after speaking with his friends, that there has been a massive flood in Indiana *with an even greater degree of warrant*. And it is this analysis of Bill's epistemic state at t_3 with which Hetherington takes issue. Granted that Bill does not know that there has been a massive flood in Indiana at t_1, Hetherington wants to say that surely Bill knows about such flooding far better at t_3 than at t_2. In other words, according to Hetherington, at t_3 Bill not only knows with a higher degree of warrant; *Bill knows to a higher degree in accord with the warrant.*

Now, why should we grant that knowledge admits degrees? What is the payoff of rejecting Epistemic Absolutism? It is not, after all, immediately apparent; indeed, the distinction that Hetherington seems to be making can, at first blush, simply seem like a matter of semantics. Whatever reasons Hetherington gives for rejecting Epistemic Absolutism and whatever merit anti-absolutism brings to various perennial epistemic debates, we need only concern ourselves at this point with how Hetherington applies this anti-absolutism to handle the Gettier Problem.

For Hetherington, Gettier problems will be unavoidable so long as "we see knowledge as being categorical and [warrant] as being gradual"; hence, he proposes that once we see both warrant and knowledge as admitting degrees, "[t]he Gettier Problem will disappear" (Hetherington 2001, 72).[15] How so? Consider the following case:

Dog/Sheep: Standing outside a field you see what seems to you to be a normal sheep. You do not think the false thought, "That is a sheep"; instead, you think the true thought, "That looks exactly like a sheep." From this you infer that there is a sheep in the field. And you are right. But the real sheep in the field is out of sight, hidden from your gaze, eating peacefully in a distant corner of the field. What you are seeing is a dog, disguised in a sheep's fleece. (Hetherington 2001, 71)

The typical analysis of such a case would be that the given protagonist simply lacks the relevant bit of knowledge; Hetherington, however, does not concur. According to Hetherington, all Gettier cases contain what he calls a "Strange Occurrence"; that is, all Gettier cases contain something that makes the "epistemic subject . . . somewhat lucky to have his well-justified true belief" (Hetherington 2001, 73). And instead of precluding knowledge, a Strange Occurrence only weakens the strength of a given epistemic agent's purported knowledge.[16] Hetherington offers the following general elucidation:

(1) If an epistemic subject x knows that *p* within a normal (non-Gettier) situation, then none of the close—the similar—accessible worlds, as regards that knowledge of x's, are epistemic-failure worlds for x in relation to *p*. That is, in every close world were at least two of the three traditional components of x's knowing that *p* are present, the third component is present. Because (on our hypothesis), x knows that *p* in a normal way, that normality is also present within any very close worlds where at least two of those traditional components are present, with the result—the normal result, after all—being that the third component is also present. (2) On the other hand, if x knows that *p* within a Gettier situation, then there *are* some close accessible worlds, as regards that knowledge, that are epistemic-failure worlds for x in relation to *p*. This is because the close accessible worlds, as regards x's knowing that *p* within a Gettier case, are not simply worlds where at least two of the three traditional components of x's knowing that *p* are present; they are also worlds containing the Strange Occurrence from x's Gettier situation. And in some of these worlds the Strange Occurrence's presence ensures that the third traditional component of x's knowing that *p* is not present. Relative to a specific case, there need not be worlds like this for each one of the three components, but there will be some for at least one of the three. For example, the luck with which, given the Strange Occurrence, x's good evidence for *p* and his believing that *p* coincided in this world's Gettier situation with *p*'s being true might be modelled by there being some close truth-failure worlds for x in relation to *p*—some close truth-failure worlds for x in relation to *p*, that is, where the Strange Occurrence is present. (Hetherington 2001, 76–7)

Applying his degree-theoretic analysis of knowledge, Hetherington reinterprets Gettier cases like Dog/Sheep as exhibiting weak or "failable" knowledge. To put it roughly, knowledge is failable, according to Hetherington, if it nearly wasn't knowledge; in other words, S's knowledge is failable if in some close possible worlds S does not have it.[17] As such, instead of showing that the warranted true belief is insufficient for knowledge, Gettier cases simply show that knowledge might be largely (though not completely) undermined, by showing how knowledge might be very weak or failable. All this being correct, Hetherington thinks he has dissolved the Gettier Problem.

But the main problem with this proposed solution to Gettier counterexamples is that it misidentifies what is actually doing the work. Despite Hetherington's express claim that the Gettier Problem will dissolve once knowledge is acknowledged to admit degrees, Hetherington's anti-absolutism, his rejection of Epistemic Absolutism, in itself *plays absolutely no role in solving Gettier counterexamples*. Assume for the sake of argument that, while knowledge has an absolute cutoff point (i.e., a point where a given belief will either start or stop being knowledge), knowledge nevertheless admits of degrees. Let us also make the reasonable assumption that warrant, that which bridges the gap between true belief and knowledge, should bear some close but not inviolable relation to truth if a given belief is to be knowledge. With these two assumptions, Hetherington's anti-absolutist epistemology seems every bit as stymied by Gettier cases like Dog/Sheep as standard absolutist epistemologies. The protagonist's warrant for believing that "there is a sheep in the field" is critically disconnected from the belief's truth, and, as such, the relevant belief simply falls short of knowledge given our second assumption that warrant should bear some close though not inviolable relationship to truth; the anti-absolutism does not even come into play.

In accord with Chapter 1, what *is* solving the Gettier Problem for Hetherington is his tacit assumption that warrant need not bear *any* relationship to truth. Consider how he described normal (non-Gettier) epistemic circumstances versus Gettier circumstances earlier: normal (non-Gettier) epistemic circumstances are roughly those where all three components for knowledge (warrant, truth, belief) are simply "present" in all close possible worlds; Gettier circumstances are roughly those where at least one of the said components is not "present" in some close possible worlds. Knowledge, for Hetherington, is seemingly like a recipe; simply add equal parts truth and belief and a sufficient amount of warrant, stir, and then you will have knowledge (to some degree). Indeed, if warrant can be completely divorced from truth, we may wonder whether warrant was really necessary for knowledge in the first place; as such, it should come as no surprise that this is exactly the sort of view that Hetherington eventually endorses. In *Good Knowledge, Bad Knowledge* (2001), "Is There a World Where Knowledge

Has to Include Justification?" (2007), and "Elusive Epistemological Justification" (2010), Hetherington, rather shockingly, posits that mere true belief can suffice for knowledge.[18] But this is clearly a radical break from the typical understanding of knowledge. In any case, Hetherington assumes that warrant need not bear any relationship to truth. And it is this assumption that helps him solve the Gettier Problem, and it is this assumption that puts him radically at odds with the practices and intuitions of most epistemologists.

Of course, one of the main problems with such an assumed theory of knowledge is that it is *extremely* counterintuitive when it comes to Gettier-type cases. We can, to be sure, question the philosophical merit of such intuitions (and we will consider some philosophers who do just this in Section 3), but insofar as Hetherington wants to somehow honor or account for such Gettier intuitions (as I think any viable epistemology should), his proposed solution to the Gettier Problem is deeply problematic. And Hetherington does seem to try to honor or account for Gettier intuitions in at least two ways. First, Hetherington tries to defuse Gettier intuitions by arguing that to deny knowledge in Gettier scenarios is to commit what he calls *the epistemic counterfactuals fallacy*. Second, Hetherington tries to account for Gettier intuitions through his rejection of Epistemic Absolutism. We will now consider both strategies in turn.

First, in an attempt to address or at least account for the aforementioned Gettier intuitions, Hetherington argues that such intuitions rest on an easily made mistake, namely, the mistake of conflating *almost possessing knowledge* with *genuinely not possessing knowledge*—a mistake Hetherington identifies as *the epistemic counterfactual fallacy*. As Hetherington explains:

> Within each Gettier case, the epistemic subject knows, because he has a well-[warranted] true belief. But he is very lucky to have all that (and thereby the knowledge). This luck is a mark of how very failably he knows within the Gettier case. He does know—even though he almost failed to do so. He does know—even though he is very close to not doing so. Consider an analogous situation. Maybe there is luck involved in life's ever having come to exist in this universe. There are so many possible and slight differences to the universe's initial conditions that, had they been actual, would not have led to the creation of life. So, by having the initial conditions it had, the universe was close to having different initial conditions—and thereby to not containing life. Nevertheless, it did not have those different initial conditions. Most of us do not say that consequently there are no natural laws within the universe. There are, in spite of the luck involved in their obtaining. And failable knowing within a Gettier case is like that. In each such case, the epistemic subject is very close to failing to know that *p*. He almost

fails to know that *p*. And his being so close to failing to know that *p* is what misleads people into thinking that he does fail to know that *p*. Instead, we may say that his being so close to not knowing that *p* is simply part of his knowing very failably that *p*. (Hetherington 2001, 82)

Gettier cases, for Hetherington, are scenarios where at least one of the three general ingredients for knowledge (warrant, truth, and belief) is almost not present. As such, Gettier cases are, for Hetherington, simply cases where a given protagonist almost lacks knowledge: so to deny the said protagonist's knowledge is, by Hetherington's light, to commit the epistemic counterfactual fallacy. Just as we would not deny knowledge to someone who was almost struck by lightning, we should not deny knowledge to someone whose belief is almost not true, say.

But this is a confused understanding of Gettier cases.[19] Gettier cases are not simply scenarios where one of the essential ingredients for knowledge is almost missing. As we saw in the previous chapter, luck regarding the existence of a given belief (Doxastic Epistemic Luck), the truth of a given belief (Content Epistemic Luck), or the warrant of a given belief (Evidential Epistemic Luck) are all epistemically benign and manifestly *not* the luck at issue in Gettier problems; Gettier cases are scenarios that exhibit luck regarding the truth of a given belief in relation to the relevant warrant (Veritic Epistemic Luck). As such, scenarios like Hetherington's existence of life example are simply *not* analogous. Given the analysis of luck provided in the previous chapter, Gettier cases are not scenarios where a given protagonist almost does not have knowledge; they are cases where, given the kind of luck at issue, the protagonist genuinely does indeed lack knowledge.

What about the aforementioned second strategy? Hetherington tries to account for Gettier intuitions through his rejection of Epistemic Absolutism by arguing that Gettier cases only *seem* to lack knowledge because they are, in fact, very bad (i.e., very failable) instances of knowledge that do indeed fail to be knowledge in close possible worlds (Hetherington 2001, 88–92). As Hetherington explains, identifying the knowledge in Gettier scenarios as *very* failable "does justice to the feeling that there must be a difference in the quality of the instances of knowing in, respectively, a normal situation where there is failable knowledge that *p*, and a Gettier situation where there is failable knowledge that *p*" (Hetherington 2001, 76). But given what has been said in the previous chapter, this strategy is now clearly defunct. Gettier cases, it has been argued, can be created for any belief that is not knowledge in all possible worlds; if luck comes in degrees (as it seemingly does), even very "good" instances of knowledge in Hetherington's estimation can be Gettiered. As such, Hetherington cannot invoke a good knowledge/bad knowledge distinction to save face when it comes to Gettier intuitions.

In the preface to *Good Knowledge, Bad Knowledge*, Hetherington says that the "main justification" for his epistemic project is its ability to solve "many of epistemology's traditional puzzles" (Hetherington 2001, vi). But insofar as (i) Hetherington's solution to that traditional puzzle of central importance, the Gettier Problem, leads to an extremely counterintuitive analysis of knowledge (an analysis that says, at best, warrant need not relate to truth at all, and at worst that mere true belief is sufficient for knowledge) and (ii) other more viable alternative solutions (such as Timothy Williamson's) are on offer, it seems Hetherington's "main justification" is undermined. As such, the infeasibility of assuming a divorced relationship between truth and warrant, the third leg of my trilemma, still holds.

Section 3: Two Meta-objections

Having defended two of the legs of Zagzebski's trilemma (the third leg being vindicated throughout the second part of this book), we now turn to consider some meta-objections against taking Gettier counterexamples seriously to begin with. While this book is largely based on the reasonable and widespread assumption that Gettier counterexamples *should* be taken seriously, it is nevertheless worth considering some such meta-objections that can be found in the literature. That said, however, my aim in this section is relatively weak; I do not intend to disprove the pertinent meta-objections wholly but simply to cast sufficient doubt on them.[20]

In this section, we will consider two such meta-objections—both focusing on the epistemic import of the Gettier intuition (e.g., the intuition that Gettier counterexamples are genuine counterexamples). The first meta-objection comes from the paper, "Normativity and Epistemic Intuitions" (2001), by Jonathan M. Weinberg, Shaun Nichols, and Stephen Stich, in which Weinberg et al. claim that the intuitions that have generated the strong response to Gettier counterexamples (e.g., earnestly trying to avoid being vulnerable to Gettier cases) are culturally relative and as such are "seriously undermined" (Weinberg, Nichols, and Stich 2001, 429). The second meta-objection comes from Brian Weatherson's paper, "What Good Are Counterexamples?" (2003), in which Weatherson argues that intuitions are regularly unreliable and particularly unreliable when it comes to Gettier counterexamples—insisting that we should champion "a simple, systematic and largely successful theory [of knowledge]" over "respecting" the Gettier intuition (Weatherson 2003, 1). We will now consider each of these objections in turn.

Section 3.1: Weinberg et al.'s Objection

In their landmark paper in experimental philosophy, Jonathan M. Weinberg, Shaun Nichols, and Stephen Stich call into question the philosophical import of intuitions (including our intuitions regarding Gettier counterexamples) through a series of empirical observations. They argue, roughly, that if key epistemic intuitions are not shared across cultures or across socioeconomic demographics, then their evidential value in our philosophical theorizing is largely undermined. In this subsection, I first briefly elucidate Weinberg et al.'s argument and consider an example of their purported empirical observation regarding intuitions in Gettier counterexamples. I will then argue that (1) we have very good reason to be extremely skeptical of Weinberg et al.'s findings, and (2) that their empirical observations, even if generally correct, are not a threat to taking epistemic intuitions very seriously in our philosophical theorizing.

Weinberg et al. argue for the following two claims:

> [F]irst . . . that a sizeable group of epistemological projects—a group which includes much of what has been done in epistemology in the analytic tradition—would be seriously undermined if one or more of a cluster of empirical hypotheses about epistemic intuitions turns out to be true. . . . [S]econd . . . that, while the jury is still out, there is now a substantial body of evidence suggesting that some of those empirical hypotheses *are* true. (Weinberg, Nichols, and Stich 2001, 429)

These two claims, of course, can be nicely summarized in a simple modus ponens argument:

P1: If one or more of a cluster of empirical hypotheses are true, a sizable group of epistemic projects would be seriously undermined.

P2: One or more of a cluster of empirical hypotheses are true.

C: Therefore, a sizable group of epistemic projects are seriously undermined.

While their goal is expressly "not to offer a conclusive argument demonstrating that . . . [such] epistemological projects . . . are untenable," they do want to force those of us who take such projects seriously to offer a defense—to put the burden of proof on those who wish to work within that given "sizable group of epistemological projects" (Weinberg, Nichols, and Stich 2001, 430).

Now, just what is this "sizable group of epistemological projects" that are so threatened by Weinberg et al.'s yet unspecified empirical hypotheses? What are the defining characteristics of the epistemic projects Weinberg et al. wish to critique? To quote, the epistemic projects Weinberg et al. have in mind will meet the following three conditions:

(i) The [project] must take epistemic intuitions as data or input. (It can also exploit various other sorts of data.)
(ii) It must produce, as output, explicitly or implicitly normative claims or principles about matters epistemic. Explicitly normative claims include regulative claims about how we ought to go about the business of belief formation, claims about the relative merits of various strategies for belief formation, and evaluative claims about the merits of various epistemic situations. Implicitly normative claims include claims to the effect that one or another process of belief formation leads to justified beliefs or to real knowledge or that a doxastic structure of a certain kind amounts to real knowledge.
(iii) The output of the [project] must depend, in part, on the epistemic intuitions it takes as input. If provided with significantly different intuitions, the strategy must yield significantly different output.
(Weinberg, Nichols, and Stich 2001, 432)

Weinberg et al. call the "sizable group of epistemological projects" that satisfy the abovementioned conditions *Intuition-Driven Romanticism* (hereafter IDR).[21] And most importantly given our purposes, one of the projects under the umbrella of IDR is the enterprise of taking the intuitions generated by Gettier-style counterexamples as of normative import in the project of defining knowledge. Subsequently, it is Weinberg et al.'s contention that if one or more of the given set of yet unspecified hypotheses is true, the strategy of using the Gettier Problem to motivate various epistemic conclusions (the very thing being done in this book) is "seriously undermined."

Just what are these volatile hypotheses that Weinberg et al. mentioned, which, if true, seriously undermine various projects in analytic epistemology (including responses to the Gettier Problem)? They are:

Hypothesis 1: Epistemic intuitions vary from culture to culture.

Hypothesis 2: Epistemic intuitions vary from one socioeconomic group to another.

Hypothesis 3: Epistemic intuitions vary as a function of how many philosophy courses a person has had.

Hypothesis 4: Epistemic intuitions depend, in part, on the order in which cases are presented. (Weinberg, Nichols, and Stich 2001, 437–8)

The general worry, here, is clear enough. If people of other demographics (i.e., people of demographics outside professional analytic epistemology) have significantly different intuitions regarding foundational epistemic issues, then, assuming we have no plausible way to champion our own intuitions over all others, the motivational force behind IDR projects seems to evaporate—IDR will be "significantly undermined."

But why think at least one of the abovementioned hypotheses is true? Why, for example, think that people in different cultures or people with different socioeconomic backgrounds have radically divergent epistemic intuitions about key issues in epistemology? Well, straightforwardly, Weinberg et al. asked people from different cultures and socioeconomic backgrounds what their intuitions are regarding key issues in epistemology and found that they do indeed differ starkly from the intuitions of highly educated Westerners (the general demographic of analytic philosophers). In other words, Weinberg et al. tested Hypothesis 1 and Hypothesis 2 using empirical experiments (which Weinberg et al. called "intuition probes"), and, while they admit their findings are not conclusive, their findings suggest that both hypotheses are quite plausibly true. Using a sociological "ethnic identification questionnaire," Weinberg et al. were able to classify people around New Brunswick, New Jersey (usually undergraduates at Rutgers University), as "Western," "East Asian," etc. (Weinberg, Nichols, and Stich 2001, 439, 457). So classified, Weinberg et al. gauged the epistemic intuitions of different ethnicities using a simple survey. For example, both East Asians and Westerners were asked whether the protagonist in the following Gettier counterexample either "Really Knows" or "Only Believes":

> **American Car:** Bob has a friend, Jill, who has driven a Buick for many years. Bob therefore thinks that Jill drives an American car. He is not aware, however, that her Buick has recently been stolen, and he is also unaware that Jill has replaced it with a Pontiac, which is a different kind of American car. Does Bob really know that Jill drives an American car, or does he only believe it? (Weinberg, Nichols, and Stich 2001, 443)

Interestingly, Weinberg et al. found that there was a stark difference here between the intuitions of Westerners and the intuitions of East Asians. Consider the graph in Figure 2.2 portraying how Westerners and East Asians responded respectively.

To quote Weinberg et al.: "The striking finding in this case is that a large majority of [Westerners] give the standard answer in the philosophical literature, viz., 'Only Believes.' But among [East Asians] this pattern is actually *reversed*! A majority of [East Asians] say that Bob really knows" (Weinberg, Nichols, and Stich 2001, 443). And given that Weinberg et al. found similar incongruity between the epistemic intuitions of various ethnic and socioeconomic groups in similar tests, doesn't that give us good reason to suspect the philosophical import of intuitions? Doesn't that undermine their use in philosophical argument?

Not necessarily. To start, we have very good reason to be skeptical of Weinberg et al.'s findings—of their empirical experiments or "intuition probes." First of all, it's worth noting that psychological surveys are tricky endeavors—fraught with perils of false data and false conclusions—even when conducted by trained psychologists. These findings were from the early days of the emerging field of experimental philosophy, and experimental philosophers were (at that time) a bit more "loosey goosey" regarding methods. For example, do East Asians operate with a significantly different conception of "knows" than Westerners do? That's a real possibility that's not accounted for in their methods.[22] Perhaps, if East Asians were to reflect on "knowledge" in the way that Westerners use "knowledge," their intuitions may not vary at all.

But what is more, the sampling done by Weinberg et al. is questionable on at least two counts: (1) surveying undergraduates at one of the researcher's (in this case Stich's) own institution is increasingly seen as a somewhat dubious way to collect data. And (2) Weinberg et al.'s sample size in their experiments is sometimes abysmally small—sometimes as few as 8 (!) individuals are surveyed to represent a population of over a billion souls. As such, the margin of error in Weinberg et al.'s findings is going to be staggeringly huge—making their results very easy to dismiss offhand.

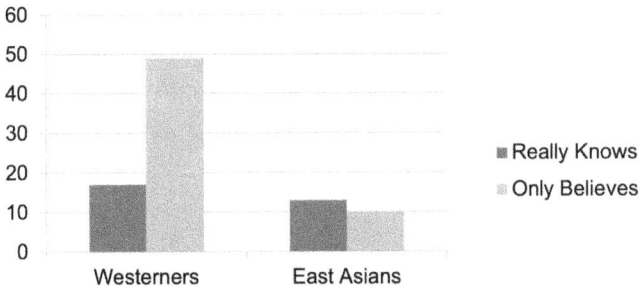

Figure 2.2 Weinberg, Nichols, and Stich Gettier results.

That said, to their credit, Weinberg et al. are quick to acknowledge that their research does not and cannot *prove* that the epistemic intuitions of East Asians genuinely differ (on average) from the epistemic intuitions of Westerners. Their goal is much more modest; they simply want to make the case that we can't take it for granted that epistemic intuitions are stable across various demographics. If philosophical intuitions do indeed diverge across various demographics, then (barring some reason to prefer one group's intuitions over others) we might legitimately worry that such intuitions shouldn't be theory guiding.[23]

And in many cases, such a worry is well-founded. Sometimes philosophical intuitions do indeed seem to diverge in ways that give us reason to pause and wonder whether we can viably take such intuitions to underwrite our philosophizing.[24] That said, when it comes to intuitions regarding the Gettier Problem—our primary focus in this book—subsequent research has found that such intuitions are remarkably stable across a wide array of demographics. Most notably, Kim and Yuan (2015) ran a replication of Weinberg et al.'s 2001 study and did not find significant variations in intuitions regarding Gettier thought experiments across the target demographics. Other research has also more broadly pointed in this direction (see, for example, Knobe 2019, 2021, Machery et al. 2015).[25] All this helps dissipate the worry that such empirical findings might undermine any project that might take Gettier intuitions seriously—projects like the one found in this book!

As a bit of an aside, even if we grant that the intuitions that underwrite Gettier counterexamples are fairly stable across various demographics, we might wonder if this empirical research could still threaten the *reductive analysis project*. In other words, while I don't think the abovementioned considerations force us to abandon Gettier cases as theory guiding, we might wonder if such empirical research might, if anything, force us to question the legitimacy of the epistemic project that gave rise to the Problem, namely the project of defining knowledge in terms of a reductive analysis.[26] We might plausibly hypothesize that treating "knowledge" like "bachelor" in that way—defining a concept in terms of necessary and jointly sufficient conditions—is psychologically bizarre when viewed across both various demographics but also the span of human history. If confirmed, such a hypothesis might give us further reason to abandon the reductive analysis project—motivating the search for other options.

Section 3.2: Weatherson's Objection

In "What Good Are Counterexamples?" (2003), Brian Weatherson calls into question the intuitions behind Gettier counterexamples—arguing that they are (at least in the case of the Gettier Problem) unreliable and should not be respected at the loss of the standard analysis of knowledge. While a large portion of the paper (over half) is devoted to elucidating the naturalness of meaning in proposed definitions of knowledge and defending the standard analysis against psychologists (see Rosch and Mervis 1975) and those who would take the standard analysis as woefully out of step with folk epistemology (see Stich 1988), our main concern in this subsection is Weatherson's critique of the Gettier intuition. I will argue (1) that Weatherson's reasons for questioning the Gettier intuition are largely misguided and (2) that following Weatherson in discrediting the Gettier intuition generalizes widely so as to lead to "an untenable kind of skepticism" (Weatherson 2003, 4).

Epistemologists, according to Weatherson, generally take intuitions regarding counterexamples far more seriously than ethicists. When an epistemologist encounters a counterexample to a given analysis of knowledge, the classic response has been to reject the given analysis—the counterexample being independently sufficient for undermining the said analysis. Ethicists, according to Weatherson, are far more inhibited regarding the ramifications for counterexamples. When a utilitarian, for example, is presented with a counterexample (perhaps a scenario that seems to suggest that torturing a few individuals to increase the happiness of the majority is, counterintuitively, the moral course of action), the typical response is *not* to dismiss utilitarianism at once. While such counterexamples are taken seriously, ethicists simply do not seem to attribute the same theoretical import to counterexamples as epistemologists do. And at the very least, Weatherson wants to argue that epistemologists should take a cue from ethicists here—considering counterexamples in light of additional factors.

After all, as Weatherson notes, "whether something seems to be true can be independent of whether we believe it to be true" (Weatherson 2003, 3). In other words, just because a given counterexample suggests that such and such, it need not necessitate our believing that such and such. For example, to quote Weatherson:

> Frege's Axiom V seems to be true though we know it is false. It does not seem to be the case, in the relevant sense, that $643 \times 721 = 463603$. Unless one is rather good at mental arithmetic, there is nothing that 643×721 seems to be; it is out of the reach of intuition.... One can judge that something seems to be the case while neither believing nor disbelieving it. This is a sensible attitude to take towards the view that one cannot *know* that a particular ticket will lose in a fair lottery. This is despite the fact that it certainly *seems* one cannot know this. (Weatherson 2003, 3)

Such a realization can seemingly help us limit the damage counterexamples do to a given theory. Just as there may be cases where utilitarianism seems to get the wrong result, we may very well go on believing in utilitarianism for other reasons. Accordingly, Gettier counterexamples may very well seem to be cases where warranted true beliefs fail to acquire knowledge, but that need not keep us from believing that the warranted true belief analysis of knowledge is correct for other reasons.

But what is more, given that intuitions (such as our intuition that Frege's Axiom V is true) are regularly mistaken, it seems as though we need independent reason to think that the intuitions at play in the relevant cases (i.e., Gettier cases) are right before we can assign them any significant philosophical importance. To quote Weatherson:

> Given . . . that the example of Axiom V shows that seemings can be mistaken, what evidence have we that they are not mistaken in cases we consider here? Arguably, we have very little indeed. Robert Cummins (1998) argues that in general intuition should not be trusted as an evidential source because it cannot be calibrated.[27] We wouldn't have trusted the evidence Galileo's telescope gave us about the moon without an independent reason for thinking his telescope reliable. Fortunately this can be done; we can point the telescope at far away terrestrial mountains, and compare its findings with the findings of examining the mountains up close and personal. There is no comparable way of calibrating intuitions. Clearly we should [be] suspicious of any method that has been tested and found unreliable, but there are tricky questions about the appropriate level of trust in methods that have not been tested. (Weatherson 2003, 4)

Regularly, people do indeed seem to have faulty intuitions regarding questions of logic (cf. the rate of error in the Wason Selection Task), and people do indeed regularly have conflicting if not contradictory intuitions regarding various moral issues (after all, we can't all be right), so the evidential role of intuitions should seemingly be duly limited until we have reason to think the given intuition is a good (i.e., a reliably truth-conducive) one.

All this is to say we should not necessarily let some pesky counterexamples get in the way of championing "a simple, systematic and largely successful theory" (Weatherson 2003, 1). In other words, given that intuitions are not necessarily belief guiding and given that intuitions are regularly mistaken, we should not, according to Weatherson, abandon the standard analysis of knowledge in the face of Gettier counterexamples. The quality of a given theory should (minus reasons to the contrary) trump counterexamples. The Gettier Problem, according to Weatherson, "is not in itself decisive" (Weatherson 2003, 2).

When determining the robustness of a given theory, we should not simply consider whether or not it is prone to counterexample (important though that may be), but we should also consider whether or not the given theory is *systematic*. According to Weatherson:

> [T]he true theory of knowledge is the one that does best at (a) accounting for as many as possible of our intuitions about knowledge while (b) remaining systematic. A "theory" that simply lists our intuitions is no theory at all, so condition (b) is vital. And it is condition (b), when fully expressed, that will do most of the work in justifying the preservation of the [standard analysis] theory in the face of the counterexamples. (Weatherson 2003, 7)

To elaborate, there are, according to Weatherson, four criteria, four tests, we should use to judge a given philosophical theory. First, as we might expect, a given theory should avoid counterexamples—"counterexamples to a theory," as Weatherson acquiesces, "count against it" (Weatherson 2003, 8). Second, a given philosophical theory should not "have too many *theoretical* consequences which are unacceptable" (Weatherson 2003, 8). Third, a given philosophical theory should analyze concepts that are "theoretically significant" and in such a way that they can be "analysed in other theoretically significant terms" (Weatherson 2003, 9). And fourth, a given philosophical theory should be appraised in accord with its simplicity—a successful philosophical theory "must be simple" (Weatherson 2003, 9).

While it is not entirely clear what these criteria amount to, the conclusion Weatherson draws from them is explicit:

> My main claim is that even once we have accepted that the [standard analysis] theory seems to say the wrong thing about Gettier cases, we should still keep an open mind to the question of whether it is true. The right theory of knowledge, the one that attributes the correct meaning to the word "knows," will do best on balance at these four tests. Granted that the [standard analysis] theory does badly on test one, it seems to do better than its rivals on tests two, three, and four, and this may be enough to make it correct. (Weatherson 2003, 10)

Why think a thing like that? Why, for example, think that the standard analysis is better at avoiding unacceptable theoretical consequences, better at elucidating significant concepts, and simpler than competing definitions of knowledge such as, say, Timothy Williamson's? Weatherson simply does not say. But without any clear reason to champion the standard analysis over rival theories using Weatherson's criteria, the standard analysis's shortcomings regarding Gettier counterexamples are uncomfortably conspicuous. Nevertheless, perhaps Weatherson's weaker point stands; perhaps we should "keep an open mind" regarding the truth of the standard analysis even in light of Gettier counterexamples. After all, if the standard analysis is, as Weatherson claims, "simple, systematic, and largely successful," perhaps we should give it more credit.

While an acquiescence that the standard analysis *may* yet be a successful philosophical theory despite the Gettier Problem is not necessarily incompatible with my proposed thesis, we should nevertheless cast some doubt on Weatherson's optimism. Is it really the case that the standard analysis is "simple, systematic, and largely successful"? Arguably, the standard analysis as we know it did not take shape until Edmund Gettier's famous paper. While no doubt the thought that knowledge involved warrant, truth, and belief can be found in pre-Gettier literature (e.g., Plato's *Meno*), we should nevertheless be skeptical as to whether or not viewing such concepts as conceptually primitive necessary and jointly sufficient conditions on knowledge has a long and illustrious history. In many ways, it seems as though the Gettier Problem gave birth to the standard analysis of knowledge, in which case calling it "largely successful" is a bit hasty, to say the least. Our contemporary understanding of the standard analysis may well be simple and systematic (though seemingly no *more* simple or *more* systematic than the rival theories), but in calling it "largely successful" when the problem that more or less birthed it has yet to be solved seems uncalled for.

While we certainly may question Weatherson's optimism regarding the virtues of the standard analysis, we can also question his pessimism regarding our intuitions in Gettier counterexamples. Weatherson contrasts the way epistemologists and ethicists typically respond to intuitions in counterexamples. Epistemologists, as shown in their response to Gettier cases, typically seem to take such intuitions as independently sufficient for rejecting the given theory of knowledge. Ethicists, says Weatherson, are more reserved. When utilitarianism faces a hypothetical scenario where it intuitively produces the wrong result (results such as "it's permissible to torture a few individuals if it benefits the majority"), utilitarianism is not at once dismissed. Ethicists, it seems, put less philosophical stock in such intuitions. But it is worth pointing out that Gettier counterexamples have important disanalogies with such counterexamples contra utilitarianism. In the case of the latter, we have conflicting intuitions; under many circumstances what seems like the right thing to do is to increase happiness (or well-being) as much as possible; we have intuitions in favor of utilitarianism *qua* utilitarianism. As such, when utilitarians face counterexamples, they usually already have strong intuitions in their favor—giving them a position from which to try to undermine or dismiss the contrary intuitions generated by the counterexample. Defenders of the standard analysis are seemingly not in the same position. Seemingly, we do not have much in the way of strong intuitions in favor of the standard analysis *qua* the standard analysis. While we surely have the intuition that knowledge involves truth, belief, and something like warrant, none of this distinctly favors the standard analysis over, say, a Williamsonian model. As such, when epistemologists see Gettier counterexamples, it seems perfectly understandable and reasonable when they dismiss the given analysis—it does not, after all, seem to have any intuitions going specifically in its favor. If an ethical theory was in such circumstances (with counterexamples against it and with nothing else clearly and specifically for it), ethicists seemingly would be every bit as cavalier as epistemologists in dismissing the given theory on those very grounds.

What about Weatherson's claim (via Cummins) that intuitions are generally not a trusted source of evidence since they cannot be calibrated? Someone certainly might worry that such a wholesale besmirching of intuitions may generalize to, say, perception and lead to a form of skepticism; perception, after all, might seem equally unable to be calibrated. Ernest Sosa (1998) levels just this sort of objection against Cummins, and Weatherson has a response in turn.[28] To quote:

> Ernest Sosa (1998) argues in response to Cummins that this kind of reasoning leads to an untenable kind of scepticism. Sosa notes that one can make the same point about perception as Cummins makes about intuition: we have no independent way of calibrating perception as a whole. There is a distinction to be drawn here, since perception divides into natural kinds, visual perception, tactile perception, etc., and we can use each of these to calibrate the others. It is hard to see how intuitions can be so divided in ways that permit us to check some kinds of intuitions against the others. In any case, the situation is probably worse than Cummins suggests, since we know that several intuitions are just false. (Weatherson 2003, 4)

But is this a sufficiently compelling response? Sosa's objection is that besmirching the evidential value of intuition because it cannot be calibrated means that we should seemingly equally besmirch the evidential value of perception *on the whole*. Given that such a conclusion puts us in the grip of skepticism, we shouldn't so besmirch intuition. And it is not entirely clear how it can be of any help to note that we can use some types of perception to gauge the accuracy of other types of perception. We seemingly have a whole host of intuitions that range across a wide range of domains; why can't we use our intuitions in certain domains to gauge the accuracy of intuitions in others? This is, after all, precisely what we sometimes seem to do. Say a contestant is trying to win a car on the Monty Hall show by guessing which of three doors has the car hidden behind it. When Monty reveals that one of the two unchosen doors does not have the car behind it, we may initially have the intuition that the contestant now has a 50/50 chance of winning the car (there are, after all, only two doors left) and would be in no better probabilistic position if he were to now switch doors. We can, however, gauge the accuracy of such an intuition by bringing to bear some of our other basic intuitions regarding probability and probabilistic reasoning; we can judge our initial intuition false while working to develop new and more robust intuitions about the contestant's chances at winning the car.[29] And pointing out that intuitions are sometimes wrong, to be sure, does nothing to assuage Sosa's worry because perceptions, clearly, are sometimes wrong too.

There is, however, another more troubling way Weatherson's besmirching (via Cummins) of the evidential value of intuitions seems to lead to an untenable kind of skepticism. There is good reason to think that the vast majority of our philosophical theorizing is critically undergirded by a vast array of intuitions, such that one should worry that sullying the evidential value of intuitions affectively takes the floor out from under us. One pressing example: if we systematically question the value of our intuitions in Gettier counterexamples, we should in the same way question Weatherson's intuition that a good theory of knowledge should, say, be systematic and simple. In questioning the Gettier intuition, Weatherson will likely have no way to champion the standard analysis because any intuition that seems to do so will be equally questionable. Not only, then, do we have a reason to think that Weatherson is leading us to a far-reaching skepticism, but we should also seemingly worry that Weatherson is leading us down a road that is ultimately self-defeating.

Both "Normativity and Epistemic Intuitions" (2001) by Jonathan M. Weinberg, Shaun Nichols, and Stephen Stich and "What Good Are Counterexamples?" (2003) by Brian Weatherson call into question the philosophical import of our intuitions, particularly our epistemic intuitions when it comes to Gettier counterexamples. Given (1) that such views are undeniably in the minority (at least for those of us working within analytic epistemology) and (2) that the current thesis is ultimately aimed at those of us who do take Gettier intuitions seriously (the majority), we are not under any great onus to respond to such views in detail. Nevertheless, we have seen in this subsection various positive reasons to reject both Weinberg et al.'s and Weatherson's arguments—leaving us all the more comfortable (and justified) in working under common post-Gettier assumptions.

Conclusion

At the end of Chapter 1, we may have felt some residual worries that questioned the parameters of the proposed diagnosis of the Gettier Problem: worries about whether or not assuming an inviolable relationship between warrant and truth really leads to radical skepticism; worries about whether assuming a close (though not inviolable) relationship between warrant and truth really leads to further Gettier counterexamples; worries about whether assuming that warrant bears no relationship to truth is, in fact, counterintuitive; and worries about the epistemic import of Gettier-styled counterexamples themselves.

In this chapter, we have considered the best the contemporary philosophical literature has to offer in promotion of these latter three concerns, and we have found them all lacking. In the first section, we considered Daniel Howard-Snyder, Frances Howard-Snyder, and Neil Feit's paper, "Infallibilism and Gettier's Legacy" (2003), which directly objected to our conclusion in the previous chapter that a close but not inviolable relationship between warrant and truth will always lead to Gettier counterexamples; and I argued that their proposed solution to the Gettier Problem is, ironically, successful only insofar as it conforms to the proposed diagnosis. In the second section, we considered recent work by Stephen Hetherington (particularly his book *Good Knowledge, Bad Knowledge* 2001), which proposed an analysis of knowledge that assumes a divorced relationship between warrant and truth; and I argue that Hetherington's epistemology is hopelessly counterintuitive and that it need not be advocated in light of viable alternatives. Finally, in Section 3, we considered landmark papers by Brian Weatherson (2003) and Jonathan M. Weinberg, Shaun Nichols, and Stephen Stich (2003), which call into question the epistemic import of Gettier counterexamples; and I argue that such criticisms either lead to intractable forms of skepticism or are ultimately incoherent or self-defeating.

But what about the first worry—the worry that assuming an inviolable relationship between warrant and truth will not really lead to radical skepticism? While it may seem very intuitive that requiring warrant to infallibly track truth will lead to skepticism, and while infallibilistic accounts of warrant indeed have a long history of doing just that, we do not have a systematic reason to think that assuming an inviolable relationship between warrant and truth will *always* lead to radical skepticism. While the diagnosis of the Gettier Problem proposed in Chapter 1 gives us reason to think that Gettier counterexamples will always occur so long as we assume a close (but not inviolable) relationship between warrant and truth, we nevertheless might doubt that skepticism *always* follows infallibilism about warrant—as intuitive as such an assumption may be. And while the accounts considered thus far (e.g., Pritchard's account, Howard-Snyder et al.'s account, etc.) have all confirmed our suspicions, perhaps virtue epistemology has something special to offer that these other accounts do not, something that allows them to endorse an inviolable connection between warrant and truth that does not lead to radical skepticism. In the next three chapters, we will put such a worry to rest. Through an examination of three eminent virtue epistemologies—(i) the agent-reliabilisms of figures like Ernest Sosa, John Greco, and John Turri, (ii) the agent-responsiblism of Linda Zagzebski, and (iii) the proper functionalism of Alvin Plantinga—we will find the proposed diagnosis of Gettier counterexamples vindicated and every instance of infallibilism leading to skepticism.

After we see how these prominent accounts of virtue epistemology flounder, the project of exploring the possibility of non-reductive virtue epistemology will be sufficiently motivated. And that will be the project we take up in the final three chapters of this book.

Part II

Applying the Diagnosis

3

Agent-reliabilism

The most prominent version of agent-reliabilism virtue epistemology in the contemporary literature—indeed, perhaps the most prominent version of any virtue epistemology in the literature—sees knowledge as a kind of *success from ability*, where (roughly) a belief is knowledge if and only if it is *true because formed by a cognitive competence*. In this chapter, we will explore this brand of virtue epistemology and how it fares against the diagnosis of the Gettier Problem developed in Chapter 1.

Starting with the seminal work of Ernest Sosa in *A Virtue Epistemology* (2007) and *Reflective Knowledge* (2009), we will introduce the view. In Section 2, we will explore how the *success from ability* account of knowledge has been challenged in the literature, particularly in regard to the Gettier Problem. I will suggest that the Gettier Problem facing analyses of knowledge has not been properly appreciated by virtue epistemologist or even virtue epistemology's most vocal critics—that the situation facing reductive accounts of knowledge is far more insidious and dire than most virtue epistemologists seem to acknowledge. In Sections 3 and 4, we will consider how some recent virtue epistemologists have tried to redevelop *success from ability* accounts of knowledge in order to defuse the Gettier Problem viably. In Section 3, we will consider John Greco's recent defense of the *knowledge as success from ability* hypothesis in "A (Different) Virtue Epistemology" (2012). We will see (i) just how the critiques elucidated in Section 2 have (mis)shaped the dialectic between virtue epistemology and what is required in solving Gettier counterexamples and (ii) how this has led to virtue epistemologists like Greco underestimating the widespread insidiousness of Gettier counterexamples. Finally, in Section 4, we will consider John Turri's virtue epistemology in "Manifest Failure: The Gettier Problem Solved" (2011), where Turri—building off of the work of Sosa—baldly claims to have solved the Gettier Problem. I argue that any success against Gettier counterexamples afforded by Turri's notion of manifestation is merely fleeting, that strengthened counterexamples can be easily produced. Tellingly, in every case—from Sosa to Greco, to Turri—we will see a recurring theme: the prominent versions of agent-reliabilist virtue epistemology cannot solve the Gettier Problem. Indeed, we will see that they fail to solve the Problem precisely along the lines predicted in Chapter 1.

Section 1: Sosa's Virtue Epistemology

While authors have been developing epistemologies that understand knowledge as something like *success from ability* for several decades, the literature has recently coalesced around Ernest Sosa's work in *A Virtue Epistemology* (2007) and *Reflective Knowledge* (2009)—providing a touchstone from which most contemporary agent-reliabilist virtue epistemologies have been developed and should be understood.[1] It behooves us, then, to elucidate the contours of Sosa's view (even if only briefly) as we dive into agent-reliabilist analyses of knowledge and their viability in the face of Gettier counterexamples.

Sosa uses the example of an archer to help us understand his theory of knowledge. In assessing an archer's shot, we will be interested in three things: (1) its accuracy—whether or not the shot hits its target; (2) its adroitness—whether or not it manifests the competence of the archer; (3) its aptness—whether or not the shot's accuracy is a result of its adroitness.[2] The question: When is the accuracy of the archer's shot attributable to him? Naturally, if the accuracy of the shot had nothing to do with the archer's competence such that it was not adroit, we would not credit the shot to him; we would not, for example, credit the accuracy of a difficult shot to an inept archer who just so happened to clumsily fire the arrow in the right direction. What is more, if a given shot is accurate and adroit though not apt (i.e., not accurate *because* adroit), we would not credit it to the archer either. Imagine a scenario where an expert archer takes a shot at a relatively easy target, a shot that in normal circumstances would have hit the target without difficulty; imagine, then, that while the arrow is still in the air it is blown off target by a sudden burst of strong wind such that it was then on an inaccurate trajectory and only lucky blown back on target by another sudden burst of strong wind in the opposite direction. While the shot indeed hits the target and seemingly manifests the archer's competence (after all, in normal circumstances it easily hits the target), it is not accurate *because of* the archer's competence—instead being accurate because of the second burst of wind. As such, we would not credit such a shot to the archer. An archer's shot, then, *is* creditable to him if and only if it is accurate as a result of its being adroit. In other words, an archer's shot is creditable to him if and only if it is apt.

Beliefs, like an archer's shots, can also be evaluated according to accuracy (i.e., truth), adroitness (whether or not it manifests the agent's epistemic competence), and aptness (whether or not the belief is true as a result of its adroitness). A given true belief is knowledge, according to Sosa, if and only if it hits upon the truth (so to speak) as a result of the given agent's epistemic competence. In other words, knowledge, for Sosa, is apt belief—belief that is "true *because* competent" (Sosa 2007, 1:23). Parallel to the archery example, if the accuracy of a given belief had nothing to do with the agent's cognitive competence such that it was not adroit, we obviously would not credit the belief to him as knowledge; if, for example, I suddenly and without reason started believing that the pope is my fourth cousin, we would not credit me with knowledge even if by some chance it turned out to be true. What is more, if a given belief is accurate and adroit though not apt (i.e., not accurate *because* adroit), we would not credit the pertinent agent with knowledge either. Imagine a Gettier-style scenario where I do a detailed investigation into my family history and come to the calculated belief that the pope is my fourth cousin; imagine, then, that while as a result of some bad luck my familial calculations were fundamentally misguided, my belief is nevertheless true—true for reasons my calculations would never have predicted. While my belief in such a case is true and adroit, the truth has nothing to do with the adroitness—it is not true because adroit, it is not apt—and, therefore, we would not credit my belief to me as knowledge.[3]

According to Sosa, S knows that *p* if and only if (i) S believes that *p* and (ii) that belief is apt, true *because of* S's cognitive competency.[4] With this initial analysis in mind, Sosa distinguishes two tiers of knowledge. The first tier of knowledge is what Sosa calls "animal knowledge," and it consists simply of apt belief; a given agent possesses animal knowledge if and only if he possesses an apt belief. The second tier of knowledge, what Sosa calls "reflective knowledge," on the other hand, is more demanding—it is, according to Sosa, not only apt belief but "defensibly apt belief," second-order apt belief that a given belief is apt (Sosa 2007, 1:24, 32). I may have apt belief that "that's a zebra," say, and therefore have animal knowledge. To have reflective knowledge, on the other hand, I need to believe aptly that my belief that "that's a zebra" is apt; I might be an expert zoologist who was able to inspect the zebra closely, for example.

Sosa's distinction between animal knowledge and reflective knowledge can be quite handy. Consider, for example, the notorious Chicken Sexer case:

Chicken Sexer: Naïve and Reflective are both chicken sexers. Their job is to look at baby chickens, determine their genders, and then segregate the chickens accordingly—putting male chicks in one box and female chicks in another. Both Naïve and Reflective are equally good at their job—both are highly reliable at determining the gender of the baby chickens. There is, however, one important difference between them: Naïve has no idea how he is able to determine the gender of the chicks correctly; he "just does it"; Reflective, on the other hand, is very much aware of how he makes such a judgment, by looking for a certain pattern in the chick's feathers. Does Naïve's ignorance affect his ability to know "that's a male chick," "that's a female chick," etc.?

The notoriety of this case comes from its divisiveness. Externalists about warrant are typically inclined to say that Naïve's ignorance is no hurdle for knowledge. Internalists, on the other hand, are likely to balk at such a suggestion because Naïve seemingly does not have the right sort of reflective access to what is grounding the pertinent belief. One way to characterize this differing opinion is through what looks like conflicting intuitions. On the one hand, Naïve obviously seems to be doing something right—he is, after all, a highly reliable judge. On the other, surely Reflective's epistemic state is preferable to Naïve's; surely they are not on equal epistemic footing. One of the nice things about Sosa's analysis is that it can account for both of these intuitions. Naïve, it seems, has apt beliefs about the genders of chicks and as such has animal knowledge; Reflective, in contrast, seems to be aptly aware of his apt beliefs concerning the gender of the chicks, and as such he enjoys the more exalted reflective knowledge. As such, Sosa's epistemology, with its distinction between animal and reflective knowledge, seems to be able to satisfy some basic internalist intuitions while nevertheless remaining decidedly externalist; it recognizes Naïve's competence all the while appreciating the superiority of Reflective's epistemic state.

Despite such merits, Sosa's analysis of knowledge as apt belief seems to run into some immediate problems. If, for example, apt belief is sufficient for knowledge, then seemingly the protagonist in the Fake Barns case has knowledge—a seemingly counterintuitive conclusion. If all it takes for a given belief to be knowledge is aptness, then it seemingly will not matter how lucky that aptness may be. Imagine an archer who is unknowingly in an absolutely terrible environment for archery—an environment that has been plagued by wild and irregular winds for thousands of years. If when he takes his shot a quasi-miracle occurs, the winds cease, and his arrow is able to fly true and hit the target, the shot is, according to Sosa, creditable to the archer; after all, it seemingly hit the target as a result of the archer's competence. And if the archer's shot hit its target because of the archer's competence (i.e., if the shot is apt), the shot is creditable to him no matter how incredibly lucky it may be that the winds died down when they did. Likewise, when a given credulous subject happens to believe "that's a barn" correctly even amid a sea of barn facades, he possesses knowledge. If his belief is true as a result of his epistemic competence, he has knowledge no matter how incredibly lucky it may be that he picked a real barn. Sosa has us consider the following case, which bears obvious similarities to Fake Barn-type scenarios just referenced:

> **Kaleidoscope**: You see a surface that looks red in ostensibly normal conditions. But it is a kaleidoscope surface controlled by a jokester who also controls the ambient light, and might as easily have presented you with a red-light+white-surface combination as with the actual white-light+red-surface combination. (Sosa 2007, 1:31)

According to Sosa, when presented with the white-light+red-surface combination, the protagonist of Kaleidoscope knows that the surface is red. In other words, so long as the protagonist's belief is true as a result of his epistemic competence, he possesses knowledge no matter how incredibly lucky it may be that the jokester was not at that moment presenting him with a red-light+white-object combination. Environmental luck of that sort does not, according to Sosa, block knowledge.

Given the broad consensus that the protagonist in cases like Kaleidoscope (including cases like Fake Barns) lacks knowledge—that his belief is at the very least somehow epistemically deficient—is not such a conclusion problematic? According to Sosa, not if we make use of the *animal knowledge/reflective knowledge* distinction. By Sosa's lights, the protagonists in such cases do indeed have first-order (or first-tier) knowledge, animal knowledge, but that is not to say that their epistemic state is not somehow deficient. They may very well have apt beliefs, but surely they lack defensible apt beliefs—in other words, surely they lack higher-order reflective knowledge. According to Sosa, when the protagonists in such cases rightly identify barns or the color of surfaces using their epistemic competencies, they should be credited for doing as much even if they could have very easily gotten it wrong. Indeed, where most accounts will simply say that something is epistemically *wrong* in cases like Kaleidoscope, perhaps it is a virtue of Sosa's account that it can also tell us what is epistemically *right*.[5]

But why does the perceiver in the Kaleidoscope case fail to have reflective knowledge? If he has animal knowledge, why should he not also have reflective knowledge? Putting aside questions as to whether or not Sosa's animal/reflective distinction solution is palatable in principle when applied to such Gettier counterexamples, let us explore the details of Sosa's solution a bit further. Consider Sosa's own explanation:

> The [Kaleidoscope] perceiver would there be said to have apt belief and animal knowledge that the seen surface is red. What he lacks ... is *reflective* knowledge, since this requires apt belief that he aptly believes the surface to be red (or at least it requires that he aptly take this for granted or assume it or presuppose it, a qualification implicit in what follows). Why should it be any less plausible to think that he aptly believes that he aptly believes than to think that he aptly believes *simpliciter*? Well, what competence might he exercise in believing that he aptly so believes, and how plausible might it be to attribute to that competence his being right in believing that he aptly believes? ... It seems a kind of default competence, whereby one automatically takes the light to be normal absent some special indication to the contrary. And that is presumably what the kaleidoscope perceiver does, absent any indication of a jokester in control. So we may suppose him to retain that competence unimpaired *and* to exercise it in taking for granted the adequacy of the ambient light, so that he can aptly take the surface to be red. Since the belief that he believes aptly is a true belief, and since it is *owed* to the exercise of a competence, how then can we suppose it not to be itself an apt belief? Well, recall: the requirement for aptly believing is not just that one's belief is true, and derived from a competence. The requirement is rather that one believes *correctly* (with truth) through the exercise of a competence in its proper conditions. What must be attributed to the competence is not just the belief's existence but its correctness. (Sosa 2007, 1:32–3)

While the protagonist in Kaleidoscope arguably has animal knowledge, he lacks reflective knowledge because the epistemic competence (that "default competence") by which he might believe his belief that the surface is red to be apt is not itself apt. Why? Because while his belief that the surface is red is apt is true and causally "owed" to the exercise of the relevant "default" competence, it is not true *because* or *through* the relevant competence. Or, as Sosa says later, the Kaleidoscope protagonist's belief that his belief is apt is not apt because the relevant competence "might ... too easily have issued a false belief that the lights are normal" (Sosa 2007, 1:33).[6]

Even if Sosa is right that the protagonists in Kaleidoscope cases possess animal knowledge but lack reflective knowledge, his explanation as to *why* this is the case (which we just considered) seems, by his own admission, to lead to a second problem. As Sosa notes, if the main character of the Kaleidoscope case fails to have reflective knowledge because the relevant competence (the default competence by which he might believe his belief that the surface is red to be apt) might too easily have produced a false belief given the close possibility of the jokester's mischief, we might worry that the close possibility of the skeptic's dream hypothesis might prevent us from *ever* having perception-based reflective knowledge. In other words, if the Kaleidoscope protagonist does not have reflective knowledge because the jokester could have easily been playing a trick on him, perhaps for similar reasons we cannot possess reflective knowledge of perceptions because we seemingly could easily be so perceiving while in a lucid dream.[7] It looks as though if we apply Sosa's response to cases like Kaleidoscope more generally, we are in the grip of radical skepticism concerning higher-order knowledge.

Before we consider how Sosa avoids such a conclusion, let us consider the Kaleidoscope case a bit further. The reason the protagonist possesses animal knowledge (i.e., apt belief) in such a case is, according to Sosa, that the protagonist's "faculty of color vision" is being exercised "in normal conditions for lighting, distance, size of surface, etc., in conditions generally appropriate for the exercise of color vision" (Sosa 2007, 1:31). Our hero in the Kaleidoscope case has a belief that is apt, a belief that is "true because competent," simply because the competence governing its production is operating in the right sort of conditions such that the given belief could not easily be false and so based (i.e., based in the given competence operating in the relevant conditions).[8] In other words, in order for a given belief to be apt, Sosa seems to require that it be produced by a cognitive competence that is operating in good conditions where "operating in good conditions" means at the very least something like "reliably based." Likewise, the reason the protagonist in the Kaleidoscope case does *not* have reflective knowledge is seemingly because the relevant competence, the "default competence" being exercised, is *not* operating under normal conditions, in conditions generally appropriate for its exercise such that it would be reliably counted on to produce a true belief. In other words, the protagonist in the Kaleidoscope case does not possess reflective knowledge because the conditions under which the given competence is operating are not a reliable basis for forming true belief given the presence of the jokester.

Now, does the possibility of the skeptic's dream-hypothesis usurp reflective knowledge in the standard case in the same way the jokester's presence usurps reflective knowledge in the Kaleidoscope case? Given what has just been said, arguably not. If (1) having an apt belief means having a belief that is produced by a cognitive competence that is operating in appropriate conditions such that the belief could not easily be so based and false, and (2) the skeptic's dream hypothesis did indeed threaten the aptness required for reflective knowledge in the standard cases, then seemingly the conditions under which our relevant competency (i.e., that "default" competency we use when we assume ourselves awake) is operating are not appropriate, that the condition for our given cognitive competency is not a good basis for reliable true belief. But why think a thing like that? Why would the possibility of a dream-hypothesis affect the appropriateness of the conditions under which my everyday cognitive competencies operate? We can arguably resist such a conclusion by simply assuming that the conditions our "default competence" is operating under when we are awake is markedly different from when we are dreaming. If we want to "appeal, with Austin, to the vividness and richness of wakeful experience, and with Descartes to its coherence, as part of the basis for our belief that we are awake," we can deny that the relevant conditions under which our cognitive faculties are operating when we are awake are the same as when we are dreaming (Sosa 2007, 1:38).[9] Given a difference in conditions, it is simply not true that my relevant default competence would be so operating in the dream scenario; it is not true that my default competence could be so based and easily lead to a corresponding false belief.

Just as we would only credit an archer with hitting the target if he hit it due to his competence as an archer, according to Sosa, we should only credit someone with knowledge if he "hit upon" the given true belief as a result of his cognitive competence. Knowledge, for Sosa, is apt belief—belief that is true because competent. And from this simple definition, Sosa specifies two tiers of knowledge. The first-tier, "animal knowledge," is simply apt belief; the second tier, "reflective knowledge," is apt belief aptly believed—an apt belief that one's (first-order) belief is apt. Among its various assets, this analysis of knowledge lets us, when faced with Chicken Sexer-style cases, satisfy both internalist and externalist intuitions; with it, we can say why the reflective Chicken Sexer's cognitive state is superior to his naive counterpart, while upholding that there is something the latter is indeed doing right. No doubt, however, when faced with cases like Kaleidoscope someone may worry about the conclusion that the given protagonist knows under such circumstances, but such worries may be assuaged by the animal/reflective distinction—by pointing out that while the Kaleidoscope protagonist may indeed have animal knowledge he surely lacks reflective knowledge. What is more, despite appearances, such a move does not (as we've just seen) lead to widespread higher-order skepticism given closeness of the skeptic's dreaming hypothesis. In fact, Sosa's analysis of knowledge seems to allow for a new and innovative virtue-theoretic solution to certain forms of dream skepticism.

Nevertheless, putting away initial worries regarding Kaleidoscope cases and dreaming, some unresolved problems remain. As we will see in the next section, the brand of agent-reliabilism virtue epistemology espoused by Ernest Sosa has come under criticism for not being able to surmount Gettier counterexamples viably.

Section 2: Knowledge as Success from Ability, Gettier, and the Critiques

According to many virtue epistemologists (e.g., Sosa 2007; Turri 2011; Greco 2009a, 2010, 2012), knowledge is a kind of success from ability. In other words, as Sosa puts it, a given belief is knowledge *if and only if* the belief is "true because competent"—belief where the truth is "derive[d] from," "attributable to," or "because [of]" a cognitive competence (Sosa 2007, 1:23, 33).[10] One of the benefits of this account is that it is meant to offer a viable solution to the Gettier Problem. And given that Gettier cases are quintessentially scenarios where a given belief is true merely by accident or dumb luck (and not because of a cognitive ability), the purported solution is easy enough to see. Consider the following straightforward Gettier case:

> **Fish Convention:** Smith, a novice ichthyologist, is attending a local fish convention. While perusing the various booths and exhibits, he comes to some fish labeled "*Cyphotilapia gibberosa*," a deep water fish from Lake Tanganyika in Africa. Smith then, excited, forms the belief that "there are *Cyphotilapia gibberosa* at this convention!" Unfortunately, the fish Smith was looking at had been misidentified—they were actually *Cyphotilapia frontosa*, fish that can easily be mistaken for *Cyphotilapia gibberosa*. Nevertheless, his belief turns out to be true—in the far corner of the convention building, unbeknownst to Smith, there are real *Cyphotilapia gibberosa* hidden amidst a very large koi exhibit.

In this case, Smith's belief is formed through an exercise of a cognitive ability, and Smith's belief is true; however, critically, Smith's belief does not hit upon the truth *because* of the cognitive competence, and the success of Smith's belief has nothing to do with his epistemic abilities. Smith's belief is only true by dumb luck; it is true for reasons that his given exercise of epistemic abilities would not have predicted. Understanding knowledge as a kind of success from ability can help us rightly predict that Smith does not know that "there are *Cyphotilapia gibberosa* at this convention." And such a solution, it seems, can be easily generalized across all Gettier cases. If knowledge requires beliefs to be true or successful *as a result of* a epistemic ability, then presumably knowledge will never be wrongly ascribed in a Gettier scenario because Gettier scenarios are (to put it roughly) those cases where a given belief is true because of luck. Agent-reliabilist virtue epistemology, it seems, has a solution to the Gettier Problem.

This solution has come under scrutiny by a number of critics, predominantly Jennifer Lackey in "Knowledge and Credit" (2009) and Krist Vaesen in "Knowledge without Credit" (2011). Both claim that virtue epistemology's success from ability account of knowledge can solve the Gettier Problem, but only at a cost. The issue, for both Lackey and Vaesen, is making sense of the distinction between (a) having a belief that is both true *and* produced by ability and (b) having a belief that is true *because* it is produced from ability. Someone can have a belief that is successful *and* produced by a cognitive ability and still be vulnerable to Gettier counterexamples; as we saw earlier, Smith, in the case of Fish Convention, has a successful belief that is also produced from an ability—in this case an ability to read signs—but that's obviously not enough to avoid being Gettiered. If knowledge requires a given belief to be true *because* it is produced from a cognitive ability, where the success *comes from* the ability, however, other problems seem to arise.

According to Lackey, if knowledge requires a belief to be true because it is produced from an ability, then Gettier problems can indeed be avoided; however, knowledge will seemingly be precluded in cases of testimony. Lackey considers the following scenario:

> **Chicago Visitor**: Having just arrived at the train station in Chicago, Morris wishes to obtain directions to the Sears Tower. He looks around, randomly approaches the first passerby that he sees, and asks how to get to his desired destination. The passerby, who happens to be a Chicago resident who knows the city extraordinarily well, provides Morris with impeccable directions to the Sears Tower. (Lackey 2009, 29)

In this scenario, is the success of Morris's belief attributable to his cognitive abilities? Is his belief true because competent? Seemingly not. As John Greco has noted, "Even if Morris is appropriately attentive to the speaker, and even if his reception of the speaker's testimony is appropriately discriminating, it seems right to say that he forms a true belief because of the speaker's testimony rather than because of his own efforts" (2012, 4). As such, it seems like virtue epistemology gives us the wrong result in cases of testimony. Intuitively, Morris *knows* where the Sears Tower is based on the impeccable directions of the passerby; however, according to the *success from ability* account of knowledge espoused by many contemporary virtue epistemologies, virtue epistemology seems to deny knowledge to Morris wrongfully, since the success of his belief seems primarily attributable to the passerby's competency rather than his own.

Of course, an advocate of virtue epistemology might be quick to object that, in the case of Chicago Visitor, Morris's cognitive abilities still play an important role in the success of his belief; after all, he wouldn't have known where the Sears Tower was had he not paid close attention. The success of Morris's belief may not be *strongly* attributable to his cognitive abilities, but it is still attributable to his cognitive abilities in a *weaker* sense. The problem, however, is that this also seems to be true in Gettier counterexamples. In the case of Fish Convention, Smith's cognitive competencies arguably play an important role in the success of his belief as well; after all, his belief that "there are *Cyphotilapia gibberosa* at this convention!" would not have been successful had he not competently read the sign. Smith's belief seems *weakly* attributable to his cognitive competencies. As Lackey points out, virtue epistemology faces a dilemma. If we understand the attribution relationship strongly—such that a belief needs to be mostly (if not entirely) true as a result of the given agent's cognitive abilities—then virtue epistemology can avoid Gettier counterexamples like Fish Convention; so understood, however, virtue epistemology will wrongfully preclude knowledge in cases of testimony. Alternatively, if we understand the attribution relation weakly—such that an agent's cognitive abilities merely need to be a contributing factor in the given belief's success—then virtue epistemology can rightly attribute knowledge in cases of testimony like that in Chicago Visitor; so understood, however, virtue epistemology will remain vulnerable to Gettier counterexamples.

In "Knowledge without Credit" (2011), Krist Vaesen levels a similar dilemma against virtue epistemology regarding extended cognition. Vaesen has us consider a scenario where an airport has recently updated their luggage security scanner. The old luggage scanner, System1, simply scanned luggage so as to allow the scanner operator to see what is inside the luggage and detect any dangerous objects. Now, since dangerous objects are exceedingly rare in pieces of luggage, anyone using a System1 security scanner will have to "stare for long uninterrupted periods of time at a monitor showing unsuspicious (and boring) goods (like toothbrushes, deodorants, computers, books)" (Vaesen 2011, 523). Such a mind-numbing and tedious task is bound eventually to result in a dramatic decrease in the vigilance of the scanner operator. To combat this, the airport has installed System2 luggage scanners, which periodically project "false signals" of dangerous objects onto luggage scans so as to keep the operator's attention. As Vaesen explains, "Whenever System2 projects a false image and the operator notices (she informs the system by, say, clicking on the image), the following message pops up: "False alarm: you were being tested!" If no message appears, the operator knows the threat is real" (2011, 523). These false alarms keep the scanner operators alert and allow them to remain far more vigilant for far longer. Vaeson has us consider the following case:

> **Sissicase:** Sissi has been a baggage inspector all her life. She used to work with an old-fashioned System1, but since 9/11, the airport she is working for introduced a System2. Her supervisor Joseph, a cognitive engineer who was actually involved in the design of the device, has informed her how it works (how its operation is almost identical to the operation of the old system). Currently Sissi is inspecting a piece of luggage which contains a bomb. She notices and forms a true belief regarding the contents of the suitcase. As such, the bomb is intercepted and a catastrophe prevented from happening. (2011, 523)

Intuitively, Sissi knows that the given piece of luggage contains a bomb; however, is her belief true because of a cognitive ability? Seemingly not. As Vaeson explains, "Note . . . that the relevant counterfactual is Sissi using the old-fashioned System1, resulting, we may reasonably suppose, in her failing to notice the bomb, and thus in her forming a false belief (rather than her just failing to form a belief)" (2011, 523). In other words, had Sissi been using the System1 scanner, her vigilance would have been so low that, chances are, she wouldn't have detected the bomb in question. The success of Sissi's belief seems largely attributable to the System2 scanner and not her cognitive abilities. And as such, virtue epistemology seems to wrongly deny that Sissi knows that the piece of luggage before her is bomb-laden.

As before, an advocate of virtue epistemology is free to object that, in the case of Sissicase, Sissi's cognitive abilities still play an important role in the success of her belief. The success of Sissi's belief may not be *strongly* attributable to her cognitive abilities, but it is still attributable to her cognitive abilities in a *weaker* sense. And again, the problem is that this also seems to be true in Gettier counterexamples. Virtue epistemology now faces a new but similar dilemma. If we understand the attribution relationship strongly—such that a belief needs to be mostly (if not entirely) true as a result of the given agent's cognitive abilities—then virtue epistemology can avoid Gettier counterexamples like Fish Convention; so understood, however, virtue epistemology will wrongfully preclude knowledge in cases of extended cognition. Alternatively, if we understand the attribution relation weakly—such that an agent's cognitive abilities merely need to be a contributing factor in the given belief's success—then virtue epistemology can rightly attribute knowledge in cases of extended cognition like that in Sissicase; so understood, however, virtue epistemology will remain vulnerable to Gettier counterexamples.

According to our diagnosis, Gettier counterexamples will be unavoidable so long as whatever takes to bridge the gap between true belief and knowledge—justification, warrant, aptness, cognitive achievement, etc.—does not necessarily *guarantee* the truth of the belief in question. This leaves reductive accounts of knowledge with a difficult dilemma: either remain vulnerable to Gettier counterexamples or adopt a view that risks falling into radical skepticism. Tellingly, this is what we are seeing in the virtue epistemology literature. Both Lackey and Vaesen have rightly pointed out that the only way virtue epistemology's *success from ability* account of knowledge will have any chance at avoiding Gettier counterexamples is if it is understood very strongly—where an agent's cognitive abilities are not just *a* contributing factor but *the* contributing factor to a given belief's success. Insofar as beliefs in Gettier counterexamples are true (at least in part) thanks to *luck* and not cognitive abilities, such an understanding of virtue epistemology will be vulnerable to Gettier counterexamples. However, as the dilemma predicts, such a strong account of knowledge faces the threat of skeptical conclusions. And, again, what Lackey and Vaesen have shown us is perfectly compatible with this. As they respectively highlighted, if an agent's cognitive abilities need to be *the* contributing factor to a given belief's success, then virtue epistemology seems to preclude knowledge wrongfully in cases of testimony and extended cognition. In other words, if (a) having a belief that is *successful because of a cognitive ability* is what bridges the gap between true belief and knowledge and (b) this is strong enough to rule out the possibility of having a belief that is successful for any other reasons (such as epistemic luck), then it will be too strong for knowledge from testimony and extended cognition. If, however, *success from ability* is weak enough to allow for success for other reasons (such as testimony or extended cognition), then it won't be strong enough to rule out Gettier counterexamples. As Lackey and Vaesen have shown us, virtue epistemology faces a dilemma: either remain vulnerable to Gettier counterexamples or adopt a view that falls into radical skepticism regarding testimony and extended cognition.

The problem, however, is that the dilemma facing virtue epistemology isn't *just* a dilemma between Gettier counterexamples and skepticism regarding testimony and extended cognition; it is (at least according to the diagnosis found in Chapter 1) a dilemma between Gettier counterexamples and radical skepticism—skepticism regarding testimony, extended cognition, *and much more*.[11] The problem isn't supposed to be that if *success from ability* is strong enough to rule out the possibility of having a belief that is successful for any other reasons (such as epistemic luck), then it be too strong for knowledge from testimony and extended cognition; the problem is supposed to be that if *success from ability* is strong enough to rule out the possibility of having a belief that is successful for any other reasons, then it is too strong, *full stop*—wrongfully ruling out knowledge in a wide range of cases. While the dilemmas raised by Lackey and Vaesen are certainly in keeping with this more general worry, the more general worry seemingly has not been fully appreciated. In particular, I suggest that the dilemma facing reductive accounts of virtue epistemology is far more insidious and dire than most virtue epistemologists seem to acknowledge.

Section 3: Greco's Virtue Epistemology

Why does it matter whether or not we see the threat facing virtue epistemology as a dilemma between Gettier counterexamples and testimonial knowledge, or as a dilemma between Gettier counterexamples and extended cognition, or (as I suggested in Section 2) a dilemma between Gettier counterexamples and radical skepticism? It matters insofar as *how the threat is perceived* will affect *the shape of proposed solutions*. To put it roughly, if the threat facing virtue epistemology is perceived to have a relatively limited scope (e.g., cases of testimony or cases of extended cognition), then any proposed solutions will likely be correspondingly limited. If the threat facing virtue epistemology is perceived to have an extremely broad scope (e.g., most instances of knowledge), however, then we should expect any proposed solutions will be correspondingly broad and far reaching.

In any case, despite the grim diagnosis explicated in Section 2, many virtue epistemologists have been optimistic about virtue epistemology's ability to provide a viable solution to the Gettier Problem. In "A (Different) Virtue Epistemology" (2012), John Greco proposes a solution to the Gettier Problem. According to Greco, the idea that knowledge is a kind of *success from ability* seems to have "surprising theoretical power," particularly with it comes to diagnosing the Gettier Problem (2012, 2). As Greco explains:

> In Gettier cases, S's belief is true and S's belief is competent, but S's belief is not true because competent. That is, S does not have a true belief because S's belief is produced by ability. . . . In cases of knowledge, true belief is no mere lucky success; rather, S's believing the truth is attributable to the exercise of ability. Put differently: Knowledge is an achievement in a sense that lucky guesses (and the like) are not. (2012, 2)

Again, if knowledge requires beliefs to be true or successful *as a result of* an epistemic ability, then presumably knowledge will never be wrongly ascribed in a Gettier scenario because Gettier scenarios are (to put it roughly) those cases where a given belief is true because of luck.

As we saw in Section 2, however, Lackey and Vaesen have pointed out that the only way virtue epistemology's *success from ability* account of knowledge will have any chance at avoiding Gettier counterexamples is if it is understood very strongly—where an agent's cognitive abilities are not just *a* contributing factor but *the* contributing factor to a given belief's success. Insofar as beliefs in Gettier counterexamples are true (at least in part) thanks to *luck* and not cognitive abilities, such an understanding of virtue epistemology will be vulnerable to Gettier counterexamples. However, as Lackey and Vaesen have shown us, if an agent's cognitive abilities need to be *the* contributing factor to a given belief's success, then virtue epistemology seems to preclude knowledge wrongfully in cases of testimony and extended cognition. In other words, if (a) having a belief that is *successful because of a cognitive ability* is what bridges the gap between true belief and knowledge and (b) this is strong enough to rule out the possibility of having a belief that is successful for any other reasons (such as epistemic luck), then it will be too strong for knowledge from testimony and extended cognition.

And while Section 2 suggested that such dilemmas are mere symptoms of a broader threat to virtue epistemology, the respective dilemmas of Lackey and Vaesen have been the guiding lights in reshaping virtue epistemology's response to the Gettier Problem. This can be most clearly seen in Greco's work in "A (Different) Virtue Epistemology" (2012). In response to the respective dilemmas posed by Lackey and Vaesen, Greco argues that the *success from ability* account of knowledge should be understood such that "A success is attributable to S's ability just in case S's ability contributes to that success in the right way" by which he means "in a way that would regularly serve relevant purposes" (2012, 14). Greco has us consider the following scenario:

> **Soccer:** Playing in a soccer game, Ted receives a brilliant, almost impossible pass. With the defense out of position and the goalie lying prostrate on the

ground, Ted kicks the ball into the net for an easy goal. . . . Compare this case with another: Ted is playing in a soccer game, but not paying attention. Never seeing the ball, a brilliant pass bounces off his head and into the goal. Here Ted does not deserve credit for the goal. He was involved in a way, but not in the right sort of way. (2012, 14–15)[12]

In the dilemmas posed by Lackey and Vaesen, the question for virtue epistemology was whether or not agent's cognitive abilities are just *a* contributing factor or *the* contributing factor to a given belief's success. Lackey and Vaesen seem to view the role of cognitive abilities play in a given belief's success as *quantitative*—concerned primarily with the extent to which a given belief is successful because of a cognitive competence. If cognitive abilities only need to be *partially* responsible for the belief's success, then virtue epistemology will be vulnerable to Gettier counterexamples; if cognitive abilities need to be entirely responsible for a belief's success, however, then virtue epistemology seems to preclude knowledge wrongly in cases of testimony and extended cognition. This *quantitative* understanding of the role of cognitive abilities, according to Greco, is misguided. Even though Ted's contribution to the scored goal (in the first instance) was extremely minimal, he still deserves credit because his contribution was of the sort (i.e., the right sort of *quality*) that deserves credit. Likewise, even though the contribution of the protagonists' respective cognitive abilities in Chicago Visitor and Sissicase is minimal, they still acquire knowledge because their cognitive abilities' contributions were of the right sort (i.e., the right sort of *quality*); the cognitive abilities of the protagonists contributed to the success of their respective beliefs "in the right way"—"in a way that would regularly serve relevant purposes" (Greco 2012, 14).

Greco's understanding of knowledge as *success from ability*—where the belief's success is attributable to the relevant cognitive abilities if those abilities contributed to the success *in the right way*—seems to prescribe knowledge rightly in cases of testimony and extended cognition; what is more, it seems to have no problem defusing garden-variety Gettier cases—Gettier cases like Fish Convention. As Greco explains:

> In cases of testimonial knowledge and knowledge involving extended cognition, but not in Gettier cases, S's believing from ability contributes to S's believing the truth in the right way—i.e., in a way that would regularly serve relevant informational needs. That is, in cases of knowledge, S's abilities exploit social practices and technologies so as to produce true belief in regular, dependable ways. In Gettier cases that does not happen. S ends up with a true belief, and S's

abilities even contribute to that, but not in a way that can be regularly exploited, not in a way that is dependable or reliable. . . . In all of the cases, S's believing from ability contributes to S's ending with a true belief—in all of the cases, the exercise of ability is part of the total causal structure leading up to the desired effect. But in Gettier cases the route . . . is not the sort of route that could be regularly exploited for relevant purposes. (2012, 17)

Greco, it seems, has given us an account of *success from ability* that can rightly handle cases of testimony without making it vulnerable to Gettier counterexamples. What is more, it seems like he has given an account of *success from ability* that handles cases of extended cognition without making it vulnerable to Gettier counterexamples. The dilemmas posed by Lackey and Vaesen respectively seem to be defused.

But what about the dilemma explicated in Chapter 1? I have suggested that the dilemmas posed by Lackey and Vaesen are merely symptoms of a broader threat facing virtue epistemology. If this is right, then perhaps any success against Gettier counterexamples afforded by Greco's understanding of *success from ability*—where the belief's success is attributable to the relevant cognitive abilities if those abilities contributed to the success *in the right way*—is merely fleeting, perhaps strengthened counterexamples are around the corner.[13] In the rest of this section, I argue that Greco's virtue epistemology—arguably the most advanced virtue-theoretic account of knowledge in the contemporary literature—fails to surmount the Gettier Problem viably: failing precisely along the lines predicted in Chapter 1, facing a dilemma between *remaining vulnerable to strengthened Gettier counterexamples or strengthening the demands of knowledge such that it is almost unattainable, paving the way to radical skepticism*.

The first point to note is that *success from ability*—even in cases where the success is attributable to the ability *in the right way*—is a matter of degree. Let's revisit Greco's soccer analogy. Consider the following three cases:

Ted1: Playing in a soccer game, Ted receives a brilliant, almost impossible pass. With the defense out of position and the goalie lying prostrate on the ground, Ted kicks the ball into the net for an easy goal. (2012, 14–15)[14]

Ted2: Playing in a soccer game, Ted receives an excellent pass. With most of the defense out of position, Ted outmaneuvers a final defender and is able to fire the ball past the goalie and into the net for an impressive goal.

Ted3: Playing in a soccer game, Ted steals the ball from an opposing player and singlehandedly runs it down the field. Ted outmaneuvers every defender and fires the ball past the goalie and into the net for a magnificent, indeed awe-inspiring, goal.

In all three cases, Ted's success in scoring the goal is attributable to his abilities, because his abilities were involved in the right way—in the sort of way that deserves credit. That said, however, the *amount* of credit Ted deserves—the extent to which his abilities are responsible for the successful goal—varies from case to case. In Ted1, Ted deserves credit, sure enough, but relatively little credit because Ted's contribution to the scored goal was minimal. In Ted2, Ted seemingly deserves more credit, because his contribution to the scored goal was more significant. And finally, in Ted3, Ted seemingly deserves even more credit, because he was singlehandedly responsible for the goal's success. In all three cases, Ted deserves credit—the successful goal is attributable to Ted's abilities in such a way that deserves credit—however, the *amount* of credit varies from case to case.

And as such, the second point to note is that Greco's shift from a quantitative understanding of the role cognitive abilities apply in a given belief's success (against environmental features like reliable informants and helpful technology) to a qualitative understanding does not mean the claim that *success from ability* admits degrees—a central claim of the dilemma posed in Chapter 1—is now moot. Since the respective dilemmas posed by Lackey and Vaesen turn on whether or not an agent's cognitive abilities are just *a* contributing factor or *the* contributing factor to a given belief's success, Greco's shift to a focus on the *quality* of the cognitive ability's contribution defused those dilemmas; however, the diagnosis of Gettier problems posed in Chapter 1 turns on success from ability admitting degrees, whatever the quality. So long as what bridges the gap between true belief and knowledge admits degrees—whether it is success from ability where the ability contributes *in the right way*, or whether it is a cognitive ability with the help of a reliable informant, or a cognitive ability with the help of technology—the dilemma posed in Chapter 1 remains intact.

Highlighting these two points helps us see just what Greco's virtue epistemology must demand if it is to handle Gettier counterexamples rightly. Consider the following case:

> **Expert Ichthyologist:** James is an expert ichthyologist who specializes in freshwater fish; indeed, he is able to distinguish competently between the over 15,000 species of known freshwater fish. James is presented with a freshwater fish and asked to identify its species. Using his amazing skill, he can clearly tell that this particular fish is either going to be a *Cyphotilapia gibberosa* or a

Cyphotilapia frontosa (which can look quite similar), and upon even further expert analysis he comes to the conclusion that it is a *Cyphotilapia gibberosa*, which it is. However, John, James's nemesis and an expert ichthyologist in his own right, decided the night before to disguise the *Cyphotilapia gibberosa* to look like a *Cyphotilapia frontosa*. Thankfully, however, Sheree, James's other expert ichthyologist nemesis (who is conveniently not on speaking terms with John), decided to try to trick James in the same way—arriving shortly after John left, mistakenly perceiving that the fish was a *Cyphotilapia frontosa*, and *disguising John's disguise* to make the fish look, once again, like a *Cyphotilapia gibberosa*.[15]

Greco is going to want to know whether or not the success of James's belief is attributable to his cognitive abilities *in the right way*——"in a way that would regularly serve relevant purposes," "in a way that would regularly serve relevant informational needs" (Greco 2012, 14, 17). But it seems clear that the success of James's belief is largely attributable to his cognitive abilities in the right way, in a way that would meet the relevant purposes and would serve relevant informational needs. James's expertise with freshwater fish is immense, and his ability to narrow down the over 15,000 possibilities was almost flawless; it'd be difficult to find someone who could satisfy the relevant informational needs any better! As such, if Greco's virtue epistemology is to rightly handle such cases, it needs to say that the success of James's belief is not attributable *enough* to his cognitive abilities—that his competency as an ichthyologist was not responsible for the truth of his belief (in the right way) to a large enough extent. However, strengthened cases could be easily produced. We can easily imagine cases where a given protagonist hits upon a true belief because of an even greater exercise of epistemic competence and ability, where the success of their belief is even more attributable to their cognitive competencies; so long as that the relevant competency is still fallible it will be possible to create more Gettier cases. As such, it looks like the only way Greco's virtue epistemology can fully avoid Gettier counterexamples is if it requires perfect *success from ability*, if it requires known beliefs to be true *entirely because* of a given cognitive ability (and in the right way), if it requires the cognitive competency at issue to guarantee, necessarily, the truth of the belief in question. That, of course, is a tall order! Very few (if any) of even our most epistemically secure beliefs are candidates for perfect *success from ability*, where the success of the belief is entirely attributable to our cognitive abilities in the right way. *Once Greco's understanding of success from ability is recognized to suit degrees, his solution to the Gettier Problem is pushed on the horns of the same dilemma explicated in*

Chapter 1: either remain vulnerable to strengthened Gettier counterexamples or strengthen the demands of knowledge such that it is almost unattainable, paving the way to radical skepticism.

Now, a defender of Greco's virtue epistemology may very well grant that *success from ability* suits degrees—that the success of a belief can be attributable to a given cognitive competency in the right way to a greater or lesser extent; however, they may want to deny that Gettier cases ever exhibit any. If Gettier cases are simply cases where a given belief is true completely divorced from the respective agent's cognitive abilities, then cases like Expert Ichthyologist are not really problematic. If a defender of virtue epistemology could show us that the truth of James's belief is (despite appearances) *completely* divorced from his competencies as a ichthyologist, then we might deny that his belief is knowledge and get the right result, defusing the case and barring any strengthened iterations.

However, that is not a viable defense against Expert Ichthyologist. Surely James's cognitive competencies *are* partially (if not largely) responsible for his belief hitting upon the truth. Surely the success of James's belief is partially (if not largely) attributable to his cognitive abilities in the right way.

Consider the following scenario:

Fish Guessing: Abbey, Jim, Debbie, and Jeff are playing a guess-the-species-of-freshwater-fish game—a game where they are presented with various types of freshwater fish and asked to identify the species. Abbey is an expert ichthyologist. When she is presented with a fish she is able to use her immense skills as a ichthyologist to narrow down the over 15,000 possibilities to the one right answer. Jim too is an expert ichthyologist; indeed, he is every bit as knowledgeable as Abbey. Using his amazing skill, he can clearly tell that the fish before him is either going to be a *Cyphotilapia gibberosa or a Cyphotilapia frontosa* (which can look quite similar), and upon even further expert analysis he comes to the conclusion that it is a *Cyphotilapia gibberosa*, which it is. However, after narrowing down the over 15,000 possibilities to just *Cyphotilapia gibberosa or a Cyphotilapia frontosa*, Jim is Gettiered about these final two options. Thirdly, Debbie is presented with a fish. She knows almost nothing about ichthyology; however, she is something of an idiot savant—having memorized the names of every single species of freshwater fish. She has no idea what species is before her, so she simply picks a species at random and just happens to get it right. Finally, Jeff is presented with a fish. He knows absolutely nothing about ichthyology. He doesn't even know the names of any species. When he goes to hazard a guess; however, he chokes on a burp and just so happens to utter the name of the species before him.

In that scenario, it is easy to assume that Abbey's belief is largely true because of her cognitive abilities; she is, after all, an expert ichthyologist and is able to identify the fish as a direct result of this expertise. Like Ted in Ted3, the success of her belief is almost entirely attributable to her abilities *in the right way*. Second, I think we can also easily assume that Debbie's belief is marginally true as a result of her cognitive abilities (though the success of her belief is certainly nowhere near attributable enough to her cognitive abilities to constitute knowledge); after all, at least she knows the names of the various species of freshwater fish. Somewhat like Ted1, the success of Debbie's belief is attributable to her abilities in the right way to some minimal extent. And third, I think we can safely assume that Jeff's correct answer is in no way a reflection of his cognitive abilities; Jeff's correct answer is well and truly devoid of *success from ability*. In no way, is Jeff's correct answer attributable to his cognitive abilities, let alone attributable to his cognitive abilities in the right way. What about Jim? To say that Jim (whose circumstances are just like James's in the case of Expert Ichthyologist) has a belief that is *in no way* true as a result of his cognitive abilities is to put it on par with Jeff's choked-on burp. But, again, that is surely wrong. Surely, the cognitive abilities of Jim (and James) are largely responsible for the truth of their belief, where the success of their belief is largely attributable to their respective cognitive competencies in such a way "that would regularly serve relevant purposes," in a way "that would regularly serve relevant informational needs" (Greco 2012, 14, 17). Even though they were eventually Gettiered in the very end, their cognitive abilities surely brought him most of the way there and got them there *in the right way*. The dilemma leveled against Greco's virtue epistemology still stands. And as such, even if Greco's account of knowledge can dissolve the respective dilemmas of Lackey and Vaesen, a far more insidious and far-reaching dilemma remains unresolved—the dilemma between *solving Gettier problems and widespread, intractable skepticism*.

Section 4: Turri

For my earlier response to Turri, see Church 2013b. In the recent article "Manifest Failure: The Gettier Problem Solved" (2011), John Turri invokes an intuitive and elegant account of manifestation not only to improve upon many seminal projects within contemporary epistemology but also to solve the Gettier Problem. This latter result, of course, is quite striking. For nearly fifty years, epistemologists have been chasing a solution for the Gettier Problem but with little to no success. If Turri is right, if he has actually solved the Gettier Problem, then he has done something that is absolutely groundbreaking and really quite remarkable.

However, if the history of epistemology has taught us anything, it is to be pessimistic regarding purported solutions to the Gettier Problem. Time and time again such solutions have been shown to either fall prey to further, strengthened counterexamples or hide dubious and unpalatable conclusions (e.g., radical skepticism). Unfortunately for Turri and his solution, in this section we will see history repeat itself. The sort of counterexamples leveled against Greco's account will be equally applicable to Turri's account. I argue that any success against Gettier counterexamples afforded by Turri's notion of manifestation is merely fleeting and that strengthened counterexamples can be easily produced.

In outlining Turri's solution to the Gettier Problem, we first need to understand his intuitive account of manifestation. Consider the following two scenarios:

> **Boil:** You place a cup of water in the microwave and press start. The magnetron generates microwaves that travel into the central compartment, penetrating the water and excite its molecules. Soon the water boils. (Turri 2011, 6)

> **Fire:** You place a cup of water in the microwave and press start. The magnetron generates microwaves that cause an insufficiently insulated wire in the control to catch fire, which fire deactivates the magnetron and spreads to the central compartment. Soon the water boils. (Turri 2011, 6)

While the result in both scenarios is the same (i.e., the cup of water boils), how that result comes about is markedly different. In Boil, the magnetron boils the cup of water. In Fire, the fire in the central compartment boils the cup of water. In the former, the boiling cup of water manifests the microwave's heating ability. In the latter, the boiling cup of water does not manifest the microwave's heating ability. And this distinction is important across a wide range of cases. To quote Turri:

> The examples highlight a general distinction between (a) an outcome manifesting a disposition and (b) an outcome happening merely because of a disposition. . . . Outcomes include conditions, events, and processes. Dispositions include powers and susceptibilities. No metaphysical theory teaches us this distinction. . . . Albert Pujols crushes home runs regularly because of his power; he also receives intentional walks regularly because of his power; his power manifests itself in the former case, but not in the latter. Roger Federer regularly smashes wicked forehands because of his skill; he is also lauded regularly because of his skill; his skill manifests itself in the former case, but not in the latter. (2011, 6)

And it is precisely this distinction between when an outcome manifests a disposition (an ability, power, competence, etc.) that Turri invokes in his proposed solution to the Gettier Problem. While there is, no doubt, more that could be said, we seem to have a good intuitive grasp of the distinction being made in his use of manifestation. Turri is willing to let us be guided by our intuitions, and, given our current purposes, so am I.

Knowledge, for Turri, is what he calls "adept belief"—true belief that manifests a cognitive competence (2011, 7). In other words, S knows that p, according to Turri, if and only if S's having a true belief that p manifests S's cognitive competence, where "cognitive competence" is used "inclusively to cover any reliable cognitive disposition, ability, power, skill, or virtue" (2011, 7).

Consider the Fish Convention case again (see Section 2), where Smith is Gettiered about there being a *Cyphotilapia gibberosa* at the local fish convention. In this case, Smith's belief is formed through an exercise of cognitive competence and Smith's belief is true; however, critically, the truth of Smith's belief does not *manifest* his competence. Smith's belief is only true by dumb luck; it is true for reasons that his given exercise of cognitive competencies would not have predicted. Turri's account rightly predicts that Smith does not know that "there is a *Cyphotilapia gibberosa* at this convention." And such a solution, it seems, can be easily generalized across all Gettier cases. If knowledge requires true beliefs to manifest the relevant agent's cognitive competencies, then presumably knowledge will never be wrongly ascribed in a Gettier scenario because Gettier scenarios are (to put it roughly) those cases where a given belief is true by sheer luck, where a belief is true but fails to manifest the competencies of the relevant agent. Gettier cases are, according to Turri, simply scenarios where there has been a "manifest failure" (2011, 7). As such, through his intuitive account of manifestation, Turri has, it may seem, given us a viable solution to the Gettier Problem.

The contours of John Turri's proposed solution to the Gettier Problem are clear. Knowledge, for Turri, is "adept belief"—true belief that *manifests* a cognitive competence (2011, 7). Such an account is meant to be immune to Gettier counterexample simply because Gettier counterexamples are quintessentially scenarios where a given belief is true out of serendipity, dumb luck, or chance—true *without* manifesting the cognitive competencies of the relevant agent. Gettier cases are quintessentially scenarios where there has been a manifest failure.

In order to see how this solution to the Gettier Problem fails, we need to appreciate (once again) the fact that manifesting competence is a matter of degree, that a given cognitive competence can be responsible for a given belief hitting upon the truth to a greater or lesser extent. Just like how the accuracy of an archer's shot can manifest her competence/abilities as an archer to a greater or lesser extent, so too can an agent's true belief manifest her cognitive competencies or intellectual abilities to a greater or lesser extent.

Highlighting degrees of manifestation helps us see just what Turri must demand if his account is to handle Gettier counterexamples rightly. Consider once again the Expert Ichthyologist case (Section 3). Parallel to what we saw with Greco, the truth of James's belief that the given fish is a *Cyphotilapia gibberosa* manifests a great deal of his cognitive competency. (He was, after all, able to narrow down the possibilities from over 15,000 to just 2.) He does not ultimately *know* that it is a *Cyphotilapia gibberosa* since he was effectively Gettiered by the combined efforts of John and Sheree.[16] As such, if Turri is to rightly handle such cases, he needs to say that the truth of James's belief does not manifest his cognitive competency *enough*, that James's skills as a ichthyologist were not responsible for the truth/success of his belief to a large enough extent. However, strengthened cases could be easily produced. We can easily imagine cases where a given protagonist has a true belief that manifests of an even greater degree of epistemic competence; so long as that the relevant competency is still fallible it will be possible to create more Gettier cases. As such, the only way Turri can fully avoid Gettier counterexamples is if he requires perfect manifestation, if he requires the cognitive competence or intellectual ability at issue to guarantee, necessarily, the truth of the belief in question. That, of course, is a tall order. Very few (if any) of even our most epistemically secure beliefs are candidates for perfectly manifesting our cognitive competency. *Once manifestation is recognized to suit degrees, John Turri's solution to the Gettier Problem (and his account of knowledge) is pushed on the horns of a familiar dilemma: either fall prey to strengthened Gettier counterexamples or strengthen the demands of knowledge such that it is almost unattainable, opening the door to radical skepticism. And insofar as neither of these options is viable, Turri's proposal cannot ultimately succeed.*[17]

Of course, while defenders of Turri's account of knowledge may very well grant that manifestation suits degrees, they may want to deny that Gettier cases ever exhibit any. If Gettier cases are simply cases where a given belief is true completely divorced from the respective agent's cognitive competency or intellectual ability, and if Gettier cases never exhibit any degree of manifestation, then cases like Expert Ichthyologist are not really problematic. If a defender of Turri's account could show us that the truth of James's belief is (despite appearances) *completely* divorced from his competencies and abilities as a ichthyologist, then Turri's epistemology could deny that it is knowledge and get the right result, defusing the case and barring any strengthened iterations.

However, again, I do not think that is a viable defense against Expert Ichthyologist; surely James's cognitive competencies or intellectual abilities *are* partially (if not largely) responsible for his belief hitting upon the truth. As we saw with the Fish Guessing case earlier, surely James's true belief manifests his cognitive competency as an ichthyologist to at least some degree.

In that scenario, it is easy to assume that Abbey's belief largely manifests her cognitive competencies; she is, after all, an expert ichthyologist and is able to identify the fish as a direct result of this expertise. Her true belief clearly manifests in her skills as an ichthyologist. Second, I think we can also easily assume that Debbie's belief is marginally true as a result of her cognitive competencies or intellectual abilities (though her belief is certainly nowhere near adept enough to constitute knowledge); after all, at least she knows the names of the various species of freshwater fish. The truth of Debbie's belief presumably manifests the faintest trace of cognitive competency. And once again, I think we can safely assume that Jeff's correct answer is in no way a reflection of his cognitive competencies or intellectual abilities; Jeff's correct answer is well and truly devoid of adeptness. Bob's correct belief in no way manifests epistemic skill. What about Jim? To say that Jim (whose circumstances are just like Abbey's in the case of Expert Ichthyologist) has a true belief that *in no way* manifests his cognitive competencies is to put it on par with Jeff's choked-on burp. But that is surely wrong. Surely, the cognitive competencies of Jim are largely responsible for the truth of his belief; surely, the truth of Jim's belief manifests a significant amount of epistemic skill; even though he was eventually Gettiered in the very end, his cognitive competencies surely brought him most of the way there. And if this is correct, then the dilemma I have leveled against Turri's solution still stands. If this is correct, then Turri's *manifest failure* solution to the Gettier Problem fails.

In "Manifest Failure: The Gettier Problem Solved," John Turri offers an account of knowledge that is meant to be immune to Gettier counterexample. Knowledge, for Turri, is adept belief—true belief that manifests cognitive competence. As cases like Expert Ichthyologist show us, however, Gettiered true beliefs can manifest cognitive competence too—and seemingly to a large degree. As such, the only way Turri's account of knowledge can fully preclude Gettier counterexample is if it demands perfect manifestation, if it requires the cognitive competence or intellectual ability at issue to necessarily guarantee the truth of the belief in question. This, of course, is a tall order. So, it seems, Turri account faces an all too familiar dilemma: either remain susceptible to Gettier counterexamples like Expert Ichthyologist or strengthen his account of knowledge such that is nearly unreachable, paving the way to radical skepticism. Sadly, the solution of "Manifest Failure" seems to fail—simply adding another iteration in the cycle we know all too well in contemporary epistemology, the cycle of purported solution to the Gettier Problem followed by further counterexample.

Conclusion

Agent-reliabilism is the most popular version of virtue epistemology in the contemporary literature. In particular, Ernest Sosa's analysis of knowledge in which knowledge is explicated as a belief being *true because competent* is arguably the seminal virtue epistemology so far in the twenty-first century—helping to usher in other, nuanced adaptations of agent-reliabilism virtue epistemology. And despite a backdrop of growing pessimism regarding the ability of reductive analyses to surmount the Gettier Problem viably, most agent-reliabilists seem remarkably sanguine in their analyses. As we've seen, this optimism is misplaced.

Ernest Sosa's seminal agent-reliabilism virtue epistemology quickly faced a series of powerful critiques—critiques by Lackey and Vaesen—that argued virtue-theoretic accounts of knowledge like Sosa's are unable to surmount the Gettier Problem viably, without, say, giving up on knowledge based on testimony or extended cognition. But without fully capturing the dilemma facing agent-reliabilism—not just a dilemma between Gettier and testimony or Gettier and extended cognition but as a dilemma between Gettier and *radical skepticism*—such critiques do not accurately or fully diagnose what it takes to surmount the Gettier Problem. As such, when other agent-reliabilists—like John Greco and John Turri—survey what is required of their respective accounts, they misjudge the situation. And as we've now seen, both Greco's account and Turri's account fall squarely on the horns of the dilemma between solving Gettier cases and facing radical, untenable skepticism.

In the next chapter, we'll explore whether or not a prominent version of agent-responsibilism will fare any better.

4

Agent-responsibilism

Agent-responsibilism (or neo-Aristotelian) virtue epistemology stands as another dominant view in the contemporary literature that aims to provide a viable reductive account of knowledge. And the seminal agent-responsibilist account of knowledge is, no doubt, Linda Zagzebski's theory of knowledge as it is explicated in *Virtues of the Mind* (1996) and "What Is Knowledge?" (1999). According to Michael Levin, Linda Zagzebski's agent-reliabilist virtue epistemology is "the only version of virtue epistemology" that "tackles the [Gettier Problem] head on" (2004, 397). Indeed, according to Levin, if Zagzebski's version of virtue epistemology fails to provide a viable analysis, then "the prospects for . . . other versions are not good" (2004, 397).

In this chapter, we will consider Zagzebski's agent-responsibilism virtue epistemology and consider whether or not it does indeed provide a viable analysis of knowledge when it comes to Gettier counterexamples. In trying to provide such an analysis, Zagzebski knows she somehow has to balance between both horns of her own dilemma—the dilemma facing all analyses of knowledge we explicated in Chapter 1, the dilemma between facing Gettier counterexamples or risk falling into radical skepticism. In §1, we will consider Michael Levin's 2004 critique of Zagzebski's analysis and explore whether striking such a balance ultimately leaves Zagzebski's analysis fundamentally incomplete. Then, in §2, I will argue that the revelation that luck suits degrees (cf. Chapter 1) radically limits the ability of Zagzebski's account—whether it is fundamentally incomplete or not—ever to offer any viable solution to the Gettier Problem.

Section1: Zagzebski's Virtue Epistemology

When Sosa defines knowledge as apt belief where aptness is understood as "true *because* competent," a casual reader may think that Sosa is saying that knowledge literally requires truth to be contingent on cognitive competencies—a view that seems overtly mistaken. Surely, for example, I can know that the earth orbits the sun even though such a fact has nothing to do with my epistemic competencies—even though the earth's movement around the sun is in no way contingent on my faculties. Such a view aside, it can nevertheless be difficult to know how exactly to understand Sosa's conception of aptness. If we should not read aptness as literally "true because competent," how *should* we read it?

Similarly, in *Virtues of the Mind* (1996) and "What Is Knowledge?" (1999), Linda Zagzebski defines knowledge as "belief arising out of acts of intellectual virtue" where a belief "arises out of" an intellectual virtue *if and only if* the belief is true "because of" or "due to" the said virtue (Zagzebski 1996, 270-1; 1999, 108-9)—an analysis of knowledge that has come under some harsh criticism because it is unclear how to understand the "because of" or "due to" relation. To be sure, while Zagzebski acknowledges that she knows "of no account of the *because of* relation that fully captures [the relevant connection]" and that "this concept is in need of further analysis and I do not know of one that is adequate," the problem is bigger than she supposes (Zagzebski 1999, 108, 111). The problem is not just that the "because of," "due to," etc. relation is under-described but that there simply is no feasible way to cash out such a relationship. To quote Michael Levin in his critique of Zagzebski, "The problem . . . is not that a gap is left in her account. In this respect the account fares no worse than any analysis of anything that takes the notion of explanation as primitive. The trouble is that there is *no* notion of explanation to fill the gap" (Levin 2004, 401).

In the paper "Virtue Epistemology: No New Cures" (2004), Michael Levin critiques Zagzebski's analysis of knowledge along these lines—providing us with a good summary of what is at issue in Zagzebski's account.[1] As we saw in Chapter 1, Zagzebski proposed that so long as we assume that truth bears a close but not inviolable connection with warrant, Gettier counterexamples are inescapable.[2] In keeping with this diagnosis, Zagzebski, in *Virtues of the Mind* (1996) and "What Is Knowledge?" (1999), proposes an analysis of knowledge where *truth is built into the warrant* (where truth and warrant are inviolably connected) and in such a way that it does not, at least at first blush, seem to lead to radical skepticism (as opposed to, say, when safety accounts establish an inviolable connection between truth and warrant). As we have already noted, Zagzebski defines knowledge as "belief arising out of acts of intellectual virtue" such that the truth of the belief is, as she says elsewhere, "due to," "because of," or "explained by" the given virtue (Zagzebski 1999, 109). That said, however, this leaves unexplained how the truth of a belief is (in any way) "explained by" acts of intellectual virtue; the problem, as Levin argues, is that simply no feasible explanation is available.³

Zagzebski's official definition of knowledge is "belief arising out of acts of intellectual virtue" or "cognitive contact with reality arising out of acts of intellectual virtue" (Zagzebski 1999, 109). To help make such a definition clearer, Levin provides us with the following notation for Zagzebski's understanding of virtue:

> Let $T(V)$ be the end or telos of virtue V. Then, for Zagzebski, act A, is an "act of V" iff (i) A expresses V-ish motives, (ii) A is the sort of thing V-ish people do, and (iii) A brings about $T(V)$ because of (i) and (ii). (Levin 2004, 399)

For example, the action of saving a child from drowning is an act of courage, say, if and only if (i) such an action expresses courageous motives, (ii) it is the sort of action that courageous people do, and (iii) if, in so doing, the child is actually saved. To be sure, according to Zagzebski, if I try so to save a child yet fail, I may very well have acted courageously, but I did not *perform an act of courage*. To use an epistemic case, the action of thinking carefully about a given inquiry is an act of scrupulousness, say, if and only if such an action (i) expresses scrupulous motives, (ii) is the sort of thing that scrupulous people would do, and (iii) if, in so doing, the given telos (which would include the truth) is reached. Again, if I am so cognizing and yet nevertheless form a false belief, I may very well have cognized scrupulously without performing an act of "cognitive scrupulousness" (Levin 2004, 399–400). As such, a given belief is knowledge for Zagzebski if and only if it arises out of a given A that (i) expresses V-ish motives, (ii) is the sort of thing that V-ish people do, and (iii) the given telos (which would include truth) is met.

Rephrased in this way, however, it looks like Zagzebski's official definition is insufficient. Seemingly there is nothing different in the cognitive character between Henry in a "Fake Barn territory" Gettier case and Henry in a "Real Barn territory" good case. In both scenarios, by hypothesis, Henry is performing identical cognitive actions—actions that have V-ish motives and that meet their telos. Seemingly, then, according to Zagzebski's official definition, Henry knows that "that's a barn" in Fake Barns—a conclusion that many of us will find counterintuitive. To be sure, other problematic cases abound; consider (once again) one of Zagzebski's own Gettier cases.

> **Lucky Mary:** Suppose that Mary has very good eyesight, but it is not perfect. It is good enough to allow her to identify her husband sitting in his usual chair in the living room from a distance of fifteen feet in somewhat dim light (the

degree of dimness can easily be specified). She has made such an identification in these circumstances many times. . . . There is nothing at all unusual about either her faculties or the environment in these cases. Her faculties may not be functioning perfectly, but they are functioning well enough, so that if she goes on to form the belief "My husband is sitting in the living room," that belief has enough warrant to constitute knowledge when true and we can assume that it is almost always true. . . . Suppose Mary simply misidentifies the chair-sitter who is, let us suppose, her husband's brother. Her faculties may be working as well as they normally do when the belief is true and when we do not hesitate to say it is warranted in a degree sufficient for knowledge. . . . Her degree of warrant is as high as it usually is when she correctly identifies her husband. . . . We can now easily emend the case as a Gettier example. Mary's husband could be sitting on the other side of the room, unseen by her. (Zagzebski 1994, 67–8)

Here again it looks like there is nothing different in the cognitive character of Mary in the abovementioned case and Mary in the nearly identical (good) case where the only difference is that she really does see her husband (call them Mary and Twin-Mary respectively). By hypothesis, Mary and Twin-Mary are performing identical cognitive actions—actions that have V-ish motives and that meet their telos. Seemingly, then, according to Zagzebski's definition, Mary knows that "My husband is sitting in the living room" in the case of Lucky Mary—again, an intuitively unacceptable conclusion.[4]

These sorts of problems arise because, according to Levin, Zagzebski's "official definition is too elaborate for its purposes" (Levin 2004, 401). On the face of it, defining knowledge as "belief arising out of acts of intellectual virtue" does not seem to incorporate truth in the right sort of way (according to Zagzebski's own diagnosis of Gettier problems)—such that what is doing the warranting in Zagzebski's account (the virtuous action) entails the truth of the target belief. Repeatedly, Zagzebski describes knowledge as belief that is true "because of" or "due to" an intellectual virtue—a noncausal "acqui[sition of] true belief through the virtues that brought it about"—and it is this feature that it seems is missing in Zagzebski's official definitions (Zagzebski 1996, 270; referenced in Levin 2004, 399). However, it is precisely this feature of her account that she invokes to surmount cases like Mary and her husband. To quote Zagzebski:

[I]n the case of Mary's belief that her husband is in the living room, she may exhibit all the relevant intellectual virtues and no intellectual vices in the process of forming the belief, but she is not led to the truth *through* those virtuous processes or motives. So even though Mary has the belief she has because of her virtues and the belief is true, she does not have the truth because of her virtues. (Zagzebski 1996, 297; emphasis mine)⁵

As Levin points out, requiring a given belief, B, to "arise from some act of virtue A, where A attains A's end, truth, via good motives A expresses" in order for it to be knowledge "interposes A between the belief and truth; neither B nor B's truth arises from motives good or bad—a result at variance with Zagzebski's plain intent that it is the *truth of the relevant belief* that must be reached via good motives (and acts) for there to be knowledge" (Levin 2004, 401; emphasis Levin's). To incorporate this feature into Zagzebski's official definition, according to Levin, we need to "bypass the middleman" and identify the given "A with the formation of B," thus restating Zagzebski's definition of knowledge as "belief whose attainment of truth arises from, or is explained by, intellectually good motives" (Levin 2004, 401).⁶

The question then becomes what this "arising from," "due to," or "through" feature of Zagzebski's account consists of. According to Zagzebski, it is not enough to form a true belief via an act of intellectual virtue—the true belief must *arise out of* such an act. As some commentators have noted, however, "[t]his distinction is obscure ... since it is not at all clear what it involves"; after all, it is not at all obvious what distinguishes Mary's cognitive act in the case where she is "Gettierized" from the case where she's not (Pritchard 2005, 197). To be clear, as Levin points out, no causal explanation is available to Zagzebski—"all causal paths from even the surest motives to belief permit double accidents" and, what is more, such a move would fundamentally change Zagzebski's account from neo-Aristotelian virtue epistemology into motive reliabilism (Levin 2004, 401).

Given Zagzebski's understanding of knowledge as "belief whose attainment of truth arises from, or is explained by, intellectually good motives," how, then, might truth "'arise noncausally from,' or be 'due noncausally to,' or 'explained noncausally by'" virtuous motives (Levin 2004, 401)? We are not told. As we have said earlier, Zagzebski admits that she "know[s] of no account of the *because of* relation that fully captures" the link between truth and virtuous motives—adding that "[w]e all have intuitions about what it means for something to happen because of something else, but this concept is in need of further analysis and I do not know of one that is adequate" (Zagzebski 1999, 111; also quoted in Levin 2004, 401). According to Levin, however, the problem with Zagzebski's account of knowledge is not just that it contains an explanatory gap (after all, as Levin notes, "any analysis of anything that takes the notion of explanation as primitive" will suffer from such problems), but rather "the trouble is that *no* notion of explanation is able to fill the gap"—that "there is no logical room for one" (Levin 2004, 401, 405).

As Levin points out, explaining a given belief will involve either (1) explaining how the belief was formed or (2) explaining why the belief is true (what makes it true). Using Levin's example, if we wanted to explain Homer's belief that he weighs 239 lbs. we might have "one of two explananda in mind"—either we will want to know how he formed such a belief (e.g., by standing on a scale) or we will want to know whether the said belief is true (i.e., does Homer really weigh 239 lbs.?) (Levin 2004, 401). Take $B(p)$ to mean "belief that p." To rephrase the current point, when asked to explain $B(p)$, we will want to provide an account of either how $B(p)$ was formed or of the truth of $B(p)$, namely, p.

Consider the first possible explanandum—explaining how the given belief was formed—what Levin calls a "presence-explanation" (Levin 2004, 401). In seeking a presence-explanation of someone's belief, we are wanting to know why he/she has such a belief—how it got into the person's head. Presence-explanations, to be sure, "are causal ... citing factors in the environment and within the subject" (Levin 2004, 402). So when we are seeking a presence-explanation for Homer's belief concerning his weight, for example, we are looking for an account of how he came to believe such a thing. Levin grants that the causal factors that led Homer to mount the scale may include virtuous motives such as "a burst of no-holds-barred honesty" for self-knowledge; however, "[t]he point to notice is that a presence-explanation of a belief $B(p)$, the sort of explanation in which mental habits generally appear, is neutral with respect to the truth of $B(p)$, i.e., of p" (Levin 2004, 402). While Homer's belief that he weighs 239 lbs. may indeed be true, Homer could have had the exact same cognitive character with exactly the same relevant stimuli and nevertheless produced a false belief. In other words, the cognitive character and stimuli that led Homer to believe that he weighs 239 lbs. would be the same in a 239 lbs. Homer or a 300 lbs. Homer. What is more, it seems as though any presence-explanation "ostensibly citing the accuracy of stimuli or the truth-conduciveness of motives" can be consistently diminished to an "internal presence-explanation that omits them" (Levin 2004, 402). As Levin points out, the presence-explanation, "Homer believes he weighs 239 lbs because the scale revealed this," for example, can be consistently diminished to "Homer believes he weighs 239 lbs. because the display read 239 lbs.," which itself can be diminished to "Homer believes [etc.] because he looked at the scale closely enough to see the display," which is also diminishable to "He looked at the scale closely enough to form the belief that it said 239 lbs." (Levin 2004, 402). This all being the case, Levin arrives at his first lemma: "While there is a sense of 'explain,' namely, presence-explain, in which motives explain belief, and these beliefs may incidentally be true, motives do not in this sense explain truth" (Levin 2004, 402–3).

Now consider the second possible explanandum—explaining what makes a given belief true—what we will call a "truth explanation." As Levin points out, it is clearly this explanandum that Zagzebski (and other virtue epistemologists) has in mind when she describes knowledge as a true belief that is "explained by" (or "due to" or "arising out of" or "because of," etc.) an intellectual virtue. Consider once again Mary and Twin-Mary. Both Mary and Twin-Mary have identical beliefs (or at least qualitatively equivalent beliefs based on "equivalent evidence from identical motives" (Levin 2004, 403). As such, Mary and Twin-Mary have identical cognitive characters concerning the belief in question. The difference between their beliefs, then, is not some psychological feature in either Mary or Twin-Mary. The one difference that Zagzebski is picking up on in her account is that, unlike Twin-Mary's belief, the motives of Mary's belief leave the truth of the belief unexplained (Levin 2004, 403). As Levin notes, however, "Shifting the explanandum to truth . . . pushes the explanans out of the believer's mind" (Levin 2004, 403). Levin explains:

> Why was Homer's belief about his weight true? Not because of whatever motives led him to form this belief, nor the merits of those motives, but because Homer does weigh 239 lbs. Whence did the truth of this belief arise? From Homer's weight, or perhaps the diet, genes, and lifestyle responsible for it. (Levin 2004, 403)

Virtuous motives, being psychological in character, in no way "explain" or "give rise to" the truth of (most) beliefs—"Insofar as truth can be explained, motives do not explain it" (Levin 2004, 403).[7] A second lemma, then: "while there is a sense in which the truth of beliefs can be explained, the truth of beliefs cannot be explained in the manner Zagzebski requires" (Levin 2004, 403).

To be sure, there may be cases where a presence-explanation seems to coincide with a truth-explanation. Consider the following:

A) "Homer was right about his weighing 239 lbs. because he forthrightly mounted a scale." (Levin 2004, 403)

In such a statement, the truth of Homer's belief seems to be directly dependent on his actions—the presence-explanation of Homer's belief seems to encompass its truth-explanation. In other words, the true belief in such a statement indeed seems to be "due to," "because of," or "explained by" the protagonist's cognitive character. As Levin points out, however, appearances deceive—"[i]n effect, (A) telescopes a nonevaluative presence-explanation of Homer's belief into a nonexplanatory characterization of that belief as true" (Levin 2004, 403–4). Once the presence-explanation and truth-explanation are isolated, however, A amounts to the following:

B) "Homer weighs 239 lbs. & he believes he does because he forthrightly mounted a scale." (Levin 2004, 404)

Leaving the two explananda telescoped, however, A amounts to this:

C) "The truth of Homer's belief that he weighs 239 lbs. is explained by his willingness to mount a scale." (Levin 2004, 404)

As Levin points out, however, while B seems plausible (certainly no less plausible than A), C seems extremely odd if not mistaken. We should not, therefore, conclude from statements like A—statements where a presence-explanation seems to coincide with a truth-explanation—that there is some middle ground where presence-explanations and truth-explanations overlap. In accord with Levin's argument, presence-explanations and truth-explanations are well and truly distinct.

Presence-explanations do not explain the truth of a given belief (lemma 1), and in the vast majority of cases truth-explanations in no way derive from the given agent's cognitive character (lemma 2). From these two lemmas, Levin summarizes the abovementioned reasoning with the following—what he calls a "quick a priori argument" (Levin 2004, 405):

> Beliefs have two sorts of properties: psychological, in virtue of occurring in minds, and semantic, in virtue of possessing content. Presence-explanations cover properties of the first sort, [truth-explanations] cover properties of the second. (The absence of mention of these two properties should not be mistaken for mention of some further one.) The two lemmas taken together, then, rule out the kind of explanation, the sort of "because" Zagzebski desires. There are, then, no other senses in which a true belief can be explained. There is no logical room for one. (Levin 2004, 405)

As such, if we, like Zagzebski, are to describe knowledge as true belief "arising out of," "due to," "because," or "explained by" virtuous motives, then we must embrace the uncomfortable conclusion of radical skepticism. To the extent that it is impossible to satisfy the "explaining" condition, it is impossible to satisfy the conditions of knowledge so defined.

Zagzebski wants to define knowledge as something like "belief whose attainment of truth arises from, or is explained by, acts of intellectual virtues";

such a definition, however, leaves us wondering how to fill in the "explained by" relation. As Levin points out, there are three ways we might explain a given true belief—*reliabilistically*: explaining causally how a given agent arrived at said true belief; *in terms of belief*: explaining why the agent believes said belief; *in terms of truth*: explaining why the given belief is true. According to Levin, we should not read Zagzebski's definition of knowledge *reliabilistically* because (1) "all causal paths from even the surest motives to belief permit double accidents" and (2) doing so would be to fundamentally change the neo-Aristotelian character of Zagzebski's account (Levin 2004, 401). We should not read Zagzebski's definition of knowledge *in terms of belief* either, because doing so is incompatible with the given definition. What is more, we should not read Zagzebski's definition of knowledge *in terms of truth* because doing so would radically limit what we know; seemingly, we would know very few things if knowledge required truth to be contingent on our intellectual virtues. This being the case, how should we understand Zagzebski's definition? Lacking any further possible filling-in, it looks as though Zagzebski's account of knowledge is fundamentally incomplete—bearing a critical gap that simply cannot be filled.[8]

Section 2: Degrees of Luck and Zagzebski's Dilemma

In "The Inescapability of Gettier Problems" (1994), Linda Zagzebski outlined a grim diagnosis of Gettier counterexamples: if whatever we take to bridge the gap between true belief and knowledge (call it warrant) assumes a close but not involuntary relationship to the truth, then Gettier problems will be unavoidable; however, if we assume warrant bears an involuntary relationship to truth, then radical skepticism looms on the horizon. Zagzebski uses her innovative virtue-theoretic account of knowledge to try to rise above her 1994 dilemma by developing an account of warrant that not only *entails* truth but is somehow *responsible* for it.[9] Such an attempt, we've now seen, doesn't seem to get off the ground; there doesn't seem to be any viable way to cash out Zagzebski's virtue epistemology as true belief *arising out of* intellectual virtue.

However, perhaps Zagzebski did not fully appreciate the direness of her own dilemma because, at least in part, she did not fully appreciate the fact that luck comes in degrees. To show that her account would fall victim to our diagnosis of Gettier counterexamples explicated in Chapter 1—which does account for degrees of luck—let's assume there *is* some viable way to explicate the *because*, *due to, arising out of* relation at the heart of account of knowledge. Assuming that Michael Levin's 2004 critique is somehow fundamentally misguided, I will argue in this section that Zagzebski's seminal virtue-reliabilist account of knowledge is still not successful at surmounting the Gettier Problem.

For Linda Zagzebski, knowledge is virtuous belief—a belief that hits its telos (truth) due to its being virtuously motivated and the sort of thing a virtuous person would do (believe). So what bridges the gap between true belief and knowledge in Zagzebski's account is this "due to" (or "arising out of," or "because of") relationship between the true belief and the virtuous motivation and virtuous action. So to see more clearly how Zagzebski's analysis of knowledge fairs against the Gettier Problem as diagnosed in Chapter 1, we need to consider whether this "due to" relation bears an inviolable connection to the truth or not. If it does, then we'd predict that Zagzebski's account of knowledge leads to radical skepticism. If it doesn't, then we'd predict that her account falls prey to further Gettier counterexamples.

Zagzebski is quite explicit on this point. She *wants* her account to bear an inviolable relationship to the truth, because she recognizes that "Gettier problems result from any definition in which the sense in which knowledge is good [the warrant] does not entail truth" (1999, 111). And as she claims, "The concept of an act of intellectual virtue does entail truth, and so [Zagzebski's] definition is not guaranteed to fail"—that is, fall victim to Gettier counterexample (1999, 111). However, insofar as an act of intellectual virtue—a belief that hits its telos (truth) due to its being virtuously motivated and the sort of thing a virtuous person would do (believe)—just *is* knowledge, the fact that an act of intellectual virtue entails truth isn't terribly important here; all accounts of knowledge that necessarily require truth (no known false beliefs) entail the truth of known beliefs. What Zagzebski needs in order to surmount the Gettier case—as she made clear in her 1994 diagnosis, and as we elaborated in Chapter 1—is a theory of *warrant* that somehow entails truth. In other words, what Zagzebski needs is her "due to" or "because of" or "arising out of" relationship between the truth of the belief and the virtuous motivation and virtuous action—the bridge between true belief and knowledge—to entail, somehow, the truth. Once this has been done, however, the diagnosis of Chapter 1 predicts that Zagzebski's account will indeed be immune to Gettier counterexamples, but only at the cost of radical and untenable skepticism.

The problem, of course, is that it is strikingly unclear how to understand Zagzebski's "due to," "because of," "arising out of" relationship. And as we saw in the previous section, it is not at all clear that is any viable way to make sense of it. However, for the sake of argument, let's assume that there is some way to make sense of such a relationship that does not do significant violence to Zagzebski's agent-responsibilism virtue epistemology.[10] What we will see is that no matter how we understand Zagzebski's "due to," "because of," "arising out of" relation at the heart of her virtue epistemology, it fails precisely in the way I predicted in Chapter 1—either falling victim to strengthened Gettier counterexamples or paving the way to radical skepticism.

To see this, the first point to appreciate is that warrant, for Zagzebski, admits degrees. In other words, the extent to which a given belief might arrive at its telos as a result of a given agent's virtuous motivation and virtuous action can be to a greater or lesser extent. We can easily imagine cases where a given agent exhibits some intellectual virtue to a greater or lesser extent. Consider the following case:

> **Holmes:** Sherlock Holmes is investigating the murder of Ronald Adair. After collecting a significant body of evidence and making various key observations, Sherlock Holmes—through his acts of intellectual courage and intellectual scrupulousness—is able to predict confidently that Colonel Sebastian Moran is the murderer. Though he is not absolutely certain that Moran is the killer, he is roughly 90% sure—accounting for some rather unlikely but nevertheless possible circumstances. While Holmes would typically prefer to be as certain as possible before having someone arrested, he learns that whoever killed Adair is going to make an attempt on Holmes's own life. Needing to move quickly, Holmes has Moran arrested immediately, only discovering much later that Moran was, without a doubt, the killer.

Holmes's belief that Moran is the killer hits the truth, it seems, largely because of (or "due to," etc.) Holmes's intellectual courage and unscrupulousness; his belief arrives at its telos (truth) by and large due to Holmes's virtuous motivation and virtuous action. Clearly enough, however, Holmes's belief could have arrived at its telos due to his virtuous motivation and virtuous action to an even greater extent—if he were, for example, able to spend more time with the case before making a conviction, to the point to where he is 99.99 percent sure that Moran is the killer.

And such a degrees-theoretic understanding of Zagzebski's account of the "because of," "due to," "arising out of" relation is confirmed by Zagzebski's own theorizing. While she is explicitly unsure as to how to cash out such a relationship—though she thinks we "all have intuitions about what it means for something to happen because of something else"—she does go on to outline the rough shape such a relationship should take (1999, 111). Consider the following quote:

Some epistemologists have attempted counterfactual accounts of the component of knowledge in addition to true belief and, up to a point, whether the believer would arrive at the truth in close counterfactual circumstances can be used as a way of determining whether the truth is reached in the actual circumstances because of virtuous activity. So, for example, we might defend our claim that you do not get to the truth in [standard Gettier cases] because of your virtuous motives and performed the same acts and failed to get to the truth.... But looking at whether the believer reaches the truth in relevantly similar counterfactual circumstances is only a rough way of determining whether the truth is reached because of designated features of the act. It is certainly not a way of explaining what is meant by saying that the truth is reached because of these features. For example, there are no counterfactual circumstances in which a bachelor is not unmarried, but it would not be true to say that he is a bachelor because he is unmarried. The concept *A because of B* is not reducible to these counterfactual conditions. At best any such definition *of because* of will be a nominal definition. (Zagzebski 1999, 111)

While Zagzebski is explicit that the "because" relation "is in need of further analysis" for which she does not "know of one that is adequate," the abovementioned quote gives us a bit more about how such a relation—which, again, is what bridges the gap between true belief and knowledge on her account—is meant to work (1999, 111). Even though Zagzebski's defense of the "because" relation above is, by her own admission, incomplete and fragmentary, it does give us a picture of the "because" relation that lends credence to cases like Holmes. Just as a given belief can arrive at the truth in close counterfactual circumstances to a greater or lesser extent—allowing the because relation to admit degrees—so too can Holmes's belief arrive at the truth to a greater or lesser extent because of his virtuous motivation and virtuous action.

Once it is clear Zagzebski's account of warrant—the "due to," "because of," "arising out of" relation—admits degrees. The fate of Zagzebski's agent-responsibilism virtue epistemology is identical to the fate of the agent-reliabilist virtue epistemologies considered in the previous chapter. Consider once again the Expert Ichthyologist case:

Expert Ichthyologist: James is an expert ichthyologist who specializes in freshwater fish; indeed, he is able to distinguish competently between the over 15,000 species of known freshwater fish. James is presented with a freshwater fish and asked to identify its species. Using his amazing skill, he can clearly tell that this particular fish is either going to be a *Cichlasoma dovii* or a *Parachromis managuensis* (which can look quite similar), and upon even further expert analysis he comes to the conclusion that it is a *Cichlasoma dovii*, which it is. However, John, James's nemesis and an expert ichthyologist in his own right, decided the night before to disguise the *Cichlasoma dovii* to look like a *Parachromis managuensis*. Thankfully, however, Sheree, James's other expert ichthyologist nemesis (who is conveniently not on speaking terms with John), decided to try to trick James in the same way—arriving shortly after John left, mistakenly perceiving that the fish was a *Parachromis managuensis*, and disguising John's disguise to make the fish look, once again, like a *Cichlasoma dovii*.[11]

Again, while James's belief that the given fish is a *Cichlasoma dovii* is largely true because of his intellectual virtue (he was, after all, scrupulously able to narrow down the possibilities from over 15,000 to just two), he does not ultimately *know* that the freshwater fish before him is a *Cichlasoma dovii* since he was effectively Gettiered by the combined efforts of John and Sheree. As such, if Zagzebski's virtue epistemology is to handle such cases rightly, it needs to say that the success of James's belief is not arising *enough* from his acts of intellectual virtue—that his competency as an ichthyologist was not responsible for the truth of his belief to a large enough extent. However, strengthened cases could be easily produced. We can easily imagine cases where a given protagonist hits upon a true belief because of an even greater exercise of intellectual virtue; so long as that the relevant competency is still fallible it will be possible to create more Gettier cases.

Zagzebski saw this, and that is why she so often stressed that her account of warrant should entail the truth of the given belief. But once we see that Zagzebski's warrant admits degrees—that a given belief can arise out of an act of intellectual virtue to a greater or lesser extent—it looks like the only way Zagzebski's virtue epistemology can fully avoid Gettier counterexamples is if it requires the given act of intellectual virtue to be *entirely responsible* for truth of the belief in question, if it requires the intellectual virtue at issue to guarantee, necessarily, the truth of the belief in question. The only way the Holmes case, for example, can be kept from turning into a Gettier counterexample is if Zagzebski demands that he, in effect, be absolutely certain (seemingly to Cartesian levels) of his belief—a tall order indeed! Very few (if any) of even our most epistemically secure beliefs are candidates for being successful entirely because of our intellectual virtue. *Once Zagzebski's agent-responsibilism virtue epistemology is recognized to suit degrees, her solution to the Gettier Problem is pushed on the horns of a serious dilemma: either remain vulnerable to strengthened Gettier counterexamples or strengthen the demands of knowledge such that it is almost unattainable, paving the way to radical skepticism.*

Of course, while defenders of Zagzebski's virtue epistemology may very well grant that the "because" relation suits degrees, they may want to deny that Gettier cases ever exhibit any. If Gettier cases are simply cases where a given belief is true completely divorced from the respective agent's intellectual abilities, then cases like Expert Ichthyologist are not really problematic. If a defender of virtue epistemology could show us that the truth of James's belief is (despite appearances) *completely* divorced from his intellectual virtues, then we might deny that his belief is knowledge and get the right result, defusing the case and barring any strengthened iterations.

However, that is not a viable defense against Expert Ichthyologist—surely James's intellectual virtues *are* partially (if not largely) responsible for his belief hitting upon the truth. Consider again the scenario of Fish Guessing:

> **Fish Guessing**: Abbey, Jim, Debbie, and Jeff are playing a guess-the-species-of-freshwater-fish game—a game where they are presented with various types of freshwater fish and asked to identify the species. Abbey is an expert ichthyologist. When she is presented with a fish she is able to use her immense skills as a ichthyologist to narrow down the over 15,000 possibilities to the one right answer. Jim too is an expert ichthyologist; indeed, he is every bit as knowledgeable as Abbey. Using his amazing skill, he can clearly tell that the fish before him is either going to be a *Cichlasoma dovii or a Parachromis managuensis* (which can look quite similar), and upon even further expert analysis he comes to the conclusion that it is a *Cichlasoma dovii*, which it is. However, after narrowing down the over 15,000 possibilities to just *Cichlasoma dovii or a Parachromis managuensis*, Jim is Gettiered about these final two options. Thirdly, Debbie is presented with a fish. She knows almost nothing about ichthyology; however, she is something of an idiot savant—having memorized the names of every single species of freshwater fish. She has no idea what species is before her, so she simply picks a species at random and just happens to get it right. Finally, Jeff is presented with a fish. He knows absolutely nothing about ichthyology. He doesn't even know the names of any species. When he goes to hazard a guess; however, he chokes on a burp and just so happens to utter the name of the species before him.

As we saw in the previous chapter, it is easy to assume that Abbey's belief is largely true because of her intellectual virtues; she is, after all, an expert ichthyologist and is able to identify the fish as a direct result of this expertise. Second, I think we can also easily assume that Debbie's belief is marginally true as a result of her intellectual virtues (though the success of her belief is certainly nowhere near attributable enough to her cognitive abilities to constitute knowledge)—after all, at least she knows the names of the various species of freshwater fish. And third, I think we can safely assume that Jeff's correct answer is in no way a reflection of intellectual virtue. What about Jim? To say that Jim (whose circumstances are just like James's in the case of Expert Ichthyologist) has a belief that is *in no way* true as a result of intellectual virtue is to put it on par with Jeff's choked-on burp. But that is surely wrong. Surely, the intellectual virtues of Jim (and James) are largely responsible for the truth of their belief; even though he was eventually Gettiered in the very end, his intellectual prowess and virtue surely brought him most of the way there. The dilemma facing Zagzebski's agent-responsibilism virtue epistemology—the exact dilemma predicted by the diagnosis explicated in Chapter 1—between Gettier counterexamples and skepticism still stands.

Conclusion

While there are several agent-responsibilism virtue epistemologies in the contemporary literature, none tackles the Gettier Problem as powerfully or as directly as Linda Zagzebski's account. When it comes to theoretically robust, agent-responsibilist analyses of knowledge, Zagzebski's account is the high water mark.[12] Nevertheless, Zagzebski's account cannot viably surmount the Gettier Problem.

Zagzebski, more so than most, knows just how challenging the Gettier Problem is—she knows that it required a theory of knowledge that not only inviolably connects warrant to truth but does so without falling into skepticism. In *Virtues of the Mind* (1996) and "What Is Knowledge?" (1999), that is a challenge that she takes up; however, as we saw in Section 1, in trying to develop such an account, Zagzebski leaves us with something that seems fundamentally incomplete—bearing a critical gap that simply cannot be filled. But even if there is some way to fill that gap, even if there is some way to viably explicate Zagzebski's seminal account of knowledge, there is still little hope that it can viably avoid Gettier counterexamples without falling into skepticism. As we saw in Section 2, no matter how we explicate Zagzebski's account of knowledge, once it becomes clear that warrant suits degrees, the Gettier Problem becomes truly inescapable.

In Chapter 1, I developed a grim diagnosis of why the Gettier Problem has been such an enduring problem, and in Chapter 2 we saw that diagnosis defended against several prominent objections. We've now seen two prominent accounts of virtue epistemology—agent-reliabilism and agent-responsibilism—fail to provide viable analyses of knowledge precisely along the lines predicted in Chapter 1. In the next chapter, we'll consider whether Alvin Plantinga's seminal account of proper functionalist virtue epistemology will fare any better (spoiler alert: it won't!).

5

Proper Functionalism

So far, we have seen that prominent agent-reliabilist and neo-Aristotelian virtue epistemologies cannot viably avoid Gettier counterexamples—failing precisely along the lines predicted in Chapter 1. There is one final account of virtue epistemology that I want to address before, in the final chapters, developing an account of non-reductive virtue epistemology: Alvin Plantinga's proper functionalism.

Alvin Plantinga's account of knowledge is one of the most iconic epistemologies of the twentieth century—offering an analysis of knowledge in terms of properly functioning cognitive faculties—a view that developed throughout his monumental warrant trilogy: *Warrant: The Current Debate* (1993a), *Warrant and Proper Function* (1993b), and *Warranted Christian Belief* (2000). While a species of agent-reliabilist virtue epistemology, Plantinga's proper functionalism is markedly different from the agent-reliabilism of Sosa, Greco, and Turri; it draws from and intersects with concepts and debates in philosophy of religion and theology and has become a touchstone for a distinct breed of virtue epistemology. In this chapter, I argue (again) that we have systematic reasons to believe that Plantinga's proper functionalism cannot viably surmount the Gettier Problem, that the future of virtue epistemology does not lie in reductive proper functionalism.

We will work toward this goal in two sections, following the chronological development of Plantinga's virtue-theoretic analysis of knowledge. In Section 1, we will elucidate and critique Plantinga's analysis of knowledge as it is found in *Warrant and Proper Function* (1993b). In Section 2, we will elucidate and critique the proposed modifications to Plantinga's original account found, first, in "Respondeo" (1996) and "Warrant and Accidentally True Belief" (1997) and, then, in *Warranted Christian Belief* (2000). In both sections, we will find our proposed diagnosis of Gettier problems vindicated, with each iteration and proposal failing precisely along the lines our diagnosis predicted.

Section 1: Plantinga's 1993 Virtue Epistemology

In *Warrant: The Current Debate* (1993a), Plantinga surveys several dominant accounts of warrant (i.e., that which bridges the gap between true belief and knowledge) in the contemporary literature and subsequently argues that each fails due to an inability to track virtue-theoretic intuitions across a range of cases. It is his particular focus on the *properly functioning* human knower that is meant to distinguish his account from all others. Plantinga's notion of proper function is meant to connect rightly a given agent to the facts (cf. René and the Gambler's Fallacy) and, of course, rightly preclude knowledge from cases of malfunction (cf. Brain Lesion). According to Plantinga, other theories of knowledge fail due to their inability to track knowledge ascription in accord with the proper functioning of the relevant cognitive faculties behind a given belief's genesis. Proper function is, for Plantinga, not only the key virtue-theoretic concept in his account; it is meant to be the "rock on which" competing theories of knowledge "founder" (Plantinga 1993b, 4).

Knowledge, for Plantinga, is warranted true belief.[1] Plantinga's 1993 theory of warrant can be approximately summarized as:

> **Plantinga's 1993 Warrant:** A belief B is warranted for S when B is formed by cognitive faculties (of S's) that are functioning properly in the right environment in accord with a good design plan aimed at truth.[2]

In other words, a given belief, B, will be warranted for Plantinga if and only if the following four conditions are met:

1) the cognitive faculties involved in the production of B are functioning properly;
2) [the] cognitive environment is sufficiently similar to the one for which [the agent's] cognitive faculties are designed;
3) the design plan governing the production of the belief in question involves, as purpose or function, the production of true beliefs;
4) the design plan is a good one: that is, there is a high statistical or objective probability that a belief produced in accordance with the relevant segment of the design plan in that sort of environment is true. (Plantinga 1993b, 194)[3]

Although such a compendious rendering of Plantinga's theory can be sufficiently understood without further elucidation, we will, for diligence sake, unpack it a bit further.

Again, it is Plantinga's focus on the epistemically virtuous agent (i.e., the agent with mechanically sound cognitive equipment) that is the cornerstone of his epistemology. But what, then, is proper function? If proper function is meant to be the cornerstone of Plantinga's account of warrant, then one may worry that the term "proper function" is every bit as enigmatic as "warrant" and that introducing the former to explain the latter is counterproductive; however, Plantinga thinks that we all have a more or less rough-and-ready understanding of what it means for something to be functioning properly or malfunctioning (Plantinga 1993b, 5–6). We all know what it means when a car cannot go in reverse because the transmission is not (mechanically) functioning properly. We know that a properly functioning human being should generally be able to walk in a straight line without tripping or swerving and how enough alcohol impairs this proper functioning. As such, Plantinga provisionally stipulates that the relevant cognitive facilities involved in a given belief's formation must be functioning properly if the belief is to have warrant. If John is on a hallucinogenic drug, his perceptual faculties will no longer be functioning as they should; hence, his belief that the sky is melting will not have any epistemic value in terms of warrant.

Although we may indeed have a sufficient rough-and-ready grasp of proper function, it will, nevertheless, be helpful to make some general clarifications. First of all, to function properly is not to function normally (as understood in the general statistical sense). Gottlob Frege may be better at logic than the normal human being, but this does not mean that his prowess in logic is the result of some cognitive malfunction. Likewise, to use one of Plantinga's examples, if due to some disaster almost everyone on earth was blinded (such blindness would be a statistically normal condition), the few sighted individuals would not be suffering from malfunctioning perceptual faculties (Plantinga 1993b, 9–10). Second, not *all* of one's cognitive faculties need to be functioning properly for them to produce warranted beliefs (Plantinga 1993b, 10). If my cognitive faculties associated with vision are faulty, that would not preclude my producing warranted beliefs with my auditory faculties. What is more, all that must be working are "the faculties (or subfaculties, or modules) involved in the production of the particular belief in question" to be warranted. For example, if I am colorblind, I can still produce all sorts of warranted visual beliefs—beliefs concerning distance, the presence of people and objects, and so on. Third and finally, proper function comes in degrees (Plantinga 1993b, 10–11). My running ability may not be functioning as well as it could (if, say, I chose to pursue athletics instead of academics in life), but that doesn't mean my running ability is somehow malfunctioning. Likewise, my cognitive faculties associated with my abilities at logic may not be as good as they could be (I could spend more time working through complex proofs, memorizing truth-tables, etc.), but I can still produce warranted beliefs based on logical deduction. How proper functioning does a given cognitive faculty need to be in order to be warrant conferring? Here, Plantinga concedes, he has no answer; however, he notes that we independently recognize that knowledge and warrant are vague to some degree—his hope, then, is that the vagueness of his theory in this instance corresponds to the vagueness of knowledge and warrant in general.

While Plantinga's focus on the mechanical proper functioning of an agent's various cognitive faculties is the cornerstone of his account, he concedes that proper function, though necessary for warrant, is not sufficient. To demonstrate, he presents us with the following case:

> **Alpha Centauri Elephants:** You have just had your annual cognitive checkup at MIT; you pass with flying colors and are in splendid epistemic condition. Suddenly and without your knowledge you are transported to an environment wholly different from earth; you awake on a planet revolving around Alpha Centauri. There conditions are quite different; elephants, we may suppose, are invisible to human beings, but emit a sort of radiation unknown on earth, a sort of radiation that causes human beings to form the belief that a trumpet is sounding nearby. An Alpha Centaurian elephant wanders by; you are subjected to the radiation, and form the belief that a trumpet is sounding nearby. (Plantinga 1993b, 6)

Your belief in such a case, though formed by properly functioning cognitive faculties, does not have warrant. What is more, even if it turned out to be true that a trumpet is sounding nearby (one is being played in a soundproof booth out of sight), your belief still wouldn't have much of any warrant.[4] Why? Because the environment on Alpha Centauri's planet is not congenial to your human cognitive faculties, properly functioning though they may be. A properly functioning toaster cannot be relied on to make toast underwater, because water is the wrong environment for toasters; likewise, properly functioning human cognitive faculties cannot be relied on to produce warranted beliefs on Alpha Centauri's planet (or in a vat, or under the influence of an evil demon, etc.), because the environment there is the wrong environment for human cognitive faculties.[5] What constitutes the right environment for human cognitive faculties? According to Plantinga, the kind of environment that our cognitive faculties were designed for (by God, evolution, or both)[6] is an environment like earth with "such ... features as the presence and properties of light and air, the presence of visible objects, of other objects detectable by cognitive systems of our kind, of some objects not so detectable, of the regularities of nature, of the existence and general nature of other people, and so on" (Plantinga 1997, 143).[7]

So, according to Plantinga, in order for the belief B to have warrant for S, it needs to be formed by cognitive faculties (of S's) that are functioning properly in the sort of environment they were designed for; however, this is not yet sufficient for warrant either. Proper function presupposes a design plan (Plantinga 1993b, 21). To assess whether or not a toaster, say, is functioning properly we need to have an idea of how it was designed to work. Likewise, in order to assess whether or not cognitive faculties are functioning properly, we need to have some idea as to how they were designed to function (by God, evolution, or both). To be sure, the design plan for human cognitive faculties is something like "a set of specifications for a well-formed, properly functioning human being—an extraordinarily complicated and highly articulated set of specifications, as any first-year medical student could tell you" (Plantinga 1993b, 14). Indeed, our cognitive faculties are so complex that they are designed to function occasionally divorced from the goal of arriving at truth. Consider how women, it seems, are designed to believe in hindsight that the pain of childbirth was less than it actually was. Similarly, people seem to be designed to optimistically believe they will survive a terrible disease far beyond what statistics vindicate. In such cases, the beliefs formed are produced by cognitive faculties that are functioning properly in the right environment according to their design plan but are nevertheless unwarranted because the cognitive faculties in question are not, at least in this instance, aimed at truth; rather, they are aimed at either propagation of the species or survival. In order for a belief to be warranted, not only does it need to be produced by cognitive faculties that are functioning properly in the right environment, but it also must be produced by cognitive faculties that are functioning properly according to a design plan that is aimed at truth (Plantinga 1993b, 11–14).

Finally, as Plantinga points out, even if S's cognitive faculties are functioning properly in a congenial environment and in accord with a design plan aimed at truth, the given belief is not necessarily warranted. Say an incompetent angel (or one of Hume's infant deities) set out to create a species of rational persons ("capable of thought, belief and knowledge"); however, due to the angel's incompetence, the vast majority of the created persons' beliefs turn out to be absurdly false (Plantinga 1993b, 17).[8] In such a case, the given people's beliefs are produced by cognitive faculties that are functioning properly in a congenial environment in accord with a design plan aimed at truth, but the design plan just turns out to be a rubbish one—despite the incompetent angel's best efforts, the subjects he created have wholly unreliable cognitive faculties. Warrant, according to Plantinga, requires reliability; more precisely, in order for a given belief to be warranted "the module of the design plan governing the production of that belief must be such that the statistical or objective probability of a belief's being true, given that it has been produced in accord with that module in a congenial cognitive environment, is high" (Plantinga 1993b, 18).[9] In other words, to use the language of Plantinga's 1993 Warrant specified earlier, the design plan of the relevant cognitive faculties must be a "good" one if a belief produced by those faculties is to have any hope for warrant.

Now that we have elucidated Plantinga's 1993 account of warrant, we are ready to consider how Plantinga's 1993 theory of knowledge, *warranted true belief*, fares against the Gettier Problem. Given the proposed diagnosis of Chapter 1, this comes down to what relationship Plantinga assumes warrant bears to truth—whether it bears an inviolable, a close, or a divorced relationship to truth. Obviously, given Plantinga's agent-reliabilism such that warrant is meant to track truth reliably, Plantinga would not endorse a divorced relationship between warrant and truth. The question then becomes: Is it possible, on Plantinga's account, to form a warranted false belief? If it is possible, then warrant is not bearing an inviolable relationship to truth. If it is not possible, then warrant is bearing an inviolable relationship to truth. Thankfully, Plantinga seems to answer this very question for us:

> On an adequate account of warrant, what counts is not whether my experience somehow *guarantees* the truth of the belief in question (and how *could* it do a thing like that?), but whether I hold it with sufficient confidence and whether it is produced in me by cognitive faculties successfully aimed at the truth and functioning properly in an appropriate environment. If so, it has warrant; and if it is also true it constitutes knowledge. (Plantinga 1993b, 55; emphasis Plantinga's)[10]

Plantinga is (reasonably) assuming that warrant bears a close but not inviolable relationship to truth. It is, on Plantinga's account, possible to have a warranted false belief. On the proposed diagnosis, then, Plantinga's 1993 theory of warrant, his 1993 epistemology, will be susceptible to Gettier counterexample.

That certainly is not a result Plantinga (in 1993) would have predicted. In *Warrant and Proper Function* (1993b), Plantinga interpreted Gettier problems *as problems specifically for internalism*; the lesson to be learned from Gettier problems, he says, is that "internalist accounts of warrant are fundamentally wanting" (1993b, 33).[11] For Plantinga, internalism requires a given agent to have some sort of special cognitive access to whatever confers warrant for a given belief if that belief is to be warranted. The point of Gettier cases for Plantinga, then, is that having special cognitive access to whatever confers warrant on my belief that, say, "that is a barn," "Jones is going to get the job," or "Smith owns a Ford" is not sufficient for that belief to be warranted. And this leads Plantinga to a rather bizarre conclusion that stands in opposition to our proposed diagnosis: "We should ... expect that an externalist account such as the present account will enjoy a certain immunity to Gettier problems" (1993b, 36–7). Thankfully for our diagnosis, however, this was a conclusion Plantinga was forced to abandon. In the Kvanvig edition, *Warrant in Contemporary Epistemology* (1996), and elsewhere, Plantinga comes face to face with Gettier counterexamples to his externalist (1993) epistemology. And in his 1996 essay, "Respondeo," Plantinga again asks "What are Gettier problems?" and though he is still quick to posit that Gettier problems show internalist theories of knowledge to be wanting, he nevertheless acknowledges that Gettier problems are not localized to such theories; instead, simply focusing on the luck involved in Gettier counterexamples—an approach that is more in line with the diagnosis offered in Chapter 1 (1996, 309).

And indeed, there was a flurry of cases that demonstrated the vulnerability of Plantinga's 1993 theory of knowledge to Gettier counterexample. For example, Linda Zagzebski, in "The Inescapability of Gettier Problems" (1994), offered the case of Lucky Mary:

> **Lucky Mary:** Suppose that Mary has very good eyesight, but it is not perfect. It is good enough to allow her to identify her husband sitting in his usual chair in the living room from a distance of fifteen feet in somewhat dim light (the degree of dimness can easily be specified). She has made such an identification in these circumstances many times. . . . There is nothing at all unusual about either her faculties or the environment in these cases. Her faculties may not be functioning perfectly, but they are functioning well enough, so that if she goes on to form the belief "My husband is sitting in the living room," that belief has enough warrant to constitute knowledge when true and we can assume that it is almost always true. . . . Suppose Mary simply misidentifies the chair-sitter who is, let us suppose, her husband's brother. Her faculties may be working as well as they normally do when the belief is true and when we do not hesitate to say it is warranted in a degree sufficient for knowledge. . . . Her degree of warrant is as high as it usually is when she correctly identifies her husband. . . . We can now easily emend the case as a Gettier example. Mary's husband could be sitting on the other side of the room, unseen by her. (Zagzebski 1994, 67–8)

Similarly, Peter Klein, in his paper "Warrant, Proper Function, Reliabilism, and Defeasibility" (1996), offered the case of Lucky Ms. Jones:

> **Lucky Ms. Jones:** Jones believes that she owns a well-functioning Ford. She forms this belief in perfectly normal circumstances using her cognitive equipment that is functioning just perfectly. But as sometimes normally happens (no deception here), unbeknownst to Jones, her Ford is hit and virtually demolished—let's say while it is parked outside her office. But also unbeknownst to Jones, she has just won a well-functioning Ford in the Well-Functioning Ford Lottery that her company runs once a year. (Klein 1996, 105)

In both of these cases, the protagonist in question seems to be using properly functioning cognitive faculties. Arguably, there is nothing wacky about the environment in these cases—the respective environments are perfectly earth-like, the cognitive faculties in question are not operating in a brain in a vat or on a planet of Alpha Centauri, and there are no liars or illusions at work. And presumably the relevant cognitive faculties in both cases are operating in accord with a design plan that is both (i) good and (ii) aimed at truth; unless we can distinguish the cognitive faculties at work in these cases from the everyday cognitive faculties of perception, memory, or credulity, denying that they meet either of these conditions will lead us directly to some unhappy skeptical conclusions.

But before we chalk one up for our proposed diagnosis of the Gettier Problem, we need to consider Plantinga's expressed methods for defending his 1993 account against Gettier cases. In *Warrant and Proper Function* (1993), Plantinga offers two distinct strategies for handling Gettier cases. Consider the second case from Edmund Gettier's original 1963 bombshell, "Is Justified True Belief Knowledge?":

> **Classic Case 2:** Smith comes to Jones bragging about his new Ford—providing manifold justification to this effect (showing Jones the bill of sale, showing Jones the title to the car, taking Jones for a ride in it, etc.). Based on this superb evidence, Jones comes to the belief "Smith owns a Ford." For whatever reason (perhaps Jones simply loves to play with logic), Jones adds to that belief the disjunct "or Brown is in Barcelona," where Brown is an acquaintance of Jones's whom he has no reason to think is in Barcelona. By chance, it turns out that Smith does not own a Ford. Also by chance, it just so happens that Brown is indeed in Barcelona. As such, Jones's belief that "Smith owns a Ford or Brown is in Barcelona" turns out to be true and highly justified (based on the aforementioned evidence),

though few would call it a case of knowledge. (paraphrased from Gettier 1963, 122–3)

On the face of it, Jones's belief could easily seem to meet all the conditions of Plantinga's theory of warrant. Jones's cognitive faculties seem to be functioning properly and the environment does not seem overly bizarre (after all, Jones is not a brain in a vat, on Alpha Centauri's planet, or anything like that), so the first two conditions on warrant seem to be met. In prudential cases where, say, a patient believes he will survive an illness against the odds, Plantinga would want to say that the relevant segment of the patient's cognitive faculties' design plan governing the production of his belief is aimed at survival and not truth, so in such cases Plantinga's second condition would not be met; however, nothing like this seems to be the case in Classic Case 2, so Plantinga's third condition on warrant seems to be met. And finally, we do not have any reason to think Plantinga's general reliability condition, the "good" design plan condition, is not met either. However, in *Warrant and Proper Function* (1993), Plantinga argues, first, that the environment in Gettier counterexamples is somehow uncongenial for the relevant cognitive faculties—that his second condition on warrant is unmet in Gettier cases like Classic Case 2. And later, Plantinga argues that the relevant segments governing the production of a Gettierized belief are not, in fact, "aimed at truth"—denying that his third condition on warrant is met. Let us consider both strategies in turn.

Consider the strategy of denying that Plantinga's second condition is met, the environmental condition on warrant. To quote Plantinga:

> The locus of infelicity, in these cases too, is not the cognitive faculties of the person forming the justified true belief that lacks warrant; they function just as they should. The locus is instead on the cognitive environment; it deviates, ordinarily to a small degree, from the paradigm situations for which the faculty in question has been designed. . . . What we have in Gettier situations is a belief's being formed in circumstances differing from the paradigm circumstances for which our faculties have been designed. (Plantinga 1993b, 35)[12]

Jones's belief is formed out of his cognitive faculty of *credulity*—"whereby for the most part we believe what our fellows tell us"—and, according to Plantinga, such a faculty is not suited for environments with liars in them (Plantinga 1993b, 33).[13] Again, to quote Plantinga:

> Still, credulity is part of our design plan. But it does not work well when our fellows lie to us or deceive us in some other manner. . . . It does not work well in the sense that the result of its proper function in those circumstances does

not or need not result in true belief. More exactly, it's not that *credulity* does not work well in these cases—after all, it may be working precisely according to its specifications in the design plan. It is rather that credulity is designed, we might say, to work in a certain kind of situation (one in which our fellows do not intend to mislead us), and designed to produce a given result (our learning something from our fellows) in that situation. But when our fellows tell us what they think is false, then credulity fails to achieve the aimed at result. (Plantinga 1993b, 34)[14]

So while we may grant that Jones's cognitive faculties are functioning properly (including the specific faculty of *credulity*) and that the relevant cognitive faculties at work are aimed at truth (even though they miss their mark in this case), Plantinga will seemingly want to deny that the environment is suitable for Jones's faculties—Plantinga's second condition for warrant.

To be sure, the environment in which Jones forms his belief must be *generally* suitable for his faculties. For example, surely Jones knows that Smith is talking to him, that Barcelona is a real place, that he is being appeared to in such and such a fashion, etc. As such, Plantinga would not want to say that the environment is bad *simpliciter* because in so doing he would be overly limiting what we can know. Instead, Plantinga will want to say that the environment is bad for the cognitive faculty of *credulity* in particular. While the cognitive faculty of credulity is not meant for an environment with liars, such as Smith, such an environment does not prohibit perceptual beliefs, say. Thus, Plantinga can sustain the intuition that Jones knows he is talking to Smith while denying that Jones's belief that "Smith owns a Ford or Brown is in Barcelona" meets the conditions for warrant.

However, as Richard Feldman notes in "Plantinga, Gettier, and Warrant," such a reply to Classic Case 2 "turns on untestable and implausible assumptions about the circumstances for which our cognitive faculties were designed and on equally questionable assumptions about the individuation of our cognitive faculties" (1996, 212). Let us say that instead of being duped by Smith, Jones is an acute cynic and able to aptly detect most liars like Smith. In other words, let us say that Jones could tell Smith was lying about owning a Ford. After all, Plantinga himself recognizes that people can "learn to believe some people under some circumstances and disbelieve others under others" (Plantinga 1993b, 33).[15] Indeed, I think we can reasonably posit that cynic-Jones is so good at detecting liars that in Classic Case 2 he would form a warranted belief that "Smith does not own a Ford." As such, Feldman levels the following dilemma-prompting question: "What faculty produced *that* warranted belief and what [environment] is it designed for?" (Feldman 1996, 212; emphasis mine). If we say that cynic-Jones's belief is formed using his faculty of *credulity*, then it looks like Plantinga is wrong to say that credulity cannot operate in an environment with liars. Alternatively, if we say that cynic-Jones formed his belief about Smith not owning a Ford using another faculty, the faculty of *incredulity*, say, then Plantinga's view begins to look more and more ad hoc.

Other cases pose an even greater challenge for this strategy—the strategy of faulting the general cognitive environment in Gettier scenarios. Consider the pre-Gettier Gettier case developed originally by Bertrand Russell:

> **Russell's Stopped Clock:** I glance at a clock, forming the opinion that it is 3:43 pm; as luck would have it, the clocked stopped precisely twenty-four hours ago. The belief I form is indeed true; again, however, it is true "just by accident" (the clock could just as well have stopped an hour earlier or later); it does not constitute knowledge. (Plantinga 2000, 157)

Naturally, Plantinga will want to deny that the protagonist in this example has a warranted belief, and, as in Classic Case 2, he will do this by denying that the environment is congenial to the formation of the belief that "it is 3:43 pm." Again, Plantinga cannot say stopped clocks are epistemically incompatible with our cognitive faculties simpliciter; after all, we can seemingly know all sorts of things in such environments (i.e., that there is a clock in the room, what time the clock says, etc.) that we would not want to deny. So, as in Classic Case 2, Plantinga will want to say that stopped clocks are epistemically incompatible with a specific cognitive faculty. But what could that specific faculty be? Our time-telling faculty? Seemingly, as Feldman points out, whatever answer we choose will come across as "entirely arbitrary and unsupportable" (1996, 213). Even if we allowed for ad hoc specific cognitive faculties, it is unclear how helpful they would be. If this is indeed the state Plantinga's account of warrant has come to, "there's little by way of a general theory and nothing that is illuminating or informative about why there is no warrant in Gettier cases" (Feldman 1996, 213).

In the second chapter of *Warrant and Proper Function*, Plantinga goes on to develop a completely different kind of Gettier-defense. Now, instead of denying the congeniality of the relevant general cognitive environments (i.e., the strategy of denying that the second condition on warrant is met), Plantinga denies that "the segment of the design plan governing the production of . . . [Gettierized] belief is aimed at the production of true beliefs" (i.e., the strategy of denying that the third condition on warrant is met). According to Plantinga, though our cognitive faculties are generally apt at acquiring true beliefs, due to limitations in our design there are times in which our beliefs are formed as a result of what Plantinga calls a "compromise" or "trade-off." For example:

[S]traight sticks look bent in water; it can falsely appear that there is an oasis just a mile away; a dry North Dakota road looks wet on a hot summer day; an artificial apple among the real apples in the bin can deceive almost anyone (at least so long as she doesn't touch it); a hologram of a ball looks just like a ball and can confuse the unwary perceiver; in those famous Müller-Lyer illusions, the shorter line looks the longer because of the direction of the arrow heads. (Plantinga 1993b, 38)

According to Plantinga, the beliefs formed as a result of such tricks and illusions, though formed by cognitive faculties operating in accord with their design plan in the appropriate environment, fail to be warrant simply because the segment governing the production of said belief is not aimed at truth. Plantinga offers the following explanation:

[C]onsider these perceptual illusion cases, and for definiteness imagine that our faculties have actually been designed; and then think about these matters from an engineering and design point of view. The designer aims at a cognitive system that delivers truth (true beliefs), of course; but he also has other constraints he means or needs to work within. He wants the system to be realized within . . . a humanoid body . . . in a certain kind of world, with certain kinds of natural laws or regularities. . . . He also wants the cognitive system to draw an amount of energy consonant with our general type of body, and to require a brain of only modest size. . . . So the designer's overall aim is at truth, but within the constraints imposed by these other factors; and this may require trade-offs. (Plantinga 1993b, 38–9)[16]

In Classic Case 2, even though Jones's cognitive faculties are generally aimed at truth, other goals in Jones's design *qua* Jones such as efficiency and modest brain size sometimes take precedence. As such, employing the second strategy, Plantinga denies that Jones's belief that "Smith owns a Ford or Brown is in Barcelona" is warranted because the segment of his cognitive faculties' design plan that produced it was not aimed at truth but rather something else (perhaps efficiency).

As Richard Feldman notes, such a response to Classic Case 2 is a bit "puzzling" (1996, 214). As we just discussed, Plantinga has already argued that a belief like Jones's fails to be warrant because the cognitive faculty that produced it, namely credulity, was operating in an improper environment; however, Plantinga now seems to be ignoring the environment proviso.[17] What is more, although Plantinga had just said that *credulity* as a faculty is aimed at truth, now it seems as though Plantinga is saying that this particular exercise of *credulity* is not aimed at truth; however, as Feldman clarifies, seemingly "what Plantinga has in mind is that the specific 'segment' of the design plan involved in producing the belief that Smith owns a Ford is not something so general as *credulity*" (Feldman 1996, 214). So though *credulity* in *general* may be aimed at truth, perhaps the particular exercise of it found in Classic Case 2 is not because of the *specific* design segment at play in the given belief's genesis.

Plantinga describes these "segments" of a given faculty's design plan in terms of triplets—composed of a circumstance, a belief, and a purpose (Plantinga 1993b, 22).[18] So in a standard (i.e., non-Gettierized) case of a belief based on testimony, the segment triplet governing its production, as Feldman notes, might be something like this:

<honest testifier, belief that *p*, truth> (Feldman 1996, 215)

In Classic Case 2, however, the segment governing the production of Jones's belief could perhaps be construed quite differently:

<dishonest testifier, belief that Jones owns a Ford, efficiency> (Feldman 1996, 214)

As such, given that the segment of Jones's cognitive faculties that produced his belief is not aimed at truth, the belief in this instance is not warranted—thus defusing the case.

To be sure, there is something to this strategy. Surely, it is the case that many of the Gettier counterexamples would dissipate if only our cognitive faculties were not so limited. If only we had faculties that were not tricked by the various deceptions we currently find ourselves tricked by, the protagonist in many Gettier cases would not be fooled into a false belief (more accurately, a luckily true belief). Indeed, as the proposed diagnosis of Gettier problems in Chapter 1 would predict, Gettier counterexamples could be avoided altogether if only our cognitive faculties infallibly (inviolably) tracked truth. However, it also seems feasible to say that if our cognitive faculties were not so limited, we would not have been able to survive as a species because, perhaps, our heads would have been too big and we would not have been able to hold them up, let alone escape from predators. However, as Feldman highlights, trying to preclude Gettier counterexamples by claiming that "the segments of our design plan that get us knowledge are . . . aimed at truth while the segments responsible for the beliefs in Gettier cases have other aims is rather implausible" (1996, 215).[19]

To see this, consider a case exactly like Classic Case 2 except that Smith is actually telling Jones the truth about owning a Ford—a case where we would typically attribute knowledge to Jones's belief that "Smith owns a Ford."[20] Seemingly, there is absolutely nothing different from Jones's perspective between this standard testimony case and Classic Case 2; however, Plantinga would have to say that while the segment governing the production of Jones's belief is aimed at truth in a case where Smith is telling the truth, in Classic Case 2, the segment governing the production of his belief must be aimed at something else. Somehow, the segment governing the production of Jones's belief in the former case is markedly different from the segment governing the production of Jones's belief in the latter case even though nothing has changed from Jones's perspective. With the ad hoc multiplication of design segments and the mystery as to what is regulating their aims, such a conclusion seems at the very least far-fetched.

To accentuate further the implausibility of the claim that "the segments of our design plan that get us knowledge are . . . aimed at truth while the segments responsible for the beliefs in Gettier cases have other aims," Feldman provides another case:

> **Newspaper:** You are reading the sports section of the newspaper. There is a list of the scores of last night's basketball games. You believe that each game did have the outcome reported in the paper. Suppose there is a misprint in one of the reports. (Feldman 1996, 216)

In such a case, you form any number of true beliefs, but you do form one false belief due to the misprint (a belief that could easily be Gettierized). According to the Gettier-defense currently under consideration, as you read through the scores the segment of your cognitive faculties' design plan that is governing the production of your beliefs is aimed at truth up until (and immediately after) you read the misprint. For the instant you read the misprinted score, the segment changes and is no longer aimed at truth. As Feldman notes, "this seems wildly ad hoc" (Feldman 1996, 216). Although such cases do not decidedly refute Plantinga's second strategy, they do nevertheless condemn it as decidedly meriting rejection (Feldman 1996, 217).[21]

To defuse cases like Classic Case 2, Plantinga offered two independent strategies: (i) deny that the given cognitive environment is suitably congenial or (ii) deny that the segment of the design plan governing the production of the Gettierized belief is aimed at truth. Unfortunately for Plantinga, such strategies simply fall flat—being intractable and unable to distinguish systematically Gettier environments from normal environments, Gettier design plans from normal design plans. Plantinga's 1993 account of warrant, Plantinga's 1993 analysis of knowledge, simply lacks the material for precluding Gettier environments and design plans without precluding from knowledge our everyday beliefs formed in normal environments and according to normal design plans aimed at truth. Both of Plantinga's proposed strategies fail because they lead to skeptical conclusions, on pain of adhocery.

Plantinga's 1993 account of warrant, his reductive virtue epistemology, takes warrant as bearing a close but not inviolable relationship to truth. As such, our proposed diagnosis of the Gettier Problem predicted that Plantinga's 1993 virtue epistemology would be susceptible to Gettier counterexample. And that is precisely what the literature has shown, and that is precisely what we have seen. Plantinga's reductive account of knowledge easily lends itself to Gettier counterexample—his proposed strategies for avoiding Gettier cases being ultimately intractable. But before we count this a victory for our proposed diagnosis of the Gettier Problem, let's briefly consider some other strategies Plantinga could have tried to invoke in his defense against cases like Lucky Mary, Lucky Ms. Jones, and now Classic Case 2.

For starters, Plantinga could have tried to deny that warrant can be transferred from a false belief. But, as Peter Klein points out in "Warrant, Proper Function, Reliabilism, and Defeasibility" (1996), such a strategy is generally accepted to be a dead end—being both too strong and too weak.[22] It is too strong because it seems to prohibit some legitimate instances of knowledge.

> For example, suppose that my belief that I have an appointment at 3:00 p.m. on April 10th is based on my warranted but false belief that my secretary told me on April 6th that I had such an appointment. If my secretary told me that I had such an appointment, but she told me that on April 7th (not the 6th) my belief that I have an appointment at 3:00 p.m. can still be knowledge, even though the belief that supports it is false. (Klein 1996, 106)

And too weak because further Gettier cases can be produced even if it is adopted. Someone could easily manipulate cases like Lucky Ms. Jones and Lucky Mary so that there is no clear inference from a false belief being made.[23]

Similarly, denying the transferability of warrant full stop would not be any more fruitful as a strategy for Plantinga to pursue. While such a strategy would indeed handle Classic Case 2, it does not seem as effective against Lucky Mary or, at least, Lucky Ms. Jones. As Klein points out, though someone might read the case of Lucky Ms. Jones as involving warrant transmission—for example, thinking Ms. Jones inferred the belief that she owns a well-functioning Ford from the prior belief that she drove a well-functioning Ford to work that morning—the case need not be read that way. Ms. Jones could simply form the given belief without drawing it from an antecedent. Just as Henry in Fake Barns sees the barn and then simply believes "there's a barn," perhaps Jones in Lucky Ms. Jones simply remembers and subsequently simply believes that she owns a well-functioning Ford. The transfer of warrant does not seem to be a necessary component of Gettier counterexamples.

What if Plantinga were to deny that the cognitive faculties at issue in the relevant cases were properly functioning to a sufficient degree—denying that condition 1 of his account of warrant is met? In other words, what if Plantinga denied that Mary's faculties of perception (in the case of Lucky Mary), or Ms. Jones's faculties of memory (in the case of Lucky Ms. Jones), or Jones's faculties of credulity (in Classic Case 2) were functioning as properly as they should if the corresponding beliefs they produce were to count as knowledge? The problem with such a response to these Gettier problems is that there is absolutely no indication that the relevant faculties at issue are not already functioning extremely well. Indeed, it seems like the only way this strategy could do Plantinga any good is if he required *cognitive faculty perfection* for warrant and correspondingly for knowledge. As Linda Zagzebski rightly points out, however, Plantinga expressly does not require perfection, nor should he (Zagzebski 1994, 68). Such a demand would simply be unreasonable—leaving us with only a precious few beliefs that we know. Without requiring perfection (which would be tantamount to requiring an inviolable relationship between warrant and truth), however, there is no way that denying that the cognitive faculties at issue in the relevant cases were properly functioning to a sufficient degree will produce any lasting success against Gettier counterexamples.

Could Plantinga instead deny that the relevant design plans governing the production of Gettierized beliefs are good? Could Plantinga deny that his fourth condition on warrant is met? Seemingly not. There does not seem to be any ground for making such a claim. There is absolutely no indication that the design plans governing the production of Gettierized beliefs (as in Lucky Mary, Lucky Ms. Jones, and Classic Case 2) are not already quite good. Indeed, it seems like the only way this strategy could do Plantinga any good is if he required not just good design plans but *perfect* (infallible) design plans for warrant and correspondingly for knowledge. We can stipulate that the design plans are as good as we like, but again it seems like so long as they are anything less than (statistically) infallible, then they will produce a false belief—a false belief that can be Gettierized. Without requiring design plan *perfection* (which would be tantamount to requiring an inviolable relationship between warrant and truth and presumably lead directly to radical skepticism), there is no way that denying that the relevant design plans governing the production of Gettierized beliefs are good will produce any lasting success against Gettier counterexamples.

According to Plantinga's reductive virtue epistemology, a belief is warranted if it is produced by properly functioning cognitive faculties that are operating in a congenial environment and in accord with a good design plan aimed at truth. And given Plantinga's 1993 reading of such a definition, warrant bears a close but not inviolable relationship to truth. And in accord with our proposed diagnosis of the Gettier Problem, Plantinga's account of knowledge fell prey to Gettier counterexample. Plantinga's expressed strategies for defusing Gettier counterexamples were found to be intractable—lacking material for sufficiently (i.e., without adhocery) distinguishing between Gettier scenarios and normal, everyday circumstances. We considered some other possible arguments Plantinga could invoke to try to save his 1993 theory, but they were ultimately no more helpful—at best, avoiding Gettier counterexamples by assuming an inviolable relationship between warrant and truth, and only then at the cost of radical skepticism. Thus far, the diagnosis of Gettier counterexamples proposed in Chapter 1 seems completely on target. However, we are far from finished with Plantinga's reductive virtue epistemology. After accepting that his 1993 account of knowledge was susceptible to counterexample, Plantinga admits that cases like Classic Case 2, Russell's Stopped Clock, Lucky Mary, and Lucky Ms. Jones show that a given belief can be produced by cognitive faculties functioning properly in the right kind of environment in accord with a good design plan aimed at truth and nevertheless fail to have warrant.[24] In the next section, we will explore the series of two modifications Plantinga proposes to his environment proviso—starting with "Respondeo" (1996) and "Warrant and Accidentally True Belief" (1997) and working our way to Plantinga's final modifications in *Warranted Christian Belief* (2000)—and discover that neither of them is any more successful at precluding Gettier counterexamples than his original 1993 account, failing precisely along the lines predicted in Chapter 1.

Section 2: Plantinga's Modifications

So, to reiterate, according to Plantinga's original 1993 conception of warrant, a belief B will be warranted for S if and only if the following four conditions are met:

1) the cognitive faculties involved in the production of B are functioning properly;

2) [the] cognitive environment is sufficiently similar to the one for which [the agent's] cognitive faculties are designed;
3) the design plan governing the production of the belief in question involves, as purpose or function, the production of true beliefs;
4) the design plan is a good one: that is, there is a high statistical or objective probability that a belief produced in accordance with the relevant segment of the design plan in that sort of environment is true. (Plantinga 1993b, 194)[25]

Or as I summarized earlier: "A belief B is warranted for S when B is formed by cognitive faculties (of S's) that are functioning properly in the right environment in accord with a good design plan aimed at truth."[26] As a number of critics pointed out, however, such conditions are not sufficient for warrant—which, given that Plantinga's 1993 account assumes a close but not inviolable relationship between warrant and truth, is precisely what our proposed diagnosis of Gettier problems would predict. In any case, Plantinga acquiesces as much in "Respondeo" (1996) and "Warrant and Accidentally True Belief" (1997)—admitting that cases like Classic Case 2, Russell's Stopped Clock, and Lucky Ms. Jones show that a given belief can be produced by cognitive faculties functioning properly in the right kind of environment in accord with a good design plan aimed at truth and nevertheless fail to have warrant. According to Plantinga, the problem with his 1993 account of warrant lies in his environment proviso. Though the beliefs formed in the aforementioned cases are formed by cognitive faculties operating within the right sort of environment, there is nevertheless some "cognitive environmental pollution," an abiding "lack of resolution" between the proper function of the given cognitive faculties and the environment in which they operate (Plantinga 1996, 309–10, 316, 327). So naturally, it is the environment condition that Plantinga seeks to expand on in his revised accounts of warrant. In his proposed modifications, Plantinga's environment condition, his second condition for warrant, is his anti-luck condition, his condition that is meant to preclude Gettier counterexamples.

Plantinga notes that in his original account the environment proviso was more or less a general environmental condition—a environmental condition that required warranted beliefs to be formed in an earth-like environment, an environment with "the presence and properties of light and air, the presence of visible objects, of other objects detectable by our kind of cognitive system, of some objects not so detectable, of regularities of nature, the existence of other people, and so on" (Plantinga 1996, 313). Plantinga has us call this notion of environment the "maxi-environment." However, as shown by the aforementioned cases, having a congenial maxi-environment alone is not sufficient for avoiding Gettier counterexamples. So Plantinga introduces the concept of what he calls a cognitive "mini-environment." Plantinga explains:

> We can think of a cognitive mini-environment of a given exercise of cognitive powers E as a *state of affairs* (or propositions)—one that includes all the relevant epistemic circumstances obtaining when that belief is formed. Consider any current belief B I hold and the exercise E of cognitive powers that produced it: the mini-environment M for E (call it "MBE") includes the state of affairs specified by my cognitive maxi-environment, but also much more specific features of my epistemic situation. (Plantinga 1996, 314)

According to Plantinga, the aforementioned "cognitive environmental pollution" and the abiding "lack of resolution" highlighted by Gettier cases like Classic Case 2, Russell's Stopped Clock, Lucky Mary, and Lucky Ms. Jones are not found in their respective maxi-environments but rather in the mini-environments of the relevant exercises of cognitive powers. In other words, the cognitive pollution and lack of resolution come from a given MBE not being favorable for said E.

As such, Plantinga adds the following Resolution Condition to his *Warrant and Proper Function* (1993) account of warrant:

Resolution Condition: A belief B produced by an exercise E of cognitive powers has warrant only if MBE is favorable for E. (Plantinga 1996, 328)

Not only does a given belief's cognitive maxi-environment need to be "sufficiently similar to the one for which [its] cognitive faculties are designed" (the original second condition on warrant), its *mini*-environment needs to be favorable for the exercise of cognitive faculties that produced it. To be sure, Plantinga goes on to say that we can make a given MBE as full and detailed as we please, with the exception of truth or falsehood of the given belief—lest mini-environments where a given belief is only luckily true, as in Gettier cases, be deemed favorable (Plantinga 1996, 314–15). As such, the relevant MBEs of cases like Classic Case 2, Russell's Stopped Clock, Lucky Mary, and Lucky Ms. Jones will, respectively, include the presence of liars, stopped clocks, visiting brothers-in-law, and Fords being unforeseeably destroyed. Plantinga's hope, then, is to explicate favorability in such a way that deems the relevant MBEs in such cases as unfavorable—precluding the corresponding beliefs from being warranted and therefore precluding their (mistakenly) being deemed knowledge by his account. At the heart of Plantinga's anti-Gettier strategy and his proposed modifications is his explication of "favorability."

Section 2.1: 1996/1997 Favorability

Just what does it mean for a mini-environment to be "favorable" for a given exercise of cognitive powers? While Plantinga is initially skeptical as to whether this kind of detail is "attainable or necessary here," nevertheless, in "Respondeo" (1996) and "Warrant and Accidentally True Belief" (1997), Plantinga posits the following definition (1996, 327):

> **1996/1997 Mini-Favorability**: MBE is favorable for E, if and only if, if S were to form a belief by way of E, S would form a true belief. (Plantinga 1997, 144; 1996, 328)

At first blush, it may seem as though Mini-Favorability is completely ineffectual. It would seem as though the mini-environment of the particular exercise of cognitive powers that produced Ms. Jones's belief that she owns a Ford is indeed favorable as the belief is true. However, Plantinga avoids this hurdle by specifying that Mini-Favorability's counterfactual semantics are non-standard (i.e., non-Lewisian, non-Stalnakerian)—"the truth of p and q is not sufficient for the truth of the counterfactual *if p then* q" (Plantinga 1996, 328).[27] Mini-Favorability is "a point where the usual semantics for counterfactuals is inadequate" (Plantinga 1996, 328–9).[28] The counterfactual semantics that Plantinga instead stipulates is one where "the counterfactual is true only if there is no *sufficiently close* possible world in which p is true but q is not" (Plantinga 1996, 329; emphasis Plantinga's). In other words, according to Plantinga, a given MBE is favorable for E, if and only if, if S were to form a belief by way of E in MBE, S would form a true belief in *all close possible worlds*. As such, the MBEs of the relevant cases are not meant to be favorable for their corresponding exercises of cognitive powers; seemingly, so it goes, in many close possible worlds, the protagonist's belief in question would be false. Subsequently, if the MBE is not favorable in such cases, then Plantinga's Resolution Condition on warrant is not met.

Perhaps realizing that Gettier cases will be unavoidable so long as warrant is not infallibly connected to truth, Plantinga's 1996/1997 account of warrant, where his new Resolution Condition is understood in terms of 1996/1997 Mini-Favorability, is meant to "[guarantee] that no false belief has warrant" (1996, 329). It is meant to be impossible for a warranted belief to be false, and as such it is supposed to be impossible for a warranted belief to only be true for reasons not captured by the warrant. As such, according to our proposed diagnosis of the Gettier Problem, Plantinga's 1996/1997 account of warrant and corresponding virtue epistemology should be immune to Gettier counterexamples but unfeasible, leading to some skeptical conclusion. At first blush, however, no such conclusion seems to be at hand. Does this mean that Plantinga has found an exception to our diagnosis of Gettier counterexamples, finding a viable reductive, virtue-theoretic solution to the Gettier Problem?

Unfortunately for Plantinga (and fortunately for the proposed diagnosis), the answer is no. Plantinga was simply wrong about his 1996/1997 account's infallibilism. Despite what Plantinga says, his 1996/1997 account of warrant simply does not "guarantee that no false belief has warrant." Consider the following familiar scenario: Ms. Jones believes that she owns a well-functioning Ford, and she forms this belief under good circumstances using properly functioning cognitive equipment. But, as it happens, a freak event occurs; Ms. Jones's car is utterly destroyed by a stray meteor. In such a scenario, Ms. Jones's belief seems to meet all of Plantinga's original 1993 conditions on warrant, and it seems to satisfy his Resolution Condition as understood in terms of 1996/1997 Mini-Favorability—presumably, in all close possible worlds, Ms. Jones's Ford is not hit by a roaming meteor. As such, Plantinga's 1996/1997 account of knowledge *does* allow for warranted false beliefs; and as such, it should, according to the proposed diagnosis, be susceptible to Gettier counterexample. And this is precisely what we find. To produce such a counterexample, simply stipulate that Ms. Jones wins that "Well-Functioning Ford Lottery" in all close possible worlds (perhaps one of her friends rigged the lottery without Ms. Jones knowing about it), and then we have produced a Lucky Ms. Jones-like counterexample to Plantinga's revised account of warrant. Again, our proposed diagnosis of Gettier problems seems to get it exactly right.

And as much is vindicated in the relevant literature. In "Gettier and Plantinga's Revised Account of Warrant" (2000), Thomas Crisp has leveled a similar Gettier counterexample against Plantinga's 1996/1997 account:

> **Prune Guessing:** Suppose your uncle runs the town's annual guess-the-number-of-prunes-in-the jar contests. Your prankish friend takes it on good authority that the jar contains 138 prunes and lets you in on the secret. Unbeknownst to both you and your friend, though, the number he is given is incorrect. Now, suppose further that your uncle has taken ill with an unusual brain fever and has come to believe that the fate of the nation hangs on your winning the contest. Since he can't remember how many prunes were in the jar to begin with, he empties it and refills it with the exact number of prunes indicated on your contest

entry card. The day of the contest arrives and the town gathers for the beloved counting of the prunes. You believe firmly that the jar contains 138 prunes. And indeed it does. But your belief is true by accident: had your uncle not taken ill with the fever, your belief would have been false. (2000, 47)

Again, the protagonist's belief in Crisp's case seemingly meets not only the original conditions for warrant but also the conditions of favorability set out in 1996/1997 Mini-Environment Favorability. The full and detailed state of affairs in the relevant MBE would include the presence of the uncle's fever and his delusional conviction about national security such that in no close possible worlds is the belief formed by the pertinent exercise of cognitive powers false, though, again, clearly the belief is still only luckily true. And indeed, by the time Plantinga wrote *Warranted Christian Belief* (2000), he seems to have realized this problem with his 1996/1997 modification.[29] According to Plantinga, his 1996/1997 account of mini-environment favorability is simply insufficient because "the relevant counterfactual itself can be true 'just by accident'"—a feature that should be simply impossible if his 1996/1997 account of warrant really was infallibilistic regarding truth (2000, 159). To illustrate as much, Plantinga provided his own Gettier counterexample to his 1996/1997 account:

> **Foggy Fake Barns:** Suppose I am driving through [fake barn territory] on an early September morning when there is a good deal of mist and fog. I glance to the right and see a real barn; as it happens, all the nearby fake barns (which outnumber the real ones) are obscured by the morning mist; I say to myself, "Now that is a fine barn!" The belief I form is true; the relevant counterfactual is also true because of the way the fake barns are obscured by mist; but the belief does not have warrant sufficient for knowledge. (Plantinga 2000, 159–60)

Once again, the protagonist's belief in Foggy Fake Barns seems to meet not only the original 1993 conditions for warrant but also the conditions of favorability set out in 1996/1997 Mini-Environment Favorability. The full and detailed state of affairs in the relevant MBE would include the presence of the fog such that in no close possible worlds is the belief formed by the pertinent exercise of cognitive powers false; though clearly the belief is still only luckily true.[30]

Stymied once again, Plantinga went back to the drawing board, so to speak, and proposed a different account of favorability in *Warranted Christian Belief* (2000).[31] If Plantinga's environmental condition on warrant, in particular his Resolution Condition on mini-environments, is meant to be his anti-Gettier condition, his 1996/1997 modification is simply insufficient. As such, in a final attempt to surmount Gettier counterexamples via reductive analysis, Plantinga tries once more to explicate mini-environment favorability.

Section 2.2: 2000 Favorability

While Plantinga is again unsure as to whether "we can say anything more definite" as to what it means for a mini-environment to be favorable for a given exercise of cognitive powers—beyond our intuition that a given mini-environment will be favorable for a given exercise insofar as that "exercise can be counted on to produce a true belief" in that mini-environment—he is, in *Warranted Christian Belief* (2000), nevertheless compelled to try (Plantinga 2000, 159). Again, Plantinga attributes the aforementioned "lack of resolution"— the lack of fit between the proper function of the given cognitive faculties and the environment in which they operate. And Plantinga characterizes this "lack of fit" in *Warranted Christian Belief* (2000) as a discrepancy between a given mini-environment as *perceived* (or detected) by the pertinent agent and the mini-environment *in full* (Plantinga 2000, 160). In other words, the discrepancy causing the "lack of resolution" is between a given MBE and the conjunct of states of affairs that are *detectible* via the said agent's exercise of cognitive powers E or DMBE (Plantinga 2000, 160). Hence, to preclude this "lack of resolution" so understood, Plantinga proposes a new conception of mini-environment favorability that aims to track warrant ascriptions along with the absence of this sort of discrepancy:

> **2000 Mini-Favorability:** MBE is favorable just if there is no state of affairs S included in MBE but not in DMBE such that the objective probability of B with respect to the conjunction of DMBE and S falls below r, where r is some real number representing a reasonably high probability. (Plantinga 2000, 160)[32]

Plantinga's hope, then, is that something like 2000 Mini-Favorability will provide not only a clearer understanding as to what is required in his Resolution Condition but also a successful defense against Gettier-style counterexamples.

According to Plantinga's analysis of knowledge, the original 1993 conditions for warrant are sufficient for warrant once the environmental condition is amended with his Resolution Condition, now understood in terms of 2000 Mini-Favorability; and warrant, so understood, is with truth and belief meant to be both necessary and jointly sufficient for knowledge.[33] In support of his second attempt at specifying MBE favorability, Plantinga has us consider another Gettier case:

> **Peter and Paul:** I am not aware that Paul's look-alike brother Peter is staying at his house; if I'm across the street, take a quick look, and form the belief that Paul is emerging from his house, I don't know that it's Paul, even if in fact it is (it could just as well have been Peter emerging); . . . if Peter would not have been in the neighborhood, I would have known. (Plantinga 2000, 157)

As Plantinga notes, the resolution problem in this case "arises because I can't (for example) distinguish Paul from Peter from across the street just by looking" (Plantinga 2000, 160). By taking a glance across the street toward Paul's house, the protagonist can detect all sorts of things ("the appearance of a person, of a man, of someone across the road, and the like"), but he cannot with such a glance tell the difference between Paul and Peter from across the street (Plantinga 2000, 160). This discrepancy between the DMBE and the MBE in the case of Peter and Paul is such that B is seemingly not probable in respect to DMBE. Likewise, cases like Russell's Stopped Clock, Lucky Ms. Jones, Lucky Mary, and Classic Case 2 seem to be defused as well. Though the protagonist in Russell's Stopped Clock can detect through his pertinent exercise of cognitive powers that there is a clock on the wall and that it says 3:43 pm, he cannot detect that the clock is broken. Though Ms. Jones in the case of Lucky Ms. Jones can detect through her pertinent exercise of cognitive powers that she had earlier driven her Ford to the office, she could not detect that the Ford she drove to the office was destroyed. Though Mary in the case of Lucky Mary can detect through her pertinent exercise of cognitive faculty that a husband-like figure is sitting in the living room, she could not detect that the figure is actually her husband's brother. Though Jones in Classic Case 2 can detect that Smith has manifold evidence to the effect that he owns a Ford, Jones could not detect that Smith was lying. In accord with Plantinga's analysis, in Russell's Stopped Clock, Lucky Ms. Jones, Lucky Mary, and Classic Case 2, just like in the case of Peter and Paul, there is a discrepancy between the respective DMBE and the MBE such that the relevant beliefs are not objectively probable in respect to their given DMBEs.

Has Plantinga finally developed a reductive virtue epistemology that avoids Gettier counterexample? According to our proposed diagnosis, this will depend on whether or not it is possible for a warranted belief, as elucidated in *Warranted Christian Belief* (2000), to be false. If it is possible, then, according to the proposed diagnosis, Plantinga's 2000 account of knowledge should still be susceptible to Gettier counterexample. If it is not possible to have a warranted false belief, then, according to the proposed diagnosis, Plantinga's 2000 account of knowledge will be Gettier-proof but unpalatable, leading to radical skepticism.

Although in *Warrant and Proper Function* (1993) Plantinga seems to expressly allow for false belief having warrant, this certainly does not seem to be his position in his revised accounts.[34] As we already noted, Plantinga fully intended for his 1996/1997 account of warrant to "[guarantee] that no false belief has warrant" (Plantinga 1996, 329). And while Plantinga is nowhere near as explicit in *Warranted Christian Belief* (2000) on this score, he nevertheless seems to imply as much. Consider the following passage:

> [T]here can be mini-environments for a given exercise of our faculties, in which it is just by accident, dumb luck, that a true belief is formed, if one is indeed formed. A true belief formed in such a mini-environment does not have warrant sufficient for knowledge, even if it has some degree of warrant. To achieve that more exalted degree of warrant, the belief must be formed in a mini-environment such that the exercise of cognitive powers producing it can be counted on to produce a true belief. (Plantinga 2000, 161)[35]

Given that "being counted on to produce a true belief" is Plantinga's synonymous lingo for mini-environment favorability, Plantinga is saying in this passage that mini-environment favorability precludes the possibility of a luckily true belief. And given that luckily true beliefs are lucky because they could just have easily been false, Plantinga seems to be saying that mini-environment favorability precludes the possibility of a false belief. In other words, Plantinga in his most recent work seems to take warrant as inviolably related to truth.[36]

And even if this is not the correct way to read such passages, we might have nevertheless *guessed* that Plantinga is assuming that warrant bears an inviolable relationship to truth simply on the grounds that it is extremely difficult to think of a false belief that could satisfy 2000 Mini-Favorability, let alone the other conditions on warrant. One seems utterly at a loss for thinking of any false belief that would not have *some* epistemically relevant state of affairs that is not detectible by the given exercise of cognitive powers that would be included in the respective mini-environment. It seems like for any given false belief there will be some state of affairs not included in the given DMBE that undermines whatever reason(s) we may have to believe said belief.

If there is not a false belief that meets Plantinga's conditions for warrant, then it will not be possible for a belief to be so warranted but true for other reasons. In other words, if there is not a false belief that meets Plantinga's conditions for warrant, then his account should be immune to Gettier counterexamples. As such, in accord with our proposed diagnosis of Gettier problems, Plantinga's account should be unpalatable, leading to skeptical conclusions. Fortunately for the proposed diagnosis (though unfortunately for Plantinga's account), this is exactly what has been noted in the literature. As critics have repeatedly pointed out, 2000 Mini-Favorability is simply too strong—for many instances that we would intuitively deem knowledge there is *some* state of affairs that would be included in the given MBE but not the DMBE that would significantly reduce the given belief's objective probability in respect to DMBE and that state of affairs.[37] Thad Botham (2003) provides the following three cases:

> **Only Paul:** Consider a version of the [Paul and Peter case] where we stipulate that Paul is an only child, thereby removing Peter from the scene. In addition, the moment before you believe the proposition "There's Paul," his uncle—unbeknownst to you—lies to a friend, telling her that Paul has an identical twin brother who's visiting Paul at that very moment and that he just spoke with each of them on the telephone. Paul's uncle asserts this falsehood while in London, thousands of miles away. (Botham 2003, 435-6)
>
> **Tiny Fake Barns:** Consider . . . [the case of Fake Barns] with the following alteration. Rather than constructing life-sized barn facades, the locals manufacture model barns so tiny that standard passersby cannot view them. Perhaps the tiny barns are only two inches in height, built to suit ant communities. As you drive through the heart of this anomalous territory, you see one of the only real barns and believe the proposition "That's a fine barn." (Botham 2003, 436)
>
> **Dalmatian:** Suppose you observe a Dalmatian by looking through a window into the backyard. You believe the proposition "There's a Dalmatian." However, there is a state of affairs [S]—being such that there are ten mechanical Dalmatians in the backyard, each of which appears like a real Dalmatian—that together with [the given DMBE] renders the objective probability of your belief less than reasonably high. Nonetheless, the owner locked all of the robotic Dalmatians in a shed in his backyard to prevent them from rusting. Indeed, they've resided in the shed for about ten years, the lock is rusted shut, and no one has known the key's whereabouts for at least two years. (Botham 2003, 436)

Andrew Chignell (2003) provides a similar case:

> **Song Sparrow:** Johnson . . . has acquired his ornithological training by reading some birding books and by listening to recordings of birdcalls. Johnson hasn't seen a song sparrow (Melospiza melodia) before, but he is familiar with their plumage, body shape, and calls. Unbeknownst to him, however, song sparrows

have suffered from a devastating virus in recent weeks, and there are now only two of them left on the entire continent. The Lincoln's sparrow (Melospiza lincolnii), which looks and sounds very similar to the song sparrow, has been unaffected by the virus and there are still quite a few of them living in Johnson's region. As Johnson strolls through the forest, he hears what seems to him to be the call of a song sparrow. He approaches the relevant tree to get an up-close look at the bird. The bird is, in fact, one of the two remaining song sparrows on the continent. Johnson studies the bird for some time: it looks to him like the song sparrow pictured in his books, and its call sounds like the recordings he has heard. On this basis these observations, Johnson assents, with a degree of strength that is just enough to put him over the threshold required for knowledge, to the proposition that the bird he is observing is a song sparrow. (Chignell 2003, 449)

In all four of these cases we intuitively think that the given protagonists possess knowledge—knowledge that "there's Paul," "that's a fine barn," "there's a Dalmatian," "that's a song sparrow," respectively; however, in all four cases there is a state of affairs that "together with [the respective DMBE] makes the objective probability of [the protagonist's] belief less than reasonably high" (Botham 2003, 436). Though the protagonists in such cases seem to know their respective beliefs, the conditions for warrant in Plantinga's 2000 account are not met, given 2000 Mini-Favorability.

And to be sure, the problem is general. Plantinga's 2000 account of warrant does not just fail to track knowledge across a limited range of cases; it seems to lead us directly into radical skepticism. Not only is it extremely difficult to think of a false belief that would satisfy Plantinga's 2000 Mini-Favorability, but it is extremely difficult to think of a true belief that satisfies it. For almost any given belief there is going to be *some* state of affairs that would reduce the objective probability of said belief in light of the perceived mini-environment (DMBE). Take my belief that grass is green, for example—a belief that is presumably quite epistemically secure. There may be any number of facts that might (either individually or in conjunction) reduce the objective probability of such a belief in light of the mini-environment as I perceive it: it might be the case that color blindness runs in my family; it might be the case that lots of people use the terms "green" and "grass" in ways that I do not;[38] I might have a personal history of getting some colors a bit mixed up, etc. As such, according to Plantinga's 2000 account of warrant, I presumably do not know that grass is green! Take my belief that I am now in pain. Again, there seem to be any number of facts that might (either individually or in conjunction) reduce the objective probability of such a belief in light of the mini-environment as I perceive it: it may be the case that I have a history of hypochondria; it may be the case that I am prone to exaggeration, etc. Again, according to Plantinga's 2000 account of warrant, I presumably do not know that I am now in pain—another radical conclusion. Given Plantinga's infallibilism about warrant, his assumption that his modified account of warrant "guarantees" truth, he can seemingly avoid Gettier counterexample, but only at the cost of skepticism—precisely as our proposed diagnosis would predict.

In response to the Gettier problems afflicting his 1993 account of warrant, Plantinga amended his environmental condition to preclude not only ill-suited maxi-environments but also unfavorable mini-environments. And in his 1996/1997 and his 2000 modifications, Plantinga tentatively tried to say a bit more about what it means for a mini-environment to be favorable for a given exercise of cognitive competence. Both attempts, as we have now seen, seem to fall flat—either leading to further Gettier counterexamples or leading to unsavory skeptical conclusions. But maybe the lesson to be learned from all this is that Plantinga should not try to explain what does not warrant or need explanation. After all, as we have already said, in "Respondeo" (1996) Plantinga worries that perhaps elucidation of mini-environment is neither "attainable or necessary" (1996, 327). In *Warranted Christian Belief* (2000) Plantinga is again unsure as to whether "we can say anything more definite" as to what it means for a mini-environment to be favorable for a given exercise of cognitive powers beyond our intuition that a given mini-environment will be favorable for a given exercise insofar as that "exercise can be counted on to produce a true belief" in that mini-environment (Plantinga 2000, 159). Perhaps Plantinga should just leave his account of warrant somewhat underdefined—omitting any explication of what precisely it means for a mini-environment to be favorable for a given exercise of cognitive faculty.

Sadly, I do not think this is viable strategy for Plantinga to take for at least two reasons. First of all, leaving his account of warrant underdefined in this way would seem negligent. For nearly fifty years, people have been wrestling with the Gettier Problem, with little success; so to say simply that Gettier counterexamples can be avoided so long as one's environment is suitably favorable, there will be deserved protests and outcries if no explication of favorability is given. Second, leaving his account of warrant underdefined in this way would simply mean that the problems that afflict it would be likewise underdefined. Even if he does not try to explain what it means for a given mini-environment to be favorable, our proposed diagnosis of Gettier problems would still apply. Assuming that Plantinga wants warrant to bear some relationship to truth, the question we need to ask is whether that relationship is inviolable or not. If it is not, if it is possible to have a warranted false belief, then presumably Plantinga's account of warrant, even left underdefined, is going to be susceptible to Gettier cases of the following form:

> **Under-Defined Plantinga Counterexample:** S forms the belief B as a result of an exercise of cognitive faculties E. S's cognitive faculties are functioning properly in accord with a good design plan aimed at truth, and the maxi and mini environments are favorable for E. By some accident B is not true for reasons related to E (since we are agreeing for the time being that this is possible), but what is more, by some other accident, B still happens to be true (divorced from E). As such, though S has a warranted true belief that B, S does not know that B.

And if warrant, left underdefined, *does* inviolably track truth, then skeptical worries will continue to loom large. Presumably, if warrant needs to guarantee the truth of the belief in question, then Plantinga's environmental proviso (his anti-luck/anti-Gettier condition) needs to preclude any possibility for a false belief, which will be tantamount to requiring a perfect cognitive environment—a condition that presumably few of even our most secure beliefs can meet.

After realizing that his fallibilistic 1993 conception of warrant was susceptible to Gettier counterexample, Plantinga proposed a series of two modifications that sought to strengthen his account of warrant so as to preclude Gettier problems. Unfortunately for Plantinga, both proposals (like his original account) failed precisely along lines predicted by our proposed diagnosis of Gettier counterexamples. Plantinga's 1996/1997 modification offered a strengthened account of warrant that was, nevertheless, ultimately still fallibilistic. As such, it fell prey to strengthened Gettier counterexamples. Plantinga's 2000 modification produced an account of warrant that seemed genuinely infallibilistic, an account of warrant where warrant inviolably tracks truth. As predicted, this led to unsavory skeptical conclusions. And in all of this, the lines taken by Plantinga's critics in the contemporary literature time and time again affirmed our verdicts and our proposed diagnosis of the Gettier Problem.

Conclusion

Alvin Plantinga's reductive account of knowledge is one of the most iconic virtue epistemologies of the twentieth century—inspiring an entire generation of epistemologists with similar theories of knowledge that are no less intricate and no less multifaceted. However, as we have seen, Plantinga's reductive analysis of knowledge in terms of virtue, in terms of properly functioning cognitive faculties, is simply unable to viably surmount the Gettier Problem. From *Warrant and Proper Function* (1993) to "Respondeo" (1996) and "Warrant and Accidentally True Belief" (1997), to *Warranted Christian Belief* (2000), Plantinga's virtue epistemology, in its various stages and iterations, fails in exactly the way our diagnosis of the Gettier Problem in Chapter 1 would predict. Whenever Plantinga's account assumed a close but not inviolable relationship between warrant and truth, he faced Gettier counterexamples. Whenever it assumed an inviolable relationship, he faced unsavory skeptical conclusions. And what is more, our proposed diagnosis explains and informs not only the development of Plantinga's virtue epistemology but also the critiques leveled against it. Time and time again, there was a revealing correspondence between our proposed diagnosis of Gettier counterexamples and the shortcomings of Plantinga's virtue epistemology as explicated in the relevant literature.[39]

Summing up the last three chapters: none of the seminal approaches to virtue epistemology in the contemporary literature have been able to provide a viable reductive analysis of knowledge, and our diagnosis of the Gettier Problem has been confirmed again and again. Not wanting to give up on virtue-theoretic approaches to knowledge, in the next chapter we'll explore some ways virtue epistemology might be non-reductive, ways virtue epistemologists might define knowledge without resorting to a reductive analysis.

Part III

Toward Non-reductive Virtue Epistemology

6

Prolegomena to Non-reductive Virtue Epistemology

Now that we've seen that the seminal, virtue-theoretic accounts of knowledge are unable to provide a viable reductive analysis (all exactly for the reasons explicated in Chapter 1), I want to explore in this chapter the possibility of adapting virtue-theoretic epistemology to suit an alternative, *non-reductive* epistemic model. In Section 1, I elucidate and outline the seminal non-reductive epistemic model to date, namely, the "knowledge-first" model of knowledge developed by Timothy Williamson in *Knowledge and Its Limits* (2000).[1] Second, in Section 2, I explore how epistemic virtue might be incorporated within a non-reductive model, generally. Finally, in Section 3, I reconsider the possibility of non-reductive virtue epistemology in light of (i) Williamson's specific non-reductive epistemology, (ii) agent-reliabilism virtue epistemology (including Plantinga's proper functionalism), (iii) and agent-responsibilism virtue epistemology.

Section 1: The Williamsonian Model

Recall Immanuel Kant's momentous claim in *The Critique of Pure Reason* to a Copernican revolution within metaphysics:

> Thus far it has been assumed that all our cognition must conform to objects. On that presupposition, however, all our attempts to establish something about them *a priori*, by means of concepts through which our cognition would be expanded, have come to nothing. Let us, therefore, try to find out whether we shall not make better progress in the problems of metaphysics if we assume that objects must conform to our cognition. This assumption already agrees better with the demanded possibility of an *a priori* cognition of objects—i.e. a cognition that is to ascertain something about them before they are given to us. The situation here is the same as was that of Copernicus when he first thought of explaining

the motions of celestial bodies. Having found it difficult to make progress there when he assumed that the entire host of stars revolved around the spectator, he tried to find out whether he might not be more successful if he had the spectator revolve around and the stars remain at rest. Now we can try something similar in metaphysics, with regard to our intuition of objects. (1998, 638)

We can see Timothy Williamson in *Knowledge and Its Limits* (2000) as initiating a similar revolution in epistemology. After all, we have "thus far ... assumed" that knowledge should be defined in terms of a reductive analysis, but as we are now seeing such a project has seemingly "come to nothing" (or at least very little). As such, "having found it difficult to make progress," perhaps, as Williamson will suggest, it is time we do away with that assumption and "[try] to find out whether [we] might not be more successful" exploring other options.[2]

The standard practice in contemporary epistemology is to provide an analysis of knowledge in terms of truth, belief, and warrant. Given (i) that truth and belief are necessary for knowledge and (ii) the widespread assumption that belief is conceptually prior to knowledge, the contemporary project of defining knowledge has for nearly fifty years taken the shape of a reductive analysis of trying to explicate what, with true belief, is sufficient for knowledge. Now, we may agree that truth and belief are indeed necessary for knowledge, but why should we assume that belief is conceptually prior to knowledge? Such an assumption is critical for the reductive analysis project, yet, as Williamson points out, it is often just "taken for granted" and "rarely supported by argument" (Williamson 2000, 2). To be sure, we might think the simple fact that "knowledge entails belief but not vice versa" is enough to get the aforementioned assumption off the ground, but this would be a mistake (Williamson 2000, 3). As Williamson explains:

> Given that knowledge entails belief, it is trivial that one knows p if and only if (i) one believes p; (ii) p is true; and (iii) if one believes p and p is true, then one knows p. But that equivalence is useless for establishing that belief is conceptually prior to knowledge, for it is circular: "know" occurs in (iii). The received idea is that we can conceptualize the factors whose conjunction with belief is necessary and sufficient for knowledge independently of knowledge; we can think of the former without already thinking of the latter, even implicitly. But the argument does not show that such independent conceptualization is possible, for a necessary but insufficient condition need not be a conjunct of a non-circular necessary and sufficient condition. Although being coloured is a necessary but insufficient condition for being red, we cannot state a necessary and sufficient condition for being red by conjoining being coloured with other properties specified without reference to red. Neither the equation "Red = coloured + X" nor the equation

"Knowledge = true belief + X" need have a non-circular solution ... belief can be a necessary but insufficient condition of knowledge even if we do not implicitly conceptualize knowledge as the conjunction of belief with that which must be added to belief to yield knowledge. (Williamson 2000, 3)

As such, the brute fact that knowledge seems to entail belief but not vice versa does not provide suitable ground on which to assume that belief is somehow conceptually prior to knowledge. Besides, the fact that knowledge seems to entail belief could just as easily support a hypothesis that sees knowledge as conceptually prior to belief. As Williamson explains, "[i]f believing p is conceptualized as being in a state sufficiently like knowing p 'from the inside' in the relevant aspects, then belief is necessary for knowledge since knowing p is sufficiently like itself in every respect, even though knowledge is conceptually prior to belief" (Williamson 2000, 3). How else, then, might someone defend the widespread assumption that belief is conceptually prior to knowledge? To be sure, if we *do not* have any good reason to suppose that belief is conceptually prior to knowledge, and if we *do* have a good reason to be pessimistic regarding any viable success against the Gettier Problem from a reductive analysis, perhaps this is simply all the more reason to give up such a project.[3]

Now someone might agree that the reductive analysis project has (at best) a lackluster history but nevertheless advocate the assumption that belief is conceptually prior to knowledge by holding out hope that a more viable analysis (after nearly fifty years) is finally on the horizon; after all, Gettier problems aside, many analyses have been at least decent approximations of knowledge. But the mere fact that p is a close approximation of q in no way entails that q can be analyzed in terms of p or that q is somehow conceptually prior to p or that q cannot be understood divorced from p. Consider Williamson's example of parenthood and ancestry. As Williamson points out, "x is an ancestor of y and x is not an ancestor of an ancestor of y" is a very close approximation of "x is a parent of y," but not perfectly so (Williamson 2000, 4). There are insurmountable counterexamples involving rare cases of incest. If a daughter bears a son by her father, that father is both a parent of the aforementioned son while also being his ancestor's ancestor. As Williamson explains, "[s]ince the father and the mother of his daughter are symmetrically related to the daughter and son in terms of and son in terms of ancestry but not in terms of parenthood, parenthood cannot be defined in terms of ancestry without extra conceptual resources" (Williamson 2000, 4). Even though parenthood can be closely approximated via ancestry, this in no way entails that "parent" can be analyzed in terms of ancestry or that the latter is in any way critical to our understanding of the former or that ancestry is somehow conceptually prior to parenthood. According to Williamson, such examples show us that "[t]he possibility of approximating knowledge in terms of belief and other concepts is not good evidence for the conceptual priority of belief over knowledge" (Williamson 2000, 4). It's not clear, then, that we have any robust theoretical reason to accept the widespread assumption that belief is somehow conceptually prior to knowledge, that knowledge should be analyzed in terms of true belief plus whatever makes true belief knowledge. Besides, as Williamson notes, generally "one would not expect the concept *knows* to have a non-trivial analysis in somehow more basic terms.... 'Bachelor' is a peculiarity not a prototype" (2000, 31).[4] If we can dispel such an assumption, then seemingly we have all the more reason to explore alternative epistemic models, specifically those that see knowledge as, at the very least, on conceptually equal footing with belief.

Williamson's is a knowledge-first epistemology. Given (i) that solving the Gettier Problem via reductive analysis seems like a Sisyphean endeavor and (ii) that we have no robust theoretical reason to assume that such an approach to knowledge is, in fact, appropriate, Williamson proposes an epistemic model that takes knowledge to be an unanalyzable primitive, where knowledge is conceptually prior to belief.[5] Instead of trying to build up (via warrant) to knowledge from true belief, Williamson starts with knowledge in hopes of exploring notions of belief, justification, and evidence in turn. Knowledge, for Williamson, is "a state of mind"; it will be our task in the rest of this section to unpack in broad strokes a bit of what that means.

While Williamson gives relatively little explanation as to what exactly a mental state is, we are presumably meant to have an intuitive enough grasp of such terminology so as to proceed without hindrance.[6] After all, it seems as though we can easily identify paradigmatic examples of mental states ("love, hate, pleasure, pain ... believing that it is so, conceiving that it is so, hoping or fearing that it is so, wondering whether it is so, intending or desiring it to be so"), so all we need to do is extrapolate from these to get a rough-and-ready understanding of how Williamson is wanting to think of knowledge (Williamson 2000, 21). An initial hurdle to doing so, however, is that, unlike paradigmatic examples of mental states, knowledge is factive; where paradigmatic examples of mental states such as "believing that p" and "hoping that p" remain neutral as to whether or not p is in fact true; "knowing that p" surely entails that "p."[7] To be sure, we could of course retreat somewhat and say that knowledge is only a mental state insofar as it necessarily involves believing, a paradigmatic mental state; such a move, however, would seemingly be a retreat into the reductive analysis project, defining knowledge as having a mental state of a certain sort that is also true. As Williamson explains:

> Someone might expect knowing to be a state of mind simply on the grounds that knowing *p* involves the paradigmatic mental state of believing that *p*. If those grounds were adequate, the claim that knowing is a state of mind would be banal. However, those grounds imply only that there is a mental state being in which is *necessary* for knowing *p*. By contrast the claim that knowing is a state of mind is to be understood as the claim that there is a mental state being in which is necessary *and sufficient* for knowing *p*. (Williamson 2000, 21; emphasis Williamson's)

When Williamson says that knowledge is a mental state, he means that knowledge is *merely* a mental state (Williamson 2000, 21). What, then, are we to make of the non-factive/factive disparity between paradigmatic mental states and knowledge? Given that knowledge requires truth, a non-mental component, how can knowledge be *merely* a state of mind? Williamson says the following:

> Our initial presumption should be that knowing is a mental state. Prior to philosophical theory-building, we learn the concept of the mental by examples. Our paradigms should include propositional attitudes such as believing and desiring, if our conception of the mental is not to be radically impoverished. But factive attitudes have so many similarities to the non-factive attitudes that we should expect them to constitute mental states too; we expect a concept to apply to whatever sufficiently resembles its paradigms. It would be strange if there were a mental state of fearing but no mental state of regretting, or a mental state of imagining but no mental state of remembering. Indeed, it is not clear that there are any pretheoretic grounds for omitting factive attitudes from the list of *paradigmatic* mental states. That the mental includes knowing and other factive attitudes is built into the natural understanding of the procedure by which the concept of the mental is acquired. Of course, that does not exclude the subsequent discovery of theoretical reasons for drawing the line between the mental and the non-mental somewhere else. But the theory behind those reasons had better be a good one. (Williamson 2000, 22)

Williamson, then, has effectively shifted the explanatory onus onto anyone who would like to deny that factivity (regarding external propositions) precludes the mental. When we ask "Why should we think that knowledge, being factive, is purely mental?" Williamson simply seems to reply "Why not?"

To see one reason why we might think the factivity of knowledge precludes its being mental, contrast knowledge with believing truly. *Believing truly* (when the proposition in question is in the external environment) is not a mental state; while *believing* is a mental state believing *truly* typically extends beyond the boundaries of the mental. And if (i) everything within the state of believing that *p* is contained within the state of believing truly that *p* and (ii) everything within believing truly that p is within the state of knowing that *p*, then it seems as though once we assume that knowledge is indeed mental we seem forced to oddly sandwich a non-mental state (believing truly that p) in between two mental states (believing that p and knowing that p). But, to quote Williamson:

> That something sandwiched between two mental states need not itself be a mental state is not as paradoxical as it may sound. Consider an analogy: the notion of a geometric property. For these purposes, we can understand geometrical properties to be properties possessed by particulars in physical space. Let π_1 be the property of being an equilateral triangle, π_2 the property of being a triangle whose sides are indiscriminable in length to the naked eye, and π_3 the property of being a triangle. Necessarily, everything that has π_1 has π_2, because lines of the same length cannot be discriminated in length; necessarily, everything that has π_2 has π_3. Nevertheless, although π_1 and π_3 are geometrical properties, π_2 is not a geometrical property, because it varies with variations in human eyesight. Something sandwiched between two geometrical properties need not itself be a geometrical property. Similarly, there is no structural reason why something sandwiched between two mental states should itself be a mental state. . . . If S is a mental state and C a non-mental condition, there need be no mental state S* such that, necessarily, one is in S* if and only if one is in S and C obtains. The non-existence of such an S* is quite consistent with the existence of a mental state S** such that, necessarily, one is in S** only if (but not: if) one is in S and C is met. A mental state can guarantee that conjunction only by guaranteeing more than that conjunction. (Williamson 2000, 27–8)

Just because knowledge seemingly requires both truth (a non-mental condition) and belief (a mental state) does not mean there needs to be a mental state *believing truly*. There is no inconsistency in taking *believing truly* to be non-mental while simultaneously taking "knowledge that *p*" to be a mental state that includes both "belief that *p*" and "*p*" (the truth that *p*). While it may initially seem strange that *believing truly* is, as it were, sandwiched between the mental states of *believing* and *knowing*, this in itself is no reason to doubt that knowledge is a mental state; the aforementioned strangeness seemingly dissipates upon reflection.[8]

There are, to be sure, a number of factive mental states: "seeing that *p*," "remembering that *p*," "hearing that *p*," etc.—such that for any given factive mental state, Φ, if "S Φ that *p*" then "*p*." Knowledge, for Williamson, is the most general factive mental state; "seeing that *p*," "remembering that *p*," "hearing that *p*," etc. are all ways of "knowing that *p*"—if "S Φ that *p*" then "S knows that *p*." Consider the following explanation:

> To picture the proposal, compare the state of knowing with the property of being coloured, the colour property which something has if it has any colour property at all. If something is coloured, then it has a more specific colour property; it is red or green or . . . . Although that specific colour may happen to lack a name in our language, we could always introduce such a name, perhaps pointing to the thing as a paradigm. We may say that being coloured is being red or green or . . . , if the list is understood as open-ended, and the concept *is coloured* is not identified with the disjunctive concept. One can grasp the concept *is coloured* without grasping the concept *is green*, therefore without grasping the disjunctive concept. Similarly, if one knows that A, then there is a specific way in which one knows; one can see or remember or . . . that A. Although that specific way may happen to lack a name in our language, we could always introduce such a name, perhaps pointing to the case as a paradigm. We may say that knowing that A is seeing or remembering or . . . that A, if the list is understood as open-ended, and the concept *knows* is not identified with the disjunctive concept. One can grasp the concept *knows* without grasping the concept *sees*, therefore without grasping the disjunctive concept. (2000, 34)

Lacking any robust theoretical reason to deny that mental states can be factive, Williamson not only describes knowledge as a factive state of mind; he describes it as *the most general* factive state of mind. In other words, "knowing," for Williamson, "is the most general factive stative attitude, which one has to a proposition if one has any factive stative attitude to it at all" (2000, 34).

Of course, for any given factive mental state there is going to be a difference between "Φ that *p*" and "Φ a situation that *p*"; as Williamson points out, "only the former requires the [agent] to grasp the proposition [*p*]" (Williamson 2000, 38). As such, using Williamson's example, there is going to be a difference between seeing people play chess and seeing a situation where people are playing chess without knowing what they are doing. "A normal observer in normal conditions who has no concept of chess can see a situation in which Olga is playing chess," says Williamson, "by looking in the right direction, but cannot see *that* Olga is playing chess because he does not know what he sees to be a situation in which Olga is playing chess" (Williamson 2000, 38; emphasis Williamson's).

Williamson's positive account of knowledge can be summarized in the following three points: for any given factive mental state, Φ:

1) "S Φ that *p*" entails that "*p*."
2) "Know" is (merely) a factive mental state.
3) "S Φ that *p*" entails "S knows that *p*."[9]

While this account of knowledge may seem relatively thin compared to the elaborate and nuanced analyses that have been produced over the past fifty years, perhaps simplicity is a virtue. As Williamson explains, on his account "the importance of knowing to us becomes as intelligible as the importance of truth. Factive mental states are important to us as states whose essence include a matching between mind and world, and knowing is important to us as the most general factive stative attitude" (2000, 39–40). "This importance," to be sure, "would be hard to understand if the concept *knows* were the more or less ad hoc sprawl that analyses have had to become" (Williamson 2000, 31).

Section 2: Non-reductive Virtue Epistemology

Having elucidated the seminal alternative to the reductive analysis of knowledge, Williamson's non-reductive model, we are now in a better position to see how virtue-theoretic concepts might be inserted within such a framework—to see how a non-reductive virtue epistemology might be developed. By way of prolegomena, it is our task in this section to map out the various ways this might be done.

As we turn to consider how virtue might be incorporated within a non-reductive model of knowledge like Williamson's, there are two axes worth tracking: (i) whether or not virtue and knowledge are primitive and (ii) whether knowledge entails or is entailed by virtue. Across these axes there are sixteen possible ways virtue might relate to knowledge.[10] Let's let "K" stand for knowledge, that "V" stands for virtue, and arrows and underscores signify entailments and conceptual priority respectively, these sixteen possibilities can be tabulated as in Table 6.1.

Table 6.1 Possible Relationships between Knowledge and Epistemic Virtue

		Conceptual Priority				
		K ∧ V	K̲ ∧ V	K ∧ V̲	K̲ ∧ V̲	
Entailments	K ⊃ V	K̲ ⊃ V	K ⊃ V̲	K̲ ⊃ V̲	K ⊃ V	A
	K ≡ V	K̲ ≡ V	K ≡ V̲	K̲ ≡ V̲	K ≡ V	B
	V ⊃ K	V ⊃ K̲	V̲ ⊃ K	V̲ ⊃ K̲	V ⊃ K	C
	K ∧ V	K̲ ∧ V	K ∧ V̲	K̲ ∧ V̲	K ∧ V	D
		1	2	3	4	

Of course, most of these options can actually be dismissed out of hand—being either incompatible with non-reductive virtue epistemology simpliciter or independently unfeasible. First of all, given that our goal is to develop a *virtue epistemology* (an epistemology that sees virtue as intimately tied to knowledge), row D can be discarded. And, given that the metaphysical priority established by entailment minimally requires *some* conceptual priority, we can discard (the rest of) column 4 as dubious, if not simply unattainable.[11] On our map of the possible relationships virtue might bear to knowledge (and vice versa), B3 designates the possibility of a reductive analysis of knowledge in terms of necessary and sufficient conditions—a project that we now hope to abandon. B1, interestingly, designates the possibility of a reductive analysis *of virtue in terms of knowledge*—a project that, lacking independent reason for thinking that virtue yields such an analysis, we presumably should be just as weary of. Under the reasonable assumption that B1 will lead to Gettier-like counterexamples about *virtue* ("Vettier" counterexamples) and similar problems parallel to those afflicting the reductive analysis of *knowledge* project, B1, too, can be discarded. Finally, I think we can also do away with C1, C2, and C3. In all three instances, virtue is merely sufficient for knowledge, not necessary; knowledge may well be necessary for virtue on these models, but nothing about virtue is necessary for knowledge. As such, whatever the virtues of epistemic virtue, C1 C2, and C3 do not allow them to be brought to bear on knowledge.[12]

If (i) we are giving up on the reductive analysis of knowledge and (ii) we still want to pursue virtue epistemology, what are our alternatives? The remaining four possibilities (A1, A2, A3, and B2) give us a map. And we can classify these remaining possibilities into three general strategies for incorporating virtue into a non-reductive model of knowledge. First, there is what I will call the *knowledge plus virtue* strategy—the strategy of adding a virtue-theoretic condition to a non-reductive epistemic model as a necessary condition on a primitive conception of knowledge (A1, A2). Second, there is what I will call the *knowledge as virtue* strategy—the strategy of explicating knowledge itself in terms of a given account of epistemic virtue (B2). Third and finally, there is what I will call the *knowledge within virtue* strategy—the strategy of adding a conceptually primitive account of virtue as a necessary condition on a conceptually subsequent account of knowledge, the strategy of explicating virtue as the richest epistemic state (A3).

Our goal in this section is to briefly explore each of these general strategies. Working from the most modest proposals (knowledge plus virtue) to the most extreme (knowledge within virtue), we will be guided by an interest in exploring just how central virtue might be within a non-reductive model of knowledge. I hope to show how (i) all three strategies might allow for the viable non-reductive virtue epistemologies and (ii) that each is compatible with Williamson's seminal non-reductive model.[13]

Section 2.1: Knowledge plus Virtue

One straightforward way to incorporate a virtue-theoretic condition into a non-reductive model is to simply identify it as a necessary condition for a primitive account of knowledge. And this is what we see happening in A1 and A2 in Table 6.1. Even as primitive, knowledge can have necessary conditions such as belief, truth, and perhaps even safety, so perhaps a virtue-theoretic condition is needed to explain and track knowledge ascriptions across a range of cases. Perhaps we can develop a non-reductive virtue epistemology by simply amending a non-reductive model with the caveat that a particular virtue condition (of our favorite stripe) is necessary for a given primitive account of knowledge. There are, to be sure, a couple of ways this might be done, contingent upon whether or not the said virtue condition is conceptually subsequent to or co-primitive with knowledge.

The weakest form of non-reductive virtue epistemology—that is, the weakest incorporation of virtue within a non-reductive model—is the one that holds a conceptually primitive account of knowledge as entailing a conceptually subsequent account of virtue but not vice versa (A1 on Table 6.1). On such an account, knowledge is sufficient for virtue and virtue is necessary for knowledge; but what is more, virtue, being conceptually subsequent to knowledge, is understood in terms of knowledge. In other words, according to this account, virtue cannot be properly comprehended apart from our (independent) understanding of knowledge.

Another form of virtue epistemology can be incorporated by simply making virtue *co-primitive* with knowledge, while keeping everything else the same (A2 on Table 6.1). On such an account, knowledge still entails virtue and not vice versa, but virtue is no longer conceptually dependent on knowledge.[14] This is, to be sure, a stronger use of virtue within a non-reductive model—allowing for an independent account of virtue alongside an independent account of knowledge. That said, however, this ultimately makes the subsequent *virtue epistemology* seem somewhat weaker—as independent concepts, virtue no longer seems as closely tied to knowledge.

Both iterations of the knowledge plus virtue proposal are, on the face of it, perfectly compatible with the Williamsonian model. As Williamson says himself, "[t]he present account of knowing makes no use of such concepts as *justified*, *caused*, and *reliable*. Yet knowing seems to be highly sensitive to such factors over a wide range of cases. Any adequate account of knowing should enable one to understand these connections" (2000, 41). Williamson acquiesces that he only "adumbrate[s] a strategy without carrying it out" in *Knowledge and Its Limits*—a project that future iterations of Williamson's epistemology should seemingly pursue (2000, 41). Supposedly, then, one set of intuitions that Williamson's epistemology should somehow explain or "be highly sensitive to" are those springing from "the wide range of cases" that help motivate virtue epistemology. It is worth keeping in mind that once Williamson recognizes that knowledge seems sensitive to safety, for example, he modifies his account accordingly— dubbing safety a necessary condition for knowledge (Williamson 2000, 41).[15] The knowledge plus virtue proposal is simply the proposal to likewise ornament Williamson's epistemology with another condition, a virtue-theoretic condition. Through his incorporation of various necessary conditions on knowledge, Williamson paved the way for our favorite epistemic concepts to piggyback on his non-reductive model via the knowledge plus virtue proposal.

But is this general strategy ultimately going to be satisfying for the lover of virtue epistemology? While the knowledge plus virtue proposals allow us to incorporate our favorite virtue-theoretic concepts into a non-reductive model, the virtue epistemology they produce may seem a bit limp wristed, spiritless, or shallow. The fact that the virtue-theoretic portion of the epistemology is reduced to a mere addendum to, at best, a conceptually co-primitive account of knowledge seems to mark its departure from prominent virtue epistemologies found in the contemporary literature. In fact, we may lose the heart and soul of virtue epistemology, namely the centrality of virtue for epistemology. For many virtue epistemologists, their notion of virtue is meant to be absolutely fundamental for epistemology, and it is hard to see how this could still be the case if the virtue condition is ultimately a caveat to a dominant account of knowledge.

Section 2.2: Knowledge as Virtue

For the lover of robust virtue epistemology, the more radical proposal of *knowledge as virtue* may satisfy (B2 on Table 6.1). The basic concept is straightforward. Simply define knowledge in terms of epistemic virtue. Instead of defining knowledge separate from virtue and subsequently adding a virtue-theoretic condition as a caveat (like we did above), define knowledge itself in terms of your favorite virtue-theoretic concept by explicating a primitive account of knowledge as both necessary and sufficient for a co-primitive account of epistemic virtue. Where the previous two accounts might be called *doubly non-reductive*—both abandoning sufficiency conditions for knowledge and holding knowledge as conceptually primitive—this account is what we might call *singularly non-reductive*. While knowledge is still held primitive in this strategy, a co-primitive conception of virtue is taken to be both necessary and *sufficient* for knowledge. The subsequent account is still non-reductive; knowledge, as a primitive, is simply defined in terms of epistemic virtue.

But what is an *epistemic virtue*? Without advocating any particular virtue-theoretic concept, we will not be able to go into any great detail in answering such a question here; however, a general sketch can certainly be provided. An act of virtue, roughly speaking, is an act that is virtuously motivated and successful in reaching its virtuous telos. So if I am to commit an act of courage by saving a drowning child from a turbulent river, say, then I need not only to be courageously motivated but also successful in my goal. If I save the child out of greed, say (hoping the child's rich parents will give me a monetary reward), then I have not committed an act of courage; I may have reached a virtuous telos, but I was not virtuously motivated. Conversely, if I courageously try to save the child but fail, I still have not committed an act of courage because the telos, saving the child, was unmet; one may act courageously without committing an act of courage. As such, an act of *epistemic* virtue, again roughly speaking, is an act that has epistemically virtuous motivation and is successful in reaching its epistemically virtuous telos (which at the very least includes truth). For example, if I believe that there is a thief in the living room as a result of drug-induced paranoia, then even if such a belief is true (the epistemically virtuous telos), it is not an act of epistemic virtue; drug-induced paranoia is presumably not epistemically virtuous motivation. Conversely, I may falsely believe that there is a thief in the living room after carefully reading reports that thieves were in my area and (having accidentally left the radio on) hearing what happens to sound very much like a thief in my living room, yet not commit an act of epistemic virtue; I may have had epistemically virtuous motives, but since I did not arrive at the truth I did not commit an act of epistemic virtue.[16]

Unlike the *knowledge plus virtue* strategy, the *knowledge as virtue* strategy allows for more robust non-reductive virtue epistemologies—virtue epistemologies that perhaps better capture the heart of virtue epistemology by placing virtue at the heart of epistemology. That said, however, being more radical, the knowledge as virtue proposal is decidedly more ambitious. Unlike the knowledge plus virtue proposal that simply attaches a virtue-theoretic condition onto a self-standing account of knowledge, the knowledge as virtue proposal forces us to carefully reconsider knowledge itself, conscientiously exploring just how a given concept of virtue can be identified with it.

Section 2.3: Knowledge within Virtue

Thus far, we have assumed that knowledge is the conceptual foundation for epistemology. Whether attaching a virtue-rich concept onto knowledge as a necessary condition (the knowledge plus virtue strategy) or redefining knowledge in terms of virtue (the knowledge as virtue strategy), we have assumed that knowledge is the richest epistemic state, that knowledge is our conceptual cornerstone. As such, another family of strategies can be developed by doing away with this assumption and placing virtue *under* knowledge, so to speak—by identifying virtue itself as epistemic bedrock, of which knowledge is merely a facet (A3 on Table 6.1). On this account, a conceptually non-primitive account of knowledge entails a primitive account of virtue; knowledge is sufficient for virtue and virtue is necessary for knowledge, but knowledge is understood in terms of virtue. Virtue is the broader, richer epistemic concept. In other words, knowledge, on this account, cannot be properly comprehended apart from our understanding of virtue. And like the knowledge as virtue proposal, the knowledge within virtue proposal is singularly non-reductive. But unlike the knowledge as virtue proposal, which was non-reductive insofar as knowledge was deemed primitive, the knowledge within virtue proposal is non-reductive insofar as the project of pursuing sufficiency conditions for knowledge has been abandoned.

Consider the following case from Williamson's *Knowledge and Its Limits* (2000), which goes toward demonstrating the richness of knowledge over other concepts like "believing truly":

Burglar: A burglar spends all night ransacking a house, risking discovery by staying so long. We ask what features of the situation when he entered the house led to that result. A reasonable answer is that he knew that there was a diamond in the house. To say that he believed truly that there was a diamond in the house would be to give a worse explanation, one whose explanans and explanandum are less closely connected. For one possibility consistent with the new explanans is that the burglar entered the house with a true belief that there was a diamond in it derived from false premises. For example, his only reason for believing that there was a diamond in the house might have been that someone told him that there was a diamond under the bed, when in fact the only diamond was in a drawer. He would then very likely have given up his true belief that there was a diamond in the house on discovering the falsity of his belief that there was a diamond under the bed, and abandoned the search. In contrast, if he *knew* that there was a diamond in the house, his knowledge was not essentially based on a false premise. Given suitable background conditions, the probability of his ransacking the house all night, conditional on his having entered it believing truly but not knowing that there was a diamond in it, will be lower than the probability of his ransacking it all night, conditional on his having entered it knowing that there was a diamond in it. (2000, 62)

While the knowledge within virtue proposal may seem bizarre and initially inscrutable, cases like Burglar help us see how such a proposal might get off the ground. Insofar as Burglar is a good argument for establishing the conceptual priority of knowledge over other concepts like believing truly, perhaps a similar story could be told to motivate the conceptual priority of virtue over knowledge. If we could come up with a case in which an agent's actions are best explained by epistemic virtue and not merely by knowledge, perhaps we could promote the richness and primacy of the former over the latter. Consider the following real-life example from Tom Wright's book, *Virtue Reborn* (2010):

> **Virtuous Pilot:** Thursday, January 15, 2009 was another ordinary day in New York City. Or so it seemed . . . Flight 1549 . . . took off . . . bound for Charlotte, North Carolina. The captain, [Sully] . . . did all the usual checks. Everything was fine in the Airbus A320. Fine until, two minutes after takeoff, the aircraft ran straight into a flock of Canada geese. . . . Almost at once both the engines were severely damaged and lost their power. The plane was at that point heading north over the Bronx, one of the most densely populated parts of the city. [Sully] and his co-pilot had to make several major decisions instantly if they were going to save the lives of people not only on board but also on the ground. They could see one or two small local airports in the distance, but quickly realized that they couldn't be sure of making it that far. If they attempted it, they might well crashland in a built-up area on the way. Likewise, the option of putting the plane down on the New Jersey Turnpike, a busy main road leading in and out of the city, would present huge problems and dangers for the plane and its occupants, let alone for cars and their drivers on the road. That left one option: the Hudson River. It's difficult to crash-land on water: one small mistake—catch the nose or one of the wings in the river, say—and the plane will turn over and over like a gymnast before breaking up and sinking. In the two or three minutes they had before landing, [Sully] and his copilot had to do [several] vital things (along with plenty of other tasks that we amateurs wouldn't understand) [which needed to

be done to safety land].... And they did it! Everyone got off safely, with [Sully] himself walking up and down the aisle a couple of times to check that everyone had escaped before leaving himself. (Wright 2010, 7–8)

What best explains Sully's successful landing on the Hudson River? No doubt, he knew what he was doing, but such an explanation does not seem to capture it. Presumably, many pilots would superficially know what to do in the same circumstances but would nevertheless fail at the task. I think the better explanation for Sully's successful landing in that emergency situation and in those extreme circumstances is that he was (is) a very good pilot, a virtuous pilot.[17] As such, if Burglar shows that knowledge is conceptually prior to true belief, then presumably cases like Virtuous Pilot can show that virtue is conceptually prior to knowledge, that virtue is the richest epistemic state—a state that, on this model, is both metaphysically necessary for and conceptually prior to knowledge.

And to be sure, insofar as we can redefine mental states in terms of epistemic virtue (as in our application of the previous proposal), there are seemingly no intrinsic obstacles within the Williamsonian model to expanding a given account of virtue to be the richest epistemic state, our conceptual cornerstone. In other words, if mental states can be reconceived in terms of virtue, they could easily be planted within a rich and broad virtue-laden context. However, insofar as Williamson's model for knowledge can be given a virtue-theoretic reading, the problem with the knowledge within virtue proposal will not come from any incompatibility with Williamson's epistemology; it will come from finding an account of virtue that will viably suit such an expansion.

This entirely pioneering approach to non-reductive virtue epistemology allows for the most extreme incorporation of virtue within a non-reductive model of knowledge; in a radical sense virtue would be at the heart of epistemology. That said, however, being radical, the knowledge within virtue proposal is extremely ambitious, requiring a substantial amount of work to adequately develop. Pursuing the knowledge within virtue proposal would not only force us to carefully reconsider knowledge itself, conscientiously exploring just how it fits within a broader concept of virtue, but it would force us to develop a thoroughgoing account of virtue to match—a formidable project that would presumably take us well away from epistemology. If it can be viably developed, the *knowledge within virtue* proposal would nevertheless be an interesting strategy for establishing a non-reductive virtue epistemology and well worth consideration.

Section 3: Rethinking Williamson and Contemporary Virtue Epistemology

Having mapped the various ways in which virtue might be incorporated within a non-reductive model of knowledge, we were able to explicate three general strategies for producing virtue epistemologies that are not committed to the analyzability of knowledge—knowledge plus virtue, knowledge as virtue, and knowledge within virtue. But in all of this, we left the relevant epistemic concepts abstract and uncommitted to any specific account of knowledge (e.g., knowledge as mental states) or any specific account of virtue (e.g., proper functioning cognitive faculties, cognitive competencies, etc.). In this section, we consider the aforementioned strategies first in light of Williamson's particular account of knowledge and then in light of the agent-reliabilism, agent-responsibilism, and the religious epistemology of the previous chapters.

On the face of it, all three strategies are compatible with Williamson's non-reductive account of knowledge. This is not to say, of course, that Williamson himself would approve of any of these strategies, just that there is nothing inherent in his epistemology that precludes them. First, consider the knowledge plus virtue proposal. As Williamson says himself, "[t]he present account of knowing makes no use of such concepts as *justified, caused*, and *reliable*. Yet knowing seems to be highly sensitive to such factors over a wide range of cases. Any adequate account of knowing should enable one to understand these connections" (2000, 41). Williamson acquiesces that he only "adumbrate[s] a strategy without carrying it out" in *Knowledge and Its Limits*—a project that future iterations of Williamson's epistemology should seemingly pursue (2000, 41). Supposedly, then, one set of intuitions that Williamson's epistemology should somehow explain or "be highly sensitive to" are those springing from "the wide range of cases" that help motivate virtue epistemology. In Section 1, we saw how Williamson ornaments his theory of knowledge with a safety condition. Once he recognizes that "knowing seems to be highly sensitive to such factors over a wide range of cases" (e.g., Fake Barn cases), Williamson is happy to amend his account accordingly—dubbing safety a necessary condition for knowledge (Williamson 2000, 41). The knowledge plus virtue proposal is simply the proposal to likewise ornament Williamson's epistemology with another condition, a virtue-theoretic condition. Again, just as safety might be key to explaining and tracking knowledge ascriptions across cases like Fake Barns and Sheep 2, perhaps a virtue-theoretic condition is needed to explain and track knowledge ascriptions across cases like René and the Gambler's Fallacy and Brain Lesion. Through his incorporation of safety,

Williamson paved the way for our favorite epistemic concepts to piggyback on his non-reductive model via the knowledge plus virtue proposal.

Applying the knowledge as virtue proposal to Williamson's account is no less straightforward; instead of defining knowledge as a mental state, simply define it as a virtuous state—explicating *mental states* in terms of *epistemic virtue*, epistemically virtuous motivation that reaches its given telos.[18] Despite being a blatant theoretical "smash and grab" job, such a move does not seem to do any violence to Williamson's epistemic framework. As was noted, Williamson says very little as to what it means for something to be a mental state; and as such, there does not seem to be any theoretical hurdles keeping us from filling in the relevant details with our favorite virtue-theoretic concepts—proper function, cognitive competencies, etc. And to be sure, we only need the *epistemic* mental states (i.e., mental states that correlate to knowledge—the *factive mental states*) to be epistemic virtues or virtuous states; we do not need to try to describe *all* mental states in virtue-theoretic terminology.[19] And what is more, in describing knowledge as a mental state by drawing parallels between knowledge and quintessential mental states, as Williamson does, we are not precluded from further elucidating epistemic mental states in terms of virtuous states. Under this proposal, knowledge remains primitive, factive, and indeed the most general factive mental state; the critical difference being that *factive mental state* is now understood using virtue-theoretic concepts. To be sure, someone might resist explicating mental states in terms of virtuous states on the grounds that, unlike quintessential mental states like *believing something is so*, virtuous states typically consist of both an internal and an external component—internal epistemically virtuous motivation and an epistemically virtuous telos that typically contains an external truth component.[20] But insofar as we lack any robust theoretical grounds to assume an overly internalistic conception of the mental, such a worry possesses no real risk.[21] Insofar as we are willing to allow for factive mental states, there is no hurdle to explicating (factive) mental states in terms of epistemic virtue and in terms of virtuous states.[22]

Finally, consider Williamson's account of knowledge in conjunction with the knowledge within virtue proposal. Insofar as we can redefine mental states in terms of epistemic virtue (as in our application of the previous proposal), there are seemingly no intrinsic obstacles within the Williamsonian model to expanding a given account of virtue to be the richest epistemic state, our conceptual cornerstone. In other words, if mental states can be reconceived in terms of virtue, they could easily be planted within a rich and broad virtue-laden context. However, insofar as Williamson's model for knowledge can be given a virtue-theoretic reading, the problem with the knowledge within virtue proposal will not come from any incompatibility with Williamson's epistemology; it will come from finding an account of virtue that will viably suit such an expansion.

Now consider once again agent-reliabilism virtue epistemology—focusing specifically on Ernest Sosa's account. In keeping with the traditional suppositions, Sosa's account took the form of an analysis of knowledge in terms of necessary and jointly sufficient conditions. And in an attempt to satisfy the high demands of such a project without producing an overly complex, intricate, and (perhaps) ad hoc account, Sosa proposed a relatively simple and elegant theory of knowledge; a belief will be knowledge by Sosa's lights if it is *apt*, if it is "true because competent," if its truth is somehow "attributable to" or "derived from" relevant cognitive faculties. From this simple definition, Sosa was able to unfold a two-tiered classification of knowledge: animal knowledge (apt belief) and reflective knowledge (apt belief aptly held). And by invoking this distinction, Sosa is able to provide new and interesting approaches to various philosophical debates (e.g., the internalism/externalism debate). Unfortunately, however, Sosa's elegant account of knowledge simply could not viably surmount the Gettier Problem. Sosa's analysis either succumbs to Gettier counterexamples or yields a radical and untenable form of skepticism.

At the heart of Sosa's definition of knowledge is his agent-reliabilist virtue-theoretic concept—cognitive competence, more specifically those cognitive competencies from which truths can somehow be "attributed to" or "derived from." And we can preserve this feature of Sosa's account by adapting it to suit the Williamsonian model using any of the general strategies explicated earlier. Sosa's virtue-theoretic concept of cognitive competency (his definition of knowledge as apt belief) is meant to connect rightly a given agent to the facts (cf. René and the Gambler's Fallacy) and rightly preclude knowledge from cases of malfunction (cf. Brain Lesion). Epistemic virtue for Sosa is the veritic exercise of cognitive competencies. *Given the knowledge plus virtue proposal*, a non-reductive virtue epistemology that is (largely) in keeping with the heart of Sosa's epistemology can be produced by simply amending Williamson's model of knowledge with the caveat that the veritic exercise of cognitive competencies is a necessary condition for knowledge. *Given the knowledge as virtue proposal*, knowledge, under a Williamsonian adaptation of Sosa's epistemology, is veritic exercise of a cognitive competence or at least the given state thereof. Of course, being veritic, the relevant cognitive competencies are factive. In other words, using my visual cognitive competency to judge that *p*, given that such a competency is veritic, entails *p*. Additionally, being in a virtuous epistemic state that *p* as a result of cognitive competency, C, will only entail knowledge that p if C is factive. There are, no doubt, many veritic epistemic states—seeing that p (via visual cognitive competencies), hearing that p (with auditory cognitive competencies), etc.—but being in any such state is sufficient for knowledge. Knowledge, again, is the most general epistemic virtue. Finally, *given the knowledge within virtue proposal*, if we can re-describe Williamson's epistemology in terms of veritic cognitive competencies, there will be no intrinsic hurdle to planting such an account within a broad and rich virtue-laden context. In other words, there is nothing about Sosa's notion of epistemic virtue that would preclude a project that would establish virtue as the richest epistemic state, being metaphysically necessary for knowledge and conceptually prior to knowledge.[23]

Now consider once again agent-responsibilism virtue epistemology—focusing specifically on Linda Zagzebki's account. Zabzeksi's account also took the form of an analysis of knowledge in terms of necessary and jointly sufficient conditions. And in an attempt to satisfy the high demands of such a project without producing an overly complex, intricate, and (perhaps) ad hoc account, Zagzebski also proposed a relatively simple and elegant theory of knowledge; a belief will be knowledge by Zagzebski's lights if it's truth is (somehow) "arisen from," "due to," or "because of" an act of intellectual virtue. Unfortunately, however, the simplicity of Zagzebski's analysis of knowledge was deceptive—hiding dubious ambiguity. As soon as we tried to elucidate *knowledge as true belief arising from intellectual virtue*, we found that under any plausible interpretation, Zagzebski's analysis, like Sosa's, either succumbs to Gettier counterexamples or yields a radical and untenable form of skepticism.

At the heart of Zagzebski's definition of knowledge is her agent-responsibilist virtue-theoretic concept: character-based intellectual virtues in terms of acts (i) that express virtuous motivation, (ii) that are the sort of things that virtuous people do, and (iii) that, as such, reach their telos (which would include truth).[24] And parallel to our treatment of Sosa's epistemology earlier, we can preserve this feature of Zagzebski's account by adapting it to suit the Williamsonian model using any of the general strategies explicated earlier. Just like Sosa's notion of cognitive competency, Zagzebski's concept of intellectual virtue is meant to connect rightly a given agent to the facts (cf. René and the Gambler's Fallacy) and rightly preclude knowledge from cases of malfunction (cf. Brain Lesion). *Given the knowledge plus virtue proposal*, a non-reductive virtue epistemology that is (largely) in keeping with the heart of Zagzebski's epistemology can be produced by simply amending Williamson's model of knowledge with the caveat that veritic, character-based intellectual virtue is a necessary condition for knowledge.²⁵ *Given the knowledge as virtue proposal,* knowledge, under a Williamsonian adaptation of Zagzebski's epistemology, is veritic, character-based intellectual virtue or at least the given state thereof. Of course, being veritic, the relevant intellectual virtues are factive. In other words, using intellectual courage to judge that *p*, given that such a virtue is veritic, entails *p*. Additionally, being in a virtuous epistemic state that *p* as a result of a character-based intellectual virtue, *C*, will only entail knowledge that *p* if *C* is factive. There are, no doubt, many veritic epistemic states—intellectual courage, open-mindedness, intellectual accuracy—but being in any such state is sufficient for knowledge. Knowledge, again, is the most general epistemic virtue. Finally, *given the knowledge within virtue proposal,* if we can re-describe Williamson's epistemology in terms of veritic character-based intellectual virtues, there will be no intrinsic hurdle to planting such an account within a broad and rich virtue-laden context. In other words, there is nothing about Zagzebski's notion of epistemic virtue that would preclude a project that would establish virtue as the richest epistemic state, being metaphysically necessary for knowledge and conceptually prior to knowledge. Indeed, given her view that epistemic normativity is a species of moral normativity, such a proposal may have broad appeal.

Now consider Plantinga's religious virtue epistemology. Again, in keeping with the traditional suppositions, Plantinga's account took the form of a reductive analysis of knowledge in terms of necessary and jointly sufficient conditions—starting with truth and belief and trying to work his way up to knowledge via warrant. And in an attempt to satisfy the high demands of such a project, Plantinga proposed an increasingly complex and intricate account of warrant. To put it roughly, a true belief will be knowledge by Plantinga's lights if it is formed by cognitive faculties that are functioning properly in the right environment (both mini-environment and maxi-environment) and in accord with a good design plan aimed at truth. Despite all of the finely tuned "bells and whistles," the demands of the reductive analysis project were simply too high; as we saw in Chapter 3, Plantinga's analysis of knowledge simply could not surmount the Gettier Problem—either falling victim to Gettier counterexamples or leading to radical and untenable skepticism.

We can preserve the heart of Plantinga's epistemology (i.e., his notion of proper function), however, by adapting it to suit the Williamsonian model using any of the general strategies explicated earlier. It is his particular focus on the *properly functioning* human knower that is meant to distinguish his account from all others. Plantinga's notion of proper function is meant to rightly connect a given agent to the facts (cf. René and the Gambler's Fallacy) and, of course, rightly preclude knowledge from cases of malfunction (cf. Brain Lesion). According to Plantinga, other theories of knowledge fail due to their inability to track knowledge ascription in accord with the proper functioning of the relevant cognitive faculties behind a given belief's genesis. Proper function is, for Plantinga, not only the key virtue-theoretic concept in his account; it is meant to be the "rock on which" competing theories of knowledge "founder" (Plantinga 1993b, 4). Epistemic virtue for Plantinga is the mechanical proper functioning of cognitive faculties. *Given the knowledge plus virtue proposal*, a non-reductive virtue epistemology that is (largely) in keeping with the heart of Plantinga's theory of knowledge can be developed by simply amending Williamson's model with a caveat that proper functioning is a necessary condition for knowledge. *Given the knowledge as virtue proposal*, knowledge, under a Williamsonian adaptation of Plantinga's epistemology, simply is properly functioning cognitive faculties or at least the state thereof. And of course, the relevant cognitive faculties at issue here are those that are factive, veritic, or (to use Plantinga's terminology) "aimed at truth." Being in a virtuous epistemic state that p as a result of cognitive faculty, F, will only entail knowledge that p if F is factive, if F is veritic, if F is aimed at truth. There are, no doubt, many veritic epistemic states—seeing that p (with properly functioning visual faculties), hearing that p (with properly functioning auditory faculties), etc.—but being in any such state is sufficient for knowledge. In other words, knowledge is the most general epistemic virtue. And of course, knowledge that p, being in a virtuous state that p, entails that p. Finally, *given the knowledge within virtue proposal*, if we can re-describe Williamson's epistemology in terms of proper function, there will be no intrinsic hurdle to planting such an account within a broader and richer virtue-laden context. In other words, there is nothing about Plantinga's notion of epistemic virtue that would preclude a project that would establish virtue as the richest epistemic state, being metaphysically necessary for knowledge and conceptually prior to knowledge.

Conclusion

In this chapter, we have laid some groundwork—exploring by way of prolegomena the possibility of endorsing non-reductive virtue epistemology. And the initial results are exciting. We have seen how there are three general strategies, *knowledge plus virtue*, *knowledge as virtue*, and *knowledge within virtue*, which can be used to develop non-reductive virtue epistemologies that will seemingly preserve our favorite virtue-theoretic concepts without committing to the analyzability of knowledge. What is more, all of these strategies are, it seems, perfectly compatible with Williamson's seminal epistemic model. But which strategy should we adopt? Do some accounts of epistemic virtue seem especially suited for certain strategies? Do we have reason to champion one account of epistemic virtue over the others? In the next chapter I will argue for a specific account of non-reductive virtue epistemology, a non-reductive proper functionalism that adopts the *knowledge as virtue* model. And then, in the final chapter, we'll consider how my proposed approach to non-reductive virtue epistemology might fare in light of two emerging challenges in the contemporary literature.

7

Knowledge as Virtue

In the previous chapter, we identified three broad strategies for developing a non-reductive account of virtue epistemology: *knowledge plus virtue*, *knowledge as virtue*, and *knowledge within virtue*. In this chapter, I will put forward some arguments in favor of one of these strategies in particular. (I'll leave it to perceptive readers to reflect on the title of this chapter and hazard a guess as to which strategy I end up advocating.)

But before we do that, we need to return to a debate that we put to the side in the previous chapter: Which account of epistemic virtue should we endorse? An agent-responsibilist account like Zagzebski's? An agent-reliabilist account like Sosa's or Greco's? Or perhaps a proper functionalist account like Plantinga's? In the previous chapter, our goal was to simply sketch general strategies for developing non-reductive accounts of virtue epistemology, regardless of the particular account of epistemic virtue someone champions; that said however, which account of epistemic virtue one advocates might constrain which non-reductive strategy seems the most plausible. For example, perhaps an agent-responsibilism like Zagzebski's, with its focus on a wide range of character virtues, is better suited for the knowledge within virtue strategy, which places virtue as the central concept within epistemology (such that epistemic virtue is taken to be more conceptually primitive than knowledge). As such, before we advocate a particular non-reductive strategy, it is worth considering, at least briefly, whether or not we have reasons to prefer a particular account of epistemic virtue.

In the first section of this chapter, we'll do just that; we'll reconsider agent-responsibilism, agent-reliabilism (of the Sosa and Greco variety), and proper functionalism,[1] and I'll make a case for my preferred account of epistemic virtue: *proper functionalism*. In Section 2, I will put forward some arguments in favor of the *knowledge as virtue* strategy for non-reductive virtue epistemology, which will leave us a non-reductive proper functionalism where epistemic virtue is co-primitive with knowledge. In Section 3, we will give a first approximation of this non-reductive proper functionalism and then explore how it might address several perennial challenges within epistemology, including the Gettier Problem, Fake Barn problems, the value of knowledge, and more.

Section 1: Which Account of Epistemic Virtue?

So how should we go about selecting an account of epistemic virtue to reenvision in terms of a non-reductive model of knowledge? To be sure, the few attempts within the contemporary philosophical literature that have tried to develop non-reductive models of knowledge—Lisa Miracchi's "Competence to Know" (2015) and Christoph Kelp's "Knowledge First Virtue Epistemology" (2017)—have done so with agent-reliabilist accounts of epistemic virtue, akin to those developed by Sosa, Greco, Turri, and others. While these accounts of epistemic virtue are, no doubt, the most popular accounts within the contemporary philosophical literature, there is no reason to think that agent-reliabilist accounts are uniquely or particularly apt for being reenvisioned in terms of a non-reductive model (at least no one has made that argument). In this section, we'll draw from some of the critiques of different accounts of epistemic virtue that we developed in Chapters 3, 4, and 5 to help justify championing proper functionalism in developing our account of non-reductive virtue epistemology in the next section. To be sure, my justification for championing proper functionalism will be far from conclusive—the literature on the different accounts of epistemic virtue and their respective virtues (no pun intended!) is extensive and we won't be able to address everything here—nevertheless, given the ground we've covered in earlier chapters, I do think we have at least material for sketching *some* reasons to champion a proper functionalist account of epistemic virtue in developing our account of non-reductive virtue epistemology in the next section.

Section 1.1: Against Agent-Responsibilism

As we saw in Chapter 4, one important strike against thinking about epistemic virtue in terms of a true belief "arising from," "due to," or "through" an act of intellectual virtue, as Linda Zagzebski does, is that it is notoriously difficult to know how to understand this "arising from," "due to," or "through" relationship.[2] (And one of the reasons I'm wanting to address Zagzebski's agent-reliabilism first is because, arguably, similar objections will apply to agent-reliabilist accounts that describe epistemic virtue in terms of beliefs being true "because" competent, say.) Such a relation, as Michael Levin (2004) argued, can be understood in three ways: *reliabilistically*: explaining causally how a given agent arrived at the target true belief; *in terms of belief*: explaining why the agent believes the target belief; and *in terms of truth*: explaining why the given belief is true.

The problem, as we saw, was that none of these readings are compatible with Zagzebski's agent-responsibilist account of epistemic virtue. According to Levin, we should not read Zagzebski's definition of knowledge *reliabilistically* because (i) "all causal paths from even the surest motives to belief permit double accidents" and (ii) doing so would be to fundamentally change the responsibilist character of Zagzebski's account (Levin 2004, 401). Additionally, we should not read Zagzebski's definition of knowledge *in terms of belief* either, because doing so is incompatible with Zagzebski's explicit definition of knowledge. (If we're only concerned with how a belief was formed, then the truth of the belief doesn't factor in.) And what is more, we should not read Zagzebski's definition of knowledge *in terms of truth* because doing so would radically limit what we know; seemingly, we would know very few things if knowledge required truth to be contingent on our intellectual virtues (e.g., the truth of my belief that the Earth orbits around the sun is in no way "arising from" or "due to" any intellectual virtue on my part).

So, as we saw in Chapter 4, it looks as though Zagzebski's account of epistemic virtue and knowledge is fundamentally incomplete—bearing a critical gap that simply cannot be filled. Given that Zagzebski's account of epistemic virtue is widely taken to be the most seminal agent-responsibilist account in the literature, we have, I think, a good reason to look elsewhere when developing our non-reductive account of virtue epistemology, at least until the aforementioned "critical gap" can be filled in.

Section 1.2: Against Agent-reliabilism

Of course, a similar worry can be leveled against the seminal accounts of agent-reliabilism in the contemporary philosophical literature. For example, Sosa thinks of knowledge in terms of a belief being "true because competent" (Sosa 2007, 1:23) and Greco defines knowledge in terms of "a kind of success from ability" (Greco 2010, 3), and, as with Zagzebski's "due to" or "through" relation between truth and epistemic virtue, we might also wonder what it means for a belief to be true "because" of our cognitive competency or successful (which includes truth) "from" of a cognitive achievement. Like Zagzebski's "due to," "because of," or "explained by" relations, such agent-reliabilist accounts can be understood in three ways: *reliabilistically*: explaining causally how a given agent arrived at said true belief; *in terms of belief*: explaining why the agent believes said belief; and *in terms of truth*: explaining why the given belief is true. Unlike Zagzebski's account, however, agent-*reliabilist* accounts can (unsurprisingly!) and presumably *should* be read reliabilistically. The danger here is that a reliabilistic understanding of "because" and "from" in Sosa and Greco's respective accounts will be vulnerable to Gettier counterexamples; as Levin warned, "all causal paths from even the surest motives to belief permit double accidents" (Levin 2004, 401). And that's what we predicted in Chapter 1 and saw fleshed out in Chapter 3. And insofar as Sosa, Greco, Turri, and others use the language of truth "because" or "from" largely as a way to try to solve the Gettier Problem (since, ostensibly, Gettiered beliefs are true because of luck and *not* because of or from any kind of cognitive competence or ability), then the motivation for so defining epistemic virtue might be significantly undercut.

That said, however, given that such agent-reliabilist virtue epistemologies are the most seminal virtue epistemologies in the contemporary literature, we might still be tempted to explore our non-reductive options while drawing from such accounts of epistemic virtue, as Miracchi (2015) and Kelp (2017) have done.[3] Unfortunately, however, as we saw in Chapter 3, *other* obstacles arise out of trying to define knowledge in terms of a belief being true "because of" or "from" a cognitive ability or competency, which might further motivate us to consider other accounts of epistemic virtue in our pursuit of a non-reductive virtue epistemology. Two such obstacles: First, as Jennifer Lackey argued in "Knowledge and Credit" (2009), such definitions struggle to viably account for testimonial knowledge. And as Krist Vaesen argued in "Knowledge without Credit" (2011), defining knowledge in terms of a belief being true "because of" or "from" a cognitive ability or competency also struggles to account for extended cognition.

Of course, these debates are ongoing and are far from settled. John Greco, for example, has powerfully responded to these objections in his article, "A (Different) Virtue Epistemology" (2012); however, as we saw in Chapter 3, Greco's defense of virtue epistemology is itself far from conclusive and faces its own significant challenges.[4] In any case, if we're tempted to define knowledge in terms of beliefs that are true "because of" or "due to" our epistemic competency or ability, then there is a serious worry that such a definition of knowledge will mistakenly preclude attributing knowledge in some cases where our cognitive abilities or competencies aren't sufficiently attributable for our hitting upon the truth (cases of testimony and extended cognition being two such examples). Add to this, lingering questions regarding how we should understand the "because of" or "due to" relation at the heart of these kinds of agent-reliabilist accounts, and I think we can find a good reason to explore an alternative account of epistemic virtue.

Section 1.3: Proper Functionalism

The third and final broad account of epistemic virtue that we've considered in this book is, of course, *proper functionalism*, particularly the proper functionalism of Alvin Plantinga. While Plantinga's virtue epistemology is best understood as a species of *agent-reliabilism*, it is markedly different from the agent-reliabilism of Ernest Sosa, John Greco, and John Turri. For one thing, unlike Zagzebski's agent-responsibilism or those other aforementioned account of agent-reliabilism, Plantinga's account of virtue epistemology isn't understood in terms of having a belief whose truth is "due to" or "arising out of" or "because of" an act of intellectual virtue (be it a character virtue, as in Zagzebski's account, or a cognitive competence or ability). Given the difficulties noted earlier attached to providing a viable understanding of such a "because of" relationship between truth and intellectual virtue, the fact that Plantinga's account doesn't rely on such a relationship is in and of itself a significant virtue of the account. Likewise, Plantinga's proper functionalism avoids mistakenly precluding attributing knowledge in cases of testimony or extended cognition. Insofar as the protagonists in cases like Chicago Visotor and Sissicase are employing cognitive faculties that are properly functioning according to a design plan that is aimed at truth in an appropriate environment, then Plantinga's account can easily attribute knowledge to the target beliefs.

The central critique of Plantinga's account of warrant in terms of proper function that we developed in Chapter 5 centrally concerned the account's inability to provide a viable answer to the Gettier Problem. Such a worry, to be sure, is addressed if we can develop an account of proper functionalism that is *non-reductive*, which doesn't aim to provide a reductive analysis of knowledge in terms of necessary and jointly sufficient conditions that are taken to be conceptually more primitive than knowledge. Where *reductive* accounts are explicitly aiming at providing a viable reductive analysis of knowledge, they'll invariably face challenges from Gettier-type cases; by going non-reductive, however, we can viably sidestep those challenges altogether. We're no longer trying to play the reductive analysis game!

To be sure, plenty of other objections have been leveled against Plantinga's account of proper functionalism over the years. Jon Kvanvig's edited volume, *Warrant in Contemporary Epistemology* (1996), includes articles highlighting a number of these objections. How should we delineate what counts as a cognitive facility?[5] How do we account for degrees of warrant within Plantinga's account of proper function?[6] How do we determine the design plan of a given cognitive faculty?[7] And, of course, is Plantinga's account of warrant in terms of proper function able to provide a viable response to the Gettier Problem?[8] That said, aside from that fourth question (which we answered in the negative in Chapter 5), we're largely going to put these issues to the side.[9] The goal in this section is *not* to provide a conclusive assessment of the different accounts of epistemic virtue on offer in the contemporary literature, while trying to weigh the pros and cons of each respective account; such a project is outside the scope of what we're able to cover in this chapter or this book. That said, however, given the accounts of epistemic virtue we've been considering in this book and the critiques of each of them that we developed in Chapters 3, 4, and 5, the goal in this section has been to provide *some* justification for championing proper functionalism as we develop our account of non-reductive virtue epistemology in the next section. And while the justification we've sketched earlier is far from conclusive, it does give us at least a sketch of *some* reasons (or at least some of *my* reasons!) to champion a proper functionalist as we move forward.

A closing question for this section: So if we're thinking about epistemic virtue merely in terms of proper function—in particular, the kind of epistemic virtue that might be incorporated within a non-reductive account of knowledge—and *not* as a bridge between true belief and knowledge, does anything change regarding how we think about proper functionalism? Maybe. For starters, and continuing with Alvin Plantinga's account of proper function as it is developed in *Warrant: The Current Debate* (1993a), *Warant and Proper Function* (1993b), and *Warranted Christian Belief* (2000), we might think about proper function in very similar terms:

> PF: A cognitive faculty will manifest epistemic virtue if and only if it is functioning properly, according to a good design plan that is aimed at truth and is operating in a suitable environment.

Given that we're talking about an agent-reliabilist account of epistemic virtue, with a focus on faculty virtues as opposed character virtues, it makes sense for cognitive faculties to be the object of epistemic virtue in this case. And each of the qualifications here—proper function, good design plan, aimed at truth, suitable environment—can be motivated and understood in the same way that they were in Chapter 5.

But given that we're no longer thinking about proper functionalism as a bridge between true belief and knowledge (as if we were pursuing a reductive analysis), a few minor revisions might be in order. Consider, for example, the *knowledge as virtue* approach to non-reductive virtue epistemology outlined in the previous chapter—where knowledge is both necessary and sufficient for epistemic virtue and vice versa. We will explore this strategy further in the next section, but for now it's worth noting that PF doesn't seem suitable for such a strategy for one simple reason: proper function, within PF does not guarantee truth. And insofar as knowledge requires truth, then epistemic virtue, so understood, cannot be sufficient for knowledge as the *knowledge as virtue* strategy requires. To accommodate the knowledge as virtue strategy, the following modification could be made:

> PF′: A cognitive faculty will manifest epistemic virtue if and only if it is functioning properly, according to a good design plan that is aimed at truth *and successful in reaching that end*, and is operating in a suitable environment.

This modification would guarantee that when a cognitive faculty manifests an epistemic virtue that it necessarily hits upon the truth.[10] We'll return to this modified account in the next section.

Section 2: Deciding on a Non-reductive Model

Now that we've tentatively landed on a specific account of epistemic virtue, we're now ready to more carefully explore the different non-reductive strategies. As we saw in the previous chapter, three broad strategies for developing a non-reductive virtue epistemology emerged: *knowledge plus virtue*, *knowledge as virtue*, and *knowledge within virtue*. Now, as we noted, all three strategies are broadly compatible with all three accounts of epistemic virtue that we've considered in this book. My goal, then, is *not* to rule out some strategies in favor of others; instead, however, my much more modest goal is simply to try to motivate my preferred strategy, *knowledge as virtue*, when developing a non-reductive proper functionalism.

In Section 2.1, I will argue that, given that a proper functionalist account of epistemic virtue like PF′ plausibly (i) already encompasses any other leading candidates for necessary conditions on knowledge (truth, safety, etc.) and (ii) itself *entails* knowledge, then we might conclude that the *knowledge plus virtue* strategy is unnecessarily weak—especially if we're attracted to a robust account of virtue epistemology.[11] Such a conclusion will lead us, in Section 2.2, to consider the *knowledge as virtue* strategy, where epistemic virtue is both co-primitive with knowledge and necessary and sufficient for knowledge. Here, I will argue that the *knowledge as virtue* is an apt strategy to employ for an account of epistemic virtue like proper functionalism. Finally, in Section 2.3, we'll consider the more ambitious strategy of *knowledge within virtue* and conclude that the resultant account of virtue epistemology would face significant challenges that might motivate us to stick with the *knowledge as virtue* strategy.

Section 2.1: The Knowledge plus Virtue Model

It makes sense to start off with the non-reductive strategy that is the easiest to develop and work from there. According to the *knowledge plus virtue* non-reductive model of virtue epistemology, all we need to do is take a non-reductive account of knowledge and identify a given virtue-theoretic condition as a necessary condition for knowledge. As we saw with Williamson's seminal non-reductive account of knowledge, even if we resist analyzing knowledge in terms of necessary and jointly sufficient conditions that are taken to be conceptually more primitive than knowledge, that doesn't mean that we can't nevertheless identify necessary conditions for knowledge. Truth, obviously enough, is necessary for knowledge, even if knowledge is understood non-reductively. And, for Williamson, a safety condition is also necessary for knowledge. As such, if we can also identify a given virtue-theoretic condition as also necessary for knowledge, then we can just add it to the list of necessary conditions—for example, truth, safe, and virtue-theoretic.

And as we saw in the previous chapter, the case can certainly be made that something like PF or PF′ is necessary for knowledge. Just as safety might be key to explaining and tracking knowledge ascriptions across cases like Fake Barns and Sheep 2, perhaps a condition like PF or PF′ is needed to explain and track knowledge ascriptions across cases like René and the Gambler's Fallacy and Brain Lesion (which we first discussed in this book's Introduction).

That said, however, if our aim is a *robust* virtue epistemology, one which strives to account for knowledge merely in virtue-theoretic conditions, then such a strategy won't satisfy. And to be sure, if we were to try to remain as faithful as possible to Plantinga's original account of knowledge, then we might plausibly want to avoid settling for anything less than a robust virtue epistemology.

After all, for Plantinga proper function—and not proper function among other conditions—is what is meant to bridge the gap between true belief and knowledge. As we noted in the last chapter, proper function is, for Plantinga, not only the key virtue-theoretic concept in his account; it is meant to be the "rock on which" competing theories of knowledge "founder" (Plantinga 1993b, 4). Proper function, someone like Plantinga might think, should not simply be one condition among many (like safety) that is necessary for knowledge; it should be *the* condition for knowledge.

And this can be *mostly* accomplished with an account of epistemic virtue like PF. If one of the central motivations for including a condition like safety as a necessary condition on knowledge is Fake Barn-styled cases, then we might plausibly think that something like PF can cover the same ground. (After all, so the argument goes, an environment that is overrun with barn facades is hardly a suitable environment for judging whether or not a given barn-appearance corresponds with an actual barn.) That said, as we noted earlier, PF can't be the *sole* condition on knowledge, since it doesn't guarantee truth. Truth is necessary for knowledge, and if that's not accounted for, then we plausibly need at least *two* necessary conditions: truth and something like PF.

But, again, insofar as we want a *robust* virtue epistemology which strives to account for knowledge *merely* in virtue-theoretic conditions, we might feel compelled to try to push further. PF' allows us to do so, because truth is built into PF' in a way that it isn't in PF. Now, there are, of course, a myriad of conditions that might plausibly be considered necessary for knowledge: sensitivity, defeasibility, character virtues, reflective access to the relevant evidence, etc. The debates surrounding these potential necessary conditions on knowledge are expansive and ongoing (Williamson was wise, in *Knowledge and Its Limits* (2000), to leave the door open to new necessary conditions); as such, trying to establish a definitive list of necessary conditions on knowledge and *then* argue that they can all be circumscribed or otherwise accounted for within a virtue-theoretic condition (e.g., like PF') is a staggeringly ambitious project—certainly not one we can take up in this book. For the sake of argument, however, let's make a generous assumption: for any given plausible necessary condition on knowledge either (i) it can be accounted for within an account of epistemic virtue like PF' (e.g., how PF' might be plausibly seen as covering the same ground as a safety condition) or (ii) it can be viably dismissed as a legitimate necessary condition on knowledge. While this is, no doubt, a generous assumption indeed, it's not an assumption that is without support in the philosophical literature; Alvin Plantinga's books *Warrant: The Current Debate* (1993a) and *Warrant and*

Proper Function (1993b) are largely arguing precisely in support of such an assumption. So, for the sake of argument, I'm asking us to assume that Plantinga is correct in arguing that proper function (and proper function alone!) is the key to understanding knowledge. What follows?

If we're taking knowledge to be an unanalyzable primitive, then what emerges is an understanding of knowledge where our target virtue condition is the *sole* condition on knowledge. Such an account of knowledge is still in keeping with the *knowledge plus virtue* strategy outlined in Chapter 6; however, it's more *robust* insofar as the virtue condition is the only necessary condition of knowledge. But as we reach this point, with our generous assumption at our back, it's difficult not to feel as though we've reached a certain escape velocity, which will lead us away from the gravitational pull, so to speak, of the *knowledge plus virtue* strategy altogether, to fly to something more ambitious. If we're assuming that proper function, as expressed in something like PF', is the only thing that's necessary for knowledge, we might wonder if a cognitive faculty can manifest proper function in the relevant sense without also being an example of knowledge. If every example of knowledge is necessarily an example of proper function according to PF', and every example of proper function according to PF' that we can think of is an example of knowledge, then an intoxicating thought emerges: What if our virtue condition and our account of knowledge are just two sides of the same coin? Without trying to provide a reductive analysis where one concept is more primitive than the other, what if we not only took proper function to be necessary for knowledge *but also took knowledge to be necessary for epistemic proper function*?

Section 2.2: The Knowledge as Virtue Strategy

According to the knowledge as virtue strategy for developing a non-reductive account of knowledge, instead of defining knowledge separate from virtue and subsequently adding a virtue-theoretic condition as a caveat (like we did with the knowledge plus virtue strategy), we are defining knowledge simply in terms of a virtue-theoretic concept, in this case proper function, by explicating a primitive account of knowledge as both necessary and sufficient for a co-primitive account of epistemic virtue (like PF'). As we noted in Chapter 6, while knowledge *plus virtue strategy* (along with Williamson's knowledge-first epistemology) might be called *doubly non-reductive*—both abandoning sufficiency conditions for knowledge and holding knowledge as conceptually primitive—the *knowledge as virtue* is what we might call *singularly non-reductive*. While knowledge is still held primitive in this strategy, a co-primitive conception of virtue is taken to be both necessary and *sufficient* for knowledge. The subsequent account is still non-reductive; knowledge, as a primitive, is simply defined in terms of epistemic virtue.

So, according to this strategy, knowledge is necessary and sufficient for epistemic virtue and vice versa. And, with PF' in hand, that means that knowledge is simply understood in terms of when a cognitive faculty manifests epistemic virtue by functioning properly, according to a good design plan that is aimed at truth (and successful in reaching that end) and is operating in a suitable environment. Analogous to Spinoza's appeals to *God or Nature*, we can, according to this strategy, refer to *epistemic virtue or knowledge*. Critically, this doesn't mean that we can't still explicate *epistemic virtue or knowledge* in terms of necessary conditions. Drawing from PF', we might say that for *epistemic virtue or knowledge*, it's necessary, for example, that one's relevant cognitive faculties are functioning properly. It's also necessary that those cognitive faculties are operating according to a good design plan that is aimed at truth (and successful in reaching that end). It's also necessary that those cognitive facilities are operating within a suitable environment. The list, theoretically, could go on; however, given the *knowledge as virtue* strategy, any additional necessary conditions would need to be both necessary for knowledge *and* for epistemic virtue.

Here's a worry: If knowledge and epistemic virtue are two sides of the same coin as we're suggesting, and if we're understanding epistemic virtue in terms of PF', then it looks like we're committed to giving a reductive analysis of, not knowledge per se, but *knowledge or epistemic virtue*. If we're saying that a cognitive faculty will manifest epistemic virtue *if and only if* it is functioning properly, according to a good design plan that is aimed at truth (and successful in reaching that end), and is operating in a suitable environment, then it looks like we're saying that *having cognitive faculties that are functioning properly according to a good design plan that is aimed at truth (and successful in reaching that end) and is operating in a suitable environment* is both necessary and jointly sufficient for *epistemic virtue or knowledge*. And if we take such conditions to be conceptually more primitive than *epistemic virtue or knowledge*, then we're functionally providing a reductive analysis of *epistemic virtue or knowledge*. And given our grim diagnosis of ever providing a viable reductive analysis of *knowledge*, we should probably be deeply pessimistic regarding our chances of ever providing viable reductive analysis of *epistemic virtue or knowledge*.

Thankfully, however, we can avoid risking accidentally proposing a reductive analysis of *epistemic virtue or knowledge* by modifying our preferred account of epistemic virtue slightly:

PF″: A cognitive faculty will manifest epistemic virtue *only if* it is functioning properly, according to a good design plan that is aimed at truth and successful in reaching that end, and is operating in a suitable environment.

In changing the "if and only if" PF′ to the "only if" in PF″, we avoid suggesting that *having cognitive faculties that are functioning properly according to a good design plan that is aimed at truth (and successful in reaching that end) and is operating in a suitable environment* is both necessary and jointly sufficient for *epistemic virtue or knowledge*. As such, according to the *knowledge as virtue* strategy, we're able to say that knowledge is necessary and sufficient for epistemic virtue and vice versa, and we can explicate that *epistemic virtue or knowledge* in terms of necessary conditions but without accidentally generating a new reductive analysis.

And I think it's worth noting that this account of knowledge shouldn't seem too unusual, given (i) our familiarity with Williamson's non-reductive account knowledge and (ii) a surprising degree of fittingness between this brand of non-reductive proper functionalism and Timothy Williamson's non-reductive account of knowledge in terms of factive, mental, and stative operators. One important criticism of Williamson's account of knowledge is that it leans heavily on what it means to be in a *factive mental state*, but without fully elucidating what factive mental states are.[12] If we understand knowledge as co-primitive with epistemic virtue while mutually necessary and sufficient for each other, then we might be able to draw from the conceptual resources of proper functionalism to further elucidate Williamson's concept of a *factive mental state* in terms of properly functioning cognitive faculties. After all, Williamson frequently points to "seeing that," "hearing that," or "remembering that" as archetypal factive mental states, and each of these can be straightforwardly understood in terms of cognitive faculties that are central to proper functionalism. According to Williamson, "[f]active mental states are important to us as states whose essence includes a matching between mind and world, and knowing is important to us as the most general factive stative attitude" (2000, 40). The species of proper functionalism we're developing in this section could help provide intuitive support for such a thesis by explicating factive mental states in terms of (i) the design plan of target cognitive faculties being aimed at truth (and successful at reaching that end) and (ii) cognitive faculties operating in suitable environments (where the fit between mind and world is possible).[13] And just as Williamson identifies knowledge as the most general factive mental state, so too might we now simply identify epistemic virtue as the most general factive mental state.[14]

Section 2.3: The Knowledge within Virtue Strategy

While *knowledge as virtue* is the strategy I ultimately want to employ and explore in the next section, it's worth at least briefly considering the third, final, and most ambitious strategy for developing non-reductive virtue epistemology: the *knowledge within virtue* strategy. As we saw in Chapter 6, we might be tempted to give epistemic virtue an even more radically central place within our virtue epistemologies, and the *knowledge within virtue* strategy certainly delivers. Thus far, we have assumed that knowledge is the conceptual foundation for epistemology. According to this strategy, in contrast, a conceptually non-primitive account of knowledge entails a primitive account of *virtue*; knowledge is sufficient for virtue and virtue is necessary for knowledge, but knowledge is understood in terms of virtue. *According to this strategy, virtue is the broader, richer epistemic concept.* In other words, knowledge, on this account, cannot be properly comprehended apart from our understanding of virtue. And like the knowledge as virtue proposal, the knowledge within virtue proposal is singularly non-reductive. But unlike the *knowledge as virtue* proposal, which was non-reductive insofar as knowledge was deemed primitive, the *knowledge within virtue* proposal is non-reductive insofar as the project of pursuing sufficiency conditions for knowledge has been abandoned.

As we saw in the previous chapter, insofar as we take the Virtuous Pilot case to be analogous to Williamson's Burglar case, we might have some motivation to explore such a non-reductive strategy. In this book, we've been primarily concerned with virtue epistemology *theories*, which, as Heather Battaly helpfully describes them, "define or otherwise ground knowledge and justified belief in terms of the intellectual virtues" (2008, 640). In other words, virtue epistemology *theories* take knowledge or justification to be the central objects of epistemological assessment, but these are understood in light of intellectual or epistemic virtues. Every virtue epistemology we've considered in this book—from Sosa to Greco, to Zagzebski, to Plantinga—has been a *theory*. For an *anti-theory* virtue epistemology, focusing on knowledge or justification is, at best, of ancillary importance (the *expansionist* view) or, at worst, a distraction from what's really important (the *eliminativism* view); anti-theorists, again according to Battaly, "shun formulaic connections between the virtues and knowledge, but argue that the intellectual virtues are the central concepts and properties in epistemology and warrant exploration in their own right" (2008, 640).[15] This distinction between virtue epistemology theories and anti-theories becomes important here, because while virtue epistemology *theories* might see a strategy like *knowledge within virtue* as radical, anti-theories (especially *expansionist* views) might see such a strategy as both apt and welcome![16] Indeed, this would likely be the case for epistemologists (or philosophers more generally) who take something like *wisdom* to be centrally important to epistemology (or all of philosophy!), or for those who see philosophy primarily as an *activity* or a way of life and not a doctrine or dogma.[17]

All that said, however, within the context of this book—where we've been chiefly interested in virtue epistemology *theories*, which tend to be the most seminal—the knowledge within virtue proposal is a significant change of pace. Indeed, with our preferred account of epistemic virtue in hand—the kind of proper functionalism defined in PF″—it may not be entirely clear what it would look like to pursue the *knowledge within virtue* strategy. While there is nothing about Plantinga's notion of epistemic virtue that would necessarily preclude a project that would establish virtue as the richest epistemic state (being metaphysically necessary for knowledge and conceptually prior to knowledge), so much about proper functionalism as we (and Plantinga) have described it is intuitively wed to knowledge that the *knowledge within virtue* strategy might seem like a bit of an awkward choice. Indeed, given that the *knowledge within virtue* strategy inverts the traditional virtue-theoretic analysis of knowledge (where virtue is necessary for knowledge), knowledge, on such a strategy, is necessary for virtue. Consider the relationship between knowledge and truth. One of the reasons we can easily see truth as necessary but not sufficient for knowledge is because we can easily think of examples where someone believes truly without possessing knowledge. The same doesn't seem to be the case when it comes to the *knowledge within virtue* strategy's claim that knowledge is necessary (but not sufficient) for virtue—especially with an account of epistemic virtue like PF″ in hand. And insofar as it's difficult to imagine an example of knowledge that where PF″ isn't satisfied (or at least where PF″ isn't supposed to be satisfied!), then, at least when it comes to accounts of epistemic virtue like PF″, the *knowledge within virtue* strategy seems unmotivated. As such, the *knowledge within virtue* strategy doesn't seem to be a good fit with our target account of epistemic virtue.

Section 3: Knowledge as Proper Function

Given a proper functionalist account of epistemic virtue—understood in terms of PF″—I have tried to argue that we can find motivation for adopting the *knowledge as virtue* strategy as we pursue our non-reductive virtue epistemology: *non-*

reductive proper functionalism. Roughly, I argued that the *knowledge plus virtue* strategy is not robust enough, and I argued that the knowledge that the *knowledge within virtue* strategy is (given PF″) largely unmotivated. The *knowledge as virtue* strategy, in contrast, affords a robust, non-reductive virtue epistemology, which allowed us to give proper function a central place within epistemology while also enjoying a significant degree of fittingness with the prominent non-reductive model in the contemporary literature, namely, Timothy Williamson's. In this section, I want to briefly elucidate this non-reductive proper functionalism a bit further and explore how such an account allows us to respond to some central perennial problems within epistemology. Our goal here is simply to provide a first approximation for the view we've landed on and to motivate future research in this direction.

But it's worth pausing for a moment to reflect on where we've been and just how much we've accomplished. The central goal of this book, as you recall, has been to try to bring together two dominant trends within contemporary epistemology: (i) the growing dissatisfaction with the reductive analysis of knowledge, the project of explicating knowledge in terms of a list of (conceptually more primitive) necessary and jointly sufficient conditions, and (ii) the enormous popularity of virtue-theoretic approaches to knowledge. The ultimate goal of this book has been to endorse *both* trends, to endorse *non-reductive virtue epistemology*. But given that almost every prominent rendition of virtue epistemology has assumed the reductive model, such a move needed to be motivated—work needed to be done to elucidate just what was wrong with the reductive analysis model, in general, and why the *reductive* accounts of virtue epistemology, in particular, are lacking.

In the *first* part of the book, we elucidated what is wrong with the reductive analysis of knowledge project by providing a grim diagnosis of the Gettier Problem—*the* central problem any particular reductive analysis faces—and defending such a diagnosis against objections. In the *second* part of the book, we applied this diagnosis to prominent versions of virtue epistemology—arguing that (i) despite the merits of virtue-theoretic accounts of knowledge, virtue epistemology offers no new cures against Gettier counterexamples and (ii) each virtue-theoretic analysis of knowledge fails precisely along the lines predicted in Chapter 1. Having paved the way for non-reductive virtue epistemology, in this *third* and final part of this book we have explored what *non-reductive* virtue epistemology might look like. In the previous chapter, we outlined three general strategies for developing non-reductive virtue epistemology, and in this chapter we've motivated a non-reductive proper functionalism, which adopts the *knowledge as virtue* strategy. Reaching the point where we can finally start to unpack such a view is, to be sure, a significant accomplishment in and of itself!

Section 3.1: Unpacking the View

According to our preferred brand of non-reductive proper functionalism in terms of the *knowledge as virtue* strategy, knowledge is necessary and sufficient for epistemic virtue and vice versa. And, with PF" in hand, that means that knowledge is simply understood in terms of when a cognitive faculty manifests epistemic virtue by functioning properly, according to a good design plan that is aimed at truth (and successful in reaching that end), and is operating in a suitable environment. As we said before, this doesn't mean that we can't still explicate what we called *epistemic virtue or knowledge* in terms of necessary conditions. Drawing from PF", we might say that for *epistemic virtue or knowledge*, it's necessary, for example, that one's relevant cognitive faculties are functioning properly. It's also necessary that those cognitive faculties are operating according to a good design plan that is aimed at truth (and successful in reaching that end). It's also necessary that those cognitive facilities are operating within a suitable environment. And as we said before, the list could theoretically go on; however, given any additional necessary conditions would need to be both necessary for knowledge *and* for epistemic virtue.

But what does it mean for cognitive faculties to be operating within a suitable environment? Or to be operating according to a good design plan? While we'll need to make a few critical adjustments, we can start from Plantinga's own elucidation of the view (as explored in Chapter 5) and work from there. Let's start with the idea of *proper function* itself. Plantinga thinks that we all have a more or less rough-and-ready understanding of what it means for something to be functioning properly or malfunctioning (Plantinga 1993b, 5–6). Plantinga seems to be willing to follow our intuitions on this score, and I'm inclined to follow suit. We all know what it means when a car cannot go in reverse because the transmission is not (mechanically) functioning properly. We know that a properly functioning human being should generally be able to walk in a straight line without tripping or swerving and how enough alcohol impairs this proper functioning. As such, with Plantinga, we might stipulate that in order for target cognitive faculties to manifest *knowledge or epistemic virtue*, they need to be functioning properly. If Sarah is on a hallucinogenic drug, her perceptual faculties will no longer be functioning as they should; hence, her belief that the sky is melting will not have any epistemic value in terms of knowledge or epistemic virtue.

Although we may indeed have a sufficient rough-and-ready grasp of proper function, it will, nevertheless, be helpful to make some general clarifications. First of all, to function properly is not to function normally (as understood in the general statistical sense). David Lewis was far better at logic than the normal human being, but this does not mean that his prowess in logic is the result of some cognitive malfunction. Likewise, to use one of Plantinga's examples, if due to some disaster almost everyone on earth was blinded (such blindness would be a statistically normal condition), the few sighted individuals would not be suffering from malfunctioning perceptual faculties (Plantinga 1993b, 9–10). Second, not *all* of one's cognitive faculties need to be functioning properly for them to produce knowledge or epistemic virtue (Plantinga 1993b, 10). If my cognitive faculties associated with vision are faulty, that would not preclude my auditory faculties manifesting knowledge or epistemic virtue. All that must be working are "the faculties (or subfaculties, or modules) involved in the production" of the particular manifestation of knowledge or epistemic virtue in question (Plantinga 1993b, 10). For example, if I am colorblind, I can still manifest all sorts of vision-based *knowledge or epistemic virtue*—knowledge concerning distance, the presence of people and objects, and so on. Third and finally, it is worth noting that proper function comes in degrees (Plantinga 1993b, 10–11). My running ability may not be functioning as well as it could (if, say, I chose to pursue athletics instead of academics), but that doesn't mean my running ability is somehow malfunctioning. Likewise, my cognitive faculties associated with my logic abilities may not be as good as they could be, but I can still manifest *knowledge or epistemic virtue* while making logical deductions. How proper functioning does a given cognitive faculty need to be in order to be able to manifest *knowledge or epistemic virtue*? Here, we might concede (with Plantinga) that we have no answer; however, following Plantinga's lead in Chapter 5, we might note that we independently recognize that knowledge and proper function are vague to some degree—our hope, then, would be that the vagueness of our theory in this instance corresponds to the vagueness of knowledge and proper function in general.[18]

Now, as we saw in Chapter 5, more is necessary for knowledge or epistemic virtue than proper functioning cognitive faculties. For one thing, our cognitive faculties will not manifest knowledge or epistemic virtue unless they are operating in an appropriate environment. My toaster, for example, might be a perfectly properly functioning toaster; however, if I try to use the toaster in an inappropriate environment—say at the bottom of the ocean—then I might not end up with toast. Likewise, my cognitive faculties might be functioning properly; however, if they're being employed in an inappropriate environment—as we saw with Plantinga's case involving Alpha Centauri elephants—then they might not manifest *knowledge or epistemic virtue*.

But what does it mean, then, for our cognitive faculties to be functioning properly in an appropriate environment? According to Plantinga's original 1993b understanding of his environmental condition, the appropriate environment is the kind of environment that our cognitive faculties were designed for (by God, evolution, or both) is an environment like earth with "such . . . features as the presence and properties of light and air, the presence of visible objects, of other objects detectable by cognitive systems of our kind, of some objects not so detectable, of the regularities of nature, of the existence and general nature of other people, and so on" (Plantinga 1997, 143). Such an account of what it means for our cognitive faculties to be functioning properly in an appropriate environment is fine for our purposes. While such an account was wholly inadequate when it comes to viably precluding Gettier counterexamples (as we saw in Chapter 5), we are now no longer trying to provide a reductive analysis of knowledge; as such, the Gettier Problem simply isn't a threat anymore, so we don't need to be driven, as Plantinga was, to develop increasingly sophisticated iterations of an environmental condition (like 1996/1997 Mini-Favorability or 2000 Mini-Favorability, discussed in Chapter 5), which might preclude Gettier counterexamples. That was a Sisyphean endeavor that we thankfully no longer need to be saddled with.

That said, regardless of how we want to think about what it means for our cognitive faculties to be functioning properly in an appropriate environment, we need to be able to say *something* about why the environment in Fake Barn-styled cases is not an appropriate environment when it comes to viably identifying genuine barns (as opposed to a façade). While the *macro*-environment in Fake Barn-styled cases is surely appropriate (it's certainly earth-like, after all), we might, following Plantinga, want to argue that there is, nevertheless, something wrong with the local or *mini*-environment. Piggy-backing off of Plantinga's 1996/1997 Mini-Favorability condition, we might think account for the favorability of a mini-environment (M) for an exercise of cognitive faculties (E) in the following way:

Modified 1996/1997 Mini-Favorability: M of E is favorable for E, if and only if, if S were to form a belief by way of E, S would form a true belief. (modified from Plantinga 1997, 144; 1996, 328)

And, following Plantinga, we will need to specify that the counterfactual semantics of Modified 1996/1997 Mini-Favorability's are non-standard (i.e., non-Lewisian, non-Stalnakerian)—"the truth of *p* and *q* is not sufficient for the truth of the counterfactual *if p then* q" (Plantinga 1996, 328).[19] Modified 1996/1997 Mini-Favorability is "a point where the usual semantics for counterfactuals is inadequate" (Plantinga 1996, 328–9).[20] The counterfactual semantics we'll instead need to stipulate is one where "the counterfactual is true only if there is no sufficiently close possible world in which *p* is true but *q* is not" (Plantinga 1996, 329). In other words, a given M is favorable for E, if and only if, if S were to form a belief by way of E in M, S would form a true belief in *all close possible worlds*.[21] As such, the mini-environments of the Fake Barn-styled cases are not meant to be favorable for their corresponding exercises of cognitive powers; seemingly, so it goes, in many close possible worlds, the protagonist's belief in question would be false. Subsequently, if the mini-environment is not favorable in such cases, then Modified 1996/1997 Mini-Favorability seems to rightly preclude knowledge in such Fake Barn-styled scenarios. This is meant to capture the common intuition that if one knows something, then they could not easily have been wrong in similar cases (see Williamson 2000, 147).

Of course, according to PF″, in order for target cognitive faculties to manifest knowledge, they not only need to function properly in an appropriate environment; they need to also hit upon the truth. In Plantinga's original proper functionalist account, he stipulated that the target cognitive faculties need to be *aimed at truth* if the belief they produced is going to enjoy warrant. As we discussed in Section 1.3 of this chapter, simply being *aimed at truth* isn't good enough. If our account of epistemic virtue is going to be co-primitive with knowledge (and necessary and sufficient for knowledge), then the truth, roughly speaking, needs to be built into our account of epistemic virtue. Epistemic virtue not only requires that the target cognitive faculties be aimed at truth but also *successful in hitting the truth*.

So far, so good. But according to PF″, more is necessary for epistemic virtue than properly functioning cognitive faculties that are aimed at truth (and successful in hitting the truth) in an appropriate environment; the target cognitive faculties also need to be operating according to *a good design plan*. While we could try to explicate good design plans in terms of a kind of fit between mind and world (or perhaps in terms of factive mental states), I think we can follow Plantinga's original account fairly closely here. To assess whether or not a toaster, say, is functioning properly, we need to have an idea of how it was designed to work. Likewise, in order to assess whether or not cognitive faculties are functioning properly, we need to have some idea as to how they were designed to function (by God, evolution, or both). To be sure, the design plan for human cognitive faculties is something like "a set of specifications for a well-formed, properly functioning human being—an extraordinarily complicated and highly articulated set of specifications, as any first-year medical student could tell you" (Plantinga 1993b, 14). But say an incompetent angel (or one of Hume's infant deities) set out to create a species of rational persons ("capable of thought, belief and knowledge"); however, due to the angel's incompetence the vast majority of the created persons' beliefs turn out to be absurdly false (Plantinga 1993b, 17).[22] In such a case, the given people's beliefs are produced by cognitive faculties that are functioning properly in a congenial environment in accord with a design plan aimed at truth, but the design plan just turns out to be a terrible one; despite the incompetent angel's best efforts, the subjects he created have wholly unreliable cognitive faculties. Even if one of these people's beliefs turned out to be true, we wouldn't want to call it knowledge. Epistemic virtue, as we're thinking about it, requires a *good* design plan. In other words, we might say that a design plan will be good if "the statistical or objective probability" is high that "the module of the design plan governing the production" of the target knowledge would be successful in actually producing knowledge (Plantinga 1993b, 18).

Section 3.2: An Application: The Value Problem

As we've already noted, one of the central "perks" of a non-reductive virtue epistemology like the non-reductive proper functionalism I've sketched earlier is the ability to entirely sidestep the Gettier Problem. By being non-reductive, we're simply not participating in the kind of activity that will yield Gettier counterexamples.[23] As we noted in the Introduction to this book, the Gettier Problem has been one of the defining issues of epistemology for nearly sixty years. Ever since 1963 when Edmund Gettier challenged the sufficiency of the standard analysis of knowledge with a series of counterexamples, all attempts to defend it have been shown either to lead to further Gettier-style counterexamples or to produce analyses of knowledge that are unfeasible. (And thanks to our diagnosis in Chapter 1, we now know why this was the case). Any view that can both (i) sidestep this entire problem while (ii) giving knowledge pride of place within epistemology already has a lot going in its favor![24]

And as we also noted earlier, the non-reductive proper functionalism on offer can also give us resources for addressing Fake Barn-style cases. Why does the protagonist driving through Fake Barn County not know that "that's a barn" when they happen to pick out the one real barn? Because the local (mini) environment is not suitable for the cognitive faculties responsible for judging that "that's a barn." The environmental luck at work in Fake Barn-style cases, in other words, pollutes the local (mini) environment relative to the target cognitive faculties.

So far, so good! But in addition to providing resources for avoiding or responding to both Gettier problems and Fake Barn-styled problems, there is one final application for the non-reductive proper functionalism we've sketched earlier that I want to consider before concluding: how the view can answer the value problem.[25]

Another virtue of non-reductive virtue epistemologies like non-reductive proper functionalism is their ability to seemingly provide us with a straightforward solution to the value problem—the problem of explaining why knowledge (and not justification, true belief, etc.) is distinctively valuable. There are, to be sure, several related issues that need to be addressed in order to *fully* explain what makes knowledge distinctively valuable. At base, addressing the value problem should "explain why knowledge is more valuable than mere true belief," what Pritchard calls *the primary value problem* (2010, 5). And naturally enough, at least for epistemologists operating from reductive analyses of knowledge, what often explains the value of knowledge over and against mere true belief is whatever bridges the gap within their analysis between true belief and knowledge—warrant, justification, epistemic virtue, etc. As Pritchard explains, however, the problem with this is that

> if the distinctive value of knowledge is due to some feature of knowledge which, with true belief, falls short of knowledge, then it seems that what we should seek is not knowledge as such, but rather that which falls short of knowledge (i.e. true belief plus the value-conferring property X, in this case justification [or warrant, epistemic virtue, etc.]). (2010, 7)

And it is this challenge—the challenge of "explaining why knowledge is more valuable than that which falls short of knowledge"—that Pritchard calls the *secondary value problem* (2010, 6). And finally, there is the question as to whether what confers value upon knowledge is a matter of degree, whether the "difference in value between knowledge and that which falls short of knowledge is not just a matter of degree, but of kind" (2010, 7). Again, as Pritchard explains:

> if one regards knowledge as being more valuable than that which falls short of knowledge merely as a matter of degree rather than kind, then this has the effect of putting knowledge on a kind of continuum of value with regard to the epistemic, albeit further up the continuum than anything that falls short of knowledge. The

problem with this "continuum" account of the value of knowledge, however, is that it fails to explain why the long history of epistemological discussion has focused specifically on the stage in this continuum of value that knowledge marks rather than some other stage. (2010, 7–8)

And it is this challenge—the challenge of explaining why knowledge has not just a greater degree but also a different kind of value or final, non-instrumental value—that Pritchard calls the *tertiary value problem* (2010, 8). These challenges—the primary value problem, the secondary value problem, and the tertiary value problem—are nested. In other words, if we are unable to address the primary value problem, then we won't have any hope of viably addressing the secondary let alone the tertiary value problems. And conversely, if we are able to viably address the tertiary value problem, then we will, in turn, have the material for addressing both the secondary and primary value problems.

To be sure, virtue epistemology—especially the species of virtue epistemology that analyses knowledge exclusively in terms of a "true belief that is the product of epistemically virtuous belief-forming process"—seems especially suited for answering the value problem (Pritchard, Millar, and Haddock 2010, 25).[26] Hitting upon a true belief as a result of one's epistemically virtuous belief-forming process is—as some virtue epistemologists consider it—a type of cognitive achievement; and if achievements are plausibly assumed to have final value as achievements, then it seems to follow that knowledge, as an achievement, has final value too. According to Pritchard, virtue epistemology, so construed, constitutes "the best—indeed the *only*—response to the value problem that [seems] able in principle to support the key claim that knowledge is finally valuable" (2010, 45).[27] That said, however, such virtue-theoretic solutions to the value problem—in particular those solutions that hinge on knowledge being a kind of cognitive achievement—have recently come under some serious scrutiny, and the defensibility of the claim that knowledge is indeed merely a cognitive achievement is, at best, uncertain.[28] In any case, virtue epistemology would benefit from having another, and potentially more viable, solution to the value problem at hand.

Non-reductive virtue epistemology like the proposed non-reductive proper functionalism can offer such a solution. An advocate of non-reductive models of knowledge will presumably be extremely attracted to the view that knowledge is the chief and fundamental epistemic good. Pritchard explains:

Consider, for example, someone like Timothy Williamson (e.g. 2000), who has explicitly argued for what he calls "knowledge-first" epistemology. Although (as far as I am aware), he has not endorsed such a view in print, presumably he would be very attracted, given his wider epistemological views, to an epistemic value monism of the following form. . . . *Knowledge is the sole fundamental epistemic good*. According to this view, there is only one fundamental epistemic good and that is knowledge, which means that the value of all other epistemic goods is to be understood along instrumental lines relevant to this fundamental good. . . . [If] knowledge is the sole fundamental epistemic value then one might plausibly contend that one can resolve the secondary value problem, and thereby the primary value problem, on account of how on this view it follows immediately that knowledge is of greater epistemic value than any epistemic standing that falls short of knowledge. Given the plausible additional claim that no lesser epistemic standing is of greater non-epistemic (e.g. practical) value than knowledge, then the second problem is completely neutralized. (2010, 18–19)

Of course, given our adoption of the *knowledge as virtue* strategy, we'd want to say that *knowledge or epistemic virtue* (and not just knowledge) is the "sole, fundamental epistemic good." That said, by incorporating virtue-theoretic concepts into a non-reductive model like Timothy Williamson's, it looks as though the resultant virtue epistemology has easy access to the non-reductive, "knowledge-first" solution to the primary and secondary value problems. Additionally, such non-reductive virtue epistemology seems, at the very least, to have the necessary tools for constructing a promising solution to the tertiary value problem as well. Since knowledge on a non-reductive model is no longer on the end of a continuum where, say, knowledge is just a true belief that has sufficient justification, warrant, or whatever, the worry driving the tertiary value problem—the worry that knowledge is just a greater degree of a similar kind of value (the value of justification, say)—seems to dissolve.[29]

8

New Horizons

In the previous chapter, I sketched a new approach to virtue epistemology—a non-reductive proper functionalism, where epistemic virtue is taken to be co-primitive with knowledge, being both necessary and sufficient for knowledge. While such an approach nicely ties together two emerging trends within the contemporary literature in epistemology (i.e., the recent flourishing of virtue epistemology with the move away from reductive analyses of knowledge), there are other developments that still need to be reckoned with: the recent "social turn" within epistemology and the recent proliferation of experimental philosophy. In this concluding chapter, I want to briefly explore these new horizons and how this new form of non-reductive proper functionalism might be positioned to face them. As we saw in Chapter 5, prominent forms of proper functional virtue epistemology will be stymied by Gettier counterexamples as long as they are committed to the reductive analysis project; freed from such a commitment, however, I'll suggest that proper functionalism is particularly adept for meeting these immerging challenges.

Section 1: Experimental Philosophy and the Grounding Problem

In Chapter 2, I argued that research from experimental philosophy does not undermine the Gettier Problem; indeed, I suggested that, if anything, the extant empirical literature on Gettier intuitions further motivates the move away from the reductive analysis project. I now want to return to experimental philosophy and highlight how it seems to raise a particular problem, what I'll call *the grounding problem*, which I'll suggest non-reductive proper functionalism is especially able to accommodate.

To start, it's worth noting that experimental philosophy is, in many ways, a traditional approach to philosophy. To quote from Joshua Knobe and Shaun Nichols' article, "An Experimental Philosophy Manifesto":

> It used to be commonplace that the discipline of philosophy was deeply concerned with questions about the human condition. Philosophers thought about human beings and how their minds worked. They took an interest in reason and passion, culture and innate ideas, the origins of people's moral and religious beliefs. On this traditional conception, it wasn't particularly important to keep philosophy clearly distinct from psychology, history, or political science. Philosophers were concerned, in a very general way, with questions about how everything fit together.
>
> The new movement of *experimental philosophy* seeks a return to this traditional vision. Like philosophers of centuries past, we are concerned with questions about how human beings actually happen to be. We recognize that such an inquiry will involve us in the study of phenomena that are messy, contingent, and highly variable across times and places, but we do not see how that fact is supposed to make the inquiry any less genuinely philosophical. On the contrary, we think that many of the deepest questions of philosophy can only be properly addressed by immersing oneself in the messy, contingent, highly variable truths about how human beings really are. (2007, 3)

Aristotle, for example, surely would have been deeply skeptical of any attempt to philosophically describe the world or human nature without carefully (empirically) observing the world and actual humans. And when later empiricists like Locke and Hume ask us to reflect on our ideas and where they come from, they're arguably doing something very similar to contemporary experimental philosophers, when they ask us to reflect on the origin and reliability of our philosophical intuitions. To quote a famous passage from Hume's *Enquiry Concerning Human Understanding*:

> The greater part of mankind are naturally apt to be affirmative and dogmatical in their opinions; and while they see objects only on one side, and have no idea of any counterpoising argument, they throw themselves precipitately into the principles, to which they are inclined; nor have they any indulgence for those who entertain opposite sentiments. . . . *But could such dogmatical reasoners become sensible of the strange infirmities of human understanding, even in its most perfect state, and when most accurate and cautious in its determinations; such a reflection would naturally inspire them with more modesty and reserve, and diminish their fond opinion of themselves, and their prejudice against antagonists.* (1975, 161; emphasis mine)

If we (i.e., philosophers) could better understand the cognitive, social, and psychological mechanisms that underwrite our beliefs (as experimental philosophy aims to supply), we *might* (as Hume sometimes suspects) find that human understanding "is by no means fitted for such remote and abstruse subjects" (1975, 12); however, more hopefully, we might simply learn a better way forward in the field—a way that's accompanied by more "modesty and reserve."

Experimental philosophers are asking us to reflect on what we philosophers are doing when we do what we do (as philosophers). More to the point, why should we think that the methods we employ within contemporary philosophy—being often driven by intuitions—are veritic or grounded in reality? The task of trying to answer such a question is what I'll call *the grounding problem*. To be sure, the Western philosophical tradition is replete with thinkers who aim to somehow ground their philosophizing in reality; however, as Helen De Cruz argues in her article, "Where Philosophical Intuitions Come From" (2015), a lot of contemporary philosophy has taken such grounding for granted. On this score, De Cruz quotes Hintikka (1999), "The vast majority of philosophical writers these days take the name 'intuition' in vain since they do not believe in Platonic anamnesis, Aristotelian forms, Cartesian innate ideas, or Kantian transcendental deductions" (131).[1] Why, for example, should I take my intuitions about some such case to be veritic? Why should I think that my idiosyncratic intuitions about some admittedly bizarre thought experiment are "cutting nature at the joints"? Experimental philosophy has, I think, nicely laid bare the grounding problem faced by contemporary philosophy.

In "Where Philosophical Intuitions Come From" (2015), Helen De Cruz proposes that contemporary philosophy might use empirical tools and resources to address the grounding problem. To quote De Cruz, "Psychological investigations of intuitions can potentially provide us with resources to gauge the evidential value of intuitions deployed in philosophical practice." Maybe we can take our philosophical intuitions about a particular case to be veritic if its cognitive genesis is known to be reliable.[2] Alternatively, if the cognitive genesis of a particular belief or intuition is known to be fraught with error, then we might not have any reason for thinking such an intuition "cuts nature at the joints."

To be sure, looking at the psychological mechanisms that underwrite our judgments, beliefs, or intuitions seems like an excellent thing to consider when we're trying to judge their veracity. After all, if someone is already committed to the belief that *p* or would personally benefit from *p* being true (maybe because they've built a career on *p*), we might not be surprised if their judgments or intuitions align with *p*; however, we would presumably look at those intuitions or judgments with a jaundiced eye.³

While a full elucidation of this psychological answer to the grounding problem is beyond the scope of this chapter, a few examples of how it might work would be helpful. To start, let's talk about nature documentaries. I'd be the first to admit that I watched too much TV when I was younger, especially nature documentaries. But with that experience in mind, I'm particularly aware of how my judgments and intuitions might be radically manipulated. Contrast the following experiences:

> **North American Bison:** Let's say I'm watching a documentary on North American bison. It's spring, the birds are singing, the sun is shining, and it's calving season. The background music is playful as we watch the incredibly cute newborn calves find their footing for the first time. But then, the music turns. Wolves are on the hunt. They're out to kill one of the adorable newborn calves as an easy meal! And when they get one, I'm compelled to cry out to the heavens that such a thing should not be! That it's an awful thing that has happened! A gratuitous evil!
>
> **Yellowstone Wolves:** But, let's say, a week later I watch a documentary on the wolves that were recently reintroduced to Yellowstone National Park. A new litter of adorable puppies has been born back at the den; the music is, again, playful and hopeful. Then, it becomes clear the pack hasn't had a successful hunt in over a week; food is scarce, and there is a real risk that if the pack doesn't make a kill soon, those cute wolf puppies won't survive. Mercifully, it's calving season for the North American Bison in the area. Now I find myself cheering as the wolves kill a vulnerable Bison calf, newly born and unable to run, because that means the puppies will survive!

Such cases might help me see that when my judgments or intuitions are formed as a result of overwhelming cuteness, moving music, etc. they are less than reliable (and, indeed, occasionally even contradictory!). While these cases are somewhat silly, they help us see that the cognitive genesis of our judgments or intuitions seems to matter. We presumably would be rightly skeptical regarding the veracity of judgments or intuitions made purely on the basis of overwhelming cuteness or moving music.

In contrast to the abovementioned cases, some scholars have suggested that we might have good reason to think that our intuitions regarding knowledge are fairly reliable. Consider De Cruz's helpful summary of that literature:

> In several papers Jennifer Nagel [e.g., Nagel 2012; Nagel et al. 2013; Boyd and Nagel 2014] advocates the reliability of epistemic intuitions. She argues that intuitions elicited by Gettier, Truetemp, and fake barn cases are underpinned by intuitive psychology. On the basis of evolutionary considerations, she proposes

that epistemic intuitions are vital to make accurate mental state attributions. Humans are a social species; successful interactions with conspecifics require that one is good at surmising what others think.

Boyd and Nagel [2014: 111] speculate that epistemic intuitions arise because it is "valuable for creatures like us to form rapid impressions about the presence or absence of knowledge." They invoke the Machiavellian Intelligence Hypothesis, which states that animals living in complex social groups gain competitive advantages by accurately attributing mental states, and by discerning good or bad intentions, including deliberate deception. However, they acknowledge that mental state attribution takes place in cooperative settings as well. One context they do not explore, but that is ecologically important, is the extensive reliance on testimony. As children depend heavily on testimony from their parents and other informants, it is unsurprising that they are sensitive to the mental states of their interlocutors. For example, four-year-olds prefer informants who are knowledgeable to those who are accurate but who have to rely on third parties to get the answer [Einav and Robinson 2011]. However, because young children typically learn from benevolent testifiers, they are better at detecting ignorance than deliberate deception. For example, three-year-olds tend to trust an adult who deliberately misled them in the past [Jaswal et al. 2010]. (2015, 11)

Our intuitions, then, regarding Gettier cases, etc.—which drove us away from the reductive analysis in the first place—might have a cognitive genesis that suggests that they're fairly reliable. Mistakes might be made, to be sure, but such naturalistic explanations might help ground our intuitions regarding knowledge in the right way.

Fine. But how does the non-reductive proper functionalism of the previous chapter come into play? While the abovementioned considerations are compatible with many epistemological positions, I'd like to suggest that they fit particularly well with proper functionalism, at least among the virtue epistemologies on offer within the contemporary literature. In other words, proper functionalism, more so than the agent-responsibilism of Zagzebski or the agent-reliabilism of Greco, Sosa, or Turri, seems straightforwardly open to the kind of psychological grounding that De Cruz recommends. Indeed, I'd suggest that this psychological grounding of proper functionalism is a natural next step in terms of lines of research.

Recall our proper functionalist account of epistemic virtue from the previous chapter (PF"): *A cognitive faculty will manifest epistemic virtue only if it is functioning properly, according to a good design plan that is aimed at truth and successful in reaching that end, and is operating in a suitable environment.* One of the obvious questions to ask here is: How do we know whether or not a cognitive faculty is, say, aimed at truth? Here it makes sense to turn to psychology and cognitive science to help us discern whether or not our beliefs are aimed at truth. Consider Alvin Plantinga's archetypal examples of cognitive faculties that might not be aimed at truth:

> Someone may remember a painful experience as less painful than it was, as is sometimes said to be the case with childbirth. You may continue to believe in your friend's honesty long after evidence and cool, objective judgment would have dictated a reluctant change of mind. I may believe that I will recover from a dread disease much more strongly than is justified by the statistics of which I am aware. William James's climber in the Alps, faced with a life or death situation, believed more strongly than the evidence warrants that he could leap the crevasse. In all of these cases, there is no cognitive dysfunction or failure to function properly; it would be a mistake, however, to say that the beliefs in question had warrant for the person in question. (1993b, 11–12)

All of these lack warrant, according to Plantinga, because "the purpose of these modules of our cognitive capacities is not to produce true beliefs" (1993b, 13). How would we know that? Surely by looking at the psychological, cognitive, and even biological mechanisms that underwrite each of them. Proper functionalism seems to cry out for the kind of addition that De Cruz recommends.

Indeed, it seems like such an empirical grounding might further elucidate some ambiguities within proper functionalist accounts on this score. If we need to know whether a cognitive faculty is aimed at truth, how do we delineate between cognitive faculties? How fine-grained should we be here? Doing this in the abstract (or from the philosophical armchair) has been deeply challenging; here it seems like work from neuroscience, psychology, and cognitive science would be particularly helpful in putting empirical flesh onto the theoretical, proper functionalist bones.[4] Relatedly, even if we can agree that a cognitive faculty is generally *aimed at the truth*, it seems like neuroscience, psychology, and cognitive science might be particularly helpful in helping us judge the conditions under which such reliability falters; helping us better distinguish general reliability from reliability in particular instances, in particular environments.[5]

Section 2: Group Epistemology and the Anthropological Challenge

In Chapter 3, we saw how the recent social turn within contemporary epistemology posed a challenge to some dominant forms of virtue epistemology—in particular the varieties of virtue-reliabilism put forward by philosophers like Greco and Sosa. (For example: If I learn that *p* via testimony, it seems like the truth of *p* is more attributable to the testifier than my own cognitive competency, right?) And in Chapter 7, I noted how proper functionalist accounts of epistemic virtue don't seem to face the same challenges. In this section, I want to briefly point to another facet of social epistemology (i.e., a new horizon) that proper functionalism seems particularly well situated to face, namely, group knowledge and group belief. In other words, Chapter 3 looked at a challenge from what Alvin Goldman calls *interpersonal social epistemology*, "where an individual epistemic subject makes use of the beliefs or assertions of others to form or revise his/her view on a certain question" (2020, 12). In this section, I want to briefly look at an issue that Goldman categorizes as *collective social epistemology*, which instead focuses on "groups or collective agents, such as juries, committees, and fact-finding bodies that have beliefs or credences" (2020, 12).

More to the point, I want to argue in this section that non-reductive proper functionalism might be particularly well suited to address what I'll call *the anthropological challenge*—a challenge that arises from some cases of group knowledge that have been identified in the field of anthropology. I'll argue that such cases don't easily fit with any dominant theories of group belief in the contemporary philosophical literature, and it's not altogether clear how the other approaches to epistemic virtue could accommodate such cases—arguing that Zagzebski's agent-responsiblism is simply (in principle) unable to accommodate these anthropology cases and that (less damningly) the fit with Sosa or Greco's form of agent-reliabilism is less than clear (though I don't think their epistemologies are, in principle, incompatible with such cases). I'll argue that proper functionalism, however, seems well positioned to accommodate such cases, pointing to an area of future research.

First, I'll provide some quick background information, before unpacking the target cases of the challenge. Then, I'll bring the competing accounts of epistemic virtue back into focus and sketch why I think proper functionalism stands in a more favorable position considering the aforementioned challenge.

Section 2.1: Some Very Brief Background on Group Belief

When we start talking about the beliefs of groups or institutions, we might naturally suspect that group-level beliefs are simply the beliefs of the individuals in that group (or key people in the group) or the individuals of an institution (or key people in that institution). Looking at Jennifer Lackey's helpful formulations, we might conservatively sketch out this idea as:

> A group G believes that p if and only if all or most of the members of G believe that p. (2020, 187)

Or more liberally as:

> A group G believes that p if and only if some of the members of G believe that p. (2020, 187)

These are what are called *summative* approaches to group belief; the beliefs of the group just are (or are a summation of) the beliefs of some or all of the individuals of that group. And one of the chief benefits of such approaches is that they're relatively straightforward. Any questions regarding how a group changes belief, where group beliefs are located, or the ontological status of group-level beliefs can seemingly be easily addressed merely in reference to the individuals of the group.

But, of course, in philosophy things are rarely that straightforward. Such summative approaches to group belief famously face serious challenges in the form of counterexamples. A few quick examples should make the point. Consider the following case from Lackey:

> **Philosophy Department:** The philosophy department at a leading university is deliberating about the final candidate to whom it will extend admission to its graduate programme. After hours of discussion, all of the members jointly agree that Jane Smith is the most qualified candidate from the pool of applicants. However, not a single member of the department actually believes this; instead, they all think that Jane Smith is the candidate who is most likely to be approved by the administration. (2020, 188)

Or consider the following similar case from Jesper Kallestrup:

> **Criminal Court:** A defendant is on trial for the crime of careless driving. The prosecution adduces evidence from the police report, as well as eyewitnesses testifying in court that the defendant was indeed driving the van that hit the victim. But the jury finds the evidence not beyond a reasonable doubt, and hence insufficient to validate criminal conviction. All the members of the jury have hearsay evidence from a reliable source that the defendant caused the accident. But the judge instructs the jurors to ignore this evidence as it fails to meet the conditions for being ruled admissible in a criminal court. Consequently, the jury, when functioning in its social office, justifiably believes the defendant is innocent, yet none of the individual jurors justifiably believes this proposition. (2016, 5239)

Both cases seem starkly at odds with sumativism, because in both cases we're inclined to assign a belief to the group (be it the department or the jury) that *none* of the members of that group hold. No individual in the department believes Jane Smith is the most qualified candidate, yet that seems to be the belief of the department. None of the individual jurors believe the defendant is innocent, yet the jury (as a group) does.

For such reasons, *non*-summativist accounts of group belief have come to dominate the contemporary philosophical literature. In her article "Group Belief: Lessons from Lies and Bullshit" (2020), Jennifer Lackey identifies two such non-summativst approaches to group belief; one being *the joint acceptance account* (JAA). For our purposes, we don't need to explore or dive into all the various non-summativist approaches; I simply want us to better see the direction some prominent non-summativist accounts have taken. According to Lackey, JAA might be briefly stated as follows:

> **JAA:** A group G believes that p if and only if the members of G jointly accept that p. (2020, 189)

Lackey then points to Gilbert (1989) to further unpack what this "joint acceptance" amounts to:

> The members of G jointly accept that p if and only if it is common knowledge in G that the members of G individually have intentionally and openly ... expressed their willingness jointly to accept that p with the other members of G. (306)[6]

It's important to note that acceptance does not entail belief. A group can accept that p without believing that p. Again, quoting from Gilbert 1989:

> It should be understood that: (1) Joint acceptance of a proposition p by a group whose members are X, Y, and Z, does not entail that there is some subset of the set comprising X, Y, and Z such that all the members of that subset individually believe that p. (2) One who participates in joint acceptance of p thereby accepts an obligation to do what he can to bring it about that any joint endeavors ... among the members of G be conducted on the assumption that p is true. He is entitled to expect others' support in bringing this about. (3) One does not have to accept an obligation to believe or to try to believe that p. However, (4) if one does believe something that is inconsistent with p, one is required at least not to express that belief baldly. (1989, 306–7)[7]

To be sure, there are other prominent formulations of the JAA (see, for example, Tuomela 1992), but Gilbert's account will suit our purposes.

All we need to see here is simply that such an account gives us straightforward ways of handling cases like Philosophy Department and Criminal Court. While no individual in the department believes that "Jane Smith is the most qualified candidate from the pool of applicants," they all jointly accept as much. As such, we can rightly say that that's what the department believes. Likewise, while no individual in the jury believes that the defendant is innocent, they jointly accept that the defendant is innocent in light of the constraints that are placed on them by the judge (i.e., ignoring the hearsay evidence). As such, we can rightly say that the jury believes the defendant is innocent.

Section 2.2: The Anthropological Challenge

Again, there are other non-summativist accounts in the literature (see, for example, List 2005 and Pettit 2003), and, again, there are other ways to refine or define JAA. Let's put all that aside. I want to highlight a challenge that, so far, has been unaccounted for in the contemporary literature, a challenge from anthropology. As virtue-theoretic approaches to knowledge participate in the "social turn" within contemporary epistemology, it's critically important that group belief and group knowledge are rightly accounted for (see, for example, Kallestrup 2016). Quintessential examples of group belief and group knowledge from anthropology might push our understanding of group epistemology in some new directions. If so, proper functionalism (I'll propose) will be in the best position to endure the shift.

Let's look at two of the cases at the heart of this challenge. In his book, *The Secret of Our Success* (2016), Joseph Henrich tells the story of how the Tukanoans of the Columbian Amazon cultivate and process manioc (or cassava), "a highly productive, starch-rich tuber that permitted relatively dense populations to inhabit drought-prone tropical environments" (2016, 97). The problem is that manioc can be toxic, if not prepared properly. Importantly, if you were starving in the Amazonian jungle and tucked into some manioc, it wouldn't have an immediate effect on you. It would be, as Henrich notes, "tasty and filling" (2016, 97). The toxin takes a long time to build up, and (if you didn't know that manioc was toxic) it would be extremely difficult to trace your symptoms back to the tuber. As Henrich explains:

> If eaten unprocessed, manioc can cause both acute and chronic cyanide poisoning. Chronic poisoning, because it emerges only gradually after years of consuming manioc that tastes fine, is particularly insidious and has been linked to neurological problems, developmental disorders, paralysis in the legs, thyroid problems (e.g., goiters), and immune suppression. (2016, 97)

In order to survive in the Columbian Amazon, the Tukanoan people needed to know a good/safe way to prepare manioc so as to somehow remove the toxin; without that starch-rich source of calories, it's not clear that there would have been enough food in that area to support any significant number of people. And, over generations, the Tukanoan people cultivated that knowledge; they learned how to process manioc.

Unfortunately, processing manioc is labor intensive, time consuming, and not at all intuitive. To quote Montell Jordan's hit song, there'd be no way of just looking at a manioc and thinking "this is how we do it." Returning to Henrich:

> [I]ndigenous Tukanoans use a multistep, multiday processing technique that involves scraping, grating, and finally washing the roots in order to separate the fiber, starch, and liquid. Once separated, the liquid is boiled into a beverage, but the fiber and starch must then sit for two more days, when they can then be baked and eaten. (2016, 97)

Such a multistep, multiday process is, according to Henrich, "long, arduous, and boring" (2016, 98). But most importantly for our purposes, this processing method is, to use Henrich's term, "causally opaque" (2016, 99). When processing manioc, they weren't aware of what they were doing when they did what they did. There were not aware of the toxin in manioc, so they couldn't have had a causal explanation for trying to remove it. Looking at the steps required to process the tuber, there is no way for "an individual [to] readily infer their functions, interrelationships, or importance" (2016, 99).[8] Indeed, just looking at manioc and the labor-intensive way in which it is processed, individuals might be extremely tempted to skip some steps (especially since there wouldn't be any immediately apparent causal connection between the eating less-than-fully-process manioc and the infirmities that would develop years later). As Henrich notes, "[i]ndividual learning does not pay here, and intuitions are misleading" (2016, 99). However, by having "faith [in] the practices handed down to [them] from earlier generations" individuals (and their families!) would be able to avoid "sickness and early death" that would otherwise be brought about by the buildup of toxins (2016, 99).

To many people with broadly Western sensibilities (like the vast majority of philosophers in the English-speaking world), such cases are deeply challenging and perhaps even a bit baffling. Such examples of group knowledge might even threaten to upend several projects at the heart of contemporary epistemology. But maybe this manioc case is a "one off" example, one which simply calls for special explanations. As it turns out; however, the abovementioned manioc case is merely an example of a much broader phenomenon. As evidence in this direction, let's consider another example.

Among the various indigenous people of Yasawa Island (Fiji) it is taboo for women to eat various large predatory marine fish (e.g., moray eel, barracuda, sharks, etc.) while pregnant or breastfeeding. Given that fish is such a large part of their diet, such a taboo is a big deal. As it turns out, however, such taboos are playing an important role in the health of those indigenous people of Yasawa Island, since the scientific literature has found such species to carry high levels of ciguatera toxin. Abstaining from such fish during pregnancy and while breastfeeding helps protect women and their children during that particularly vulnerable time.

Where did such a taboo come from? For starters, it's simply something that's passed down from one generation to the next. As Henrich explains:

> As adolescents and young women, these taboos are first learned from mothers, mothers-in-law, and grandmothers. However, this initial repertoire is then updated by a substantial portion of women who learn more taboos from village elders and prestigious local *yalewa vuku* (wise women), who are known for being knowledgeable about birthing and medicinal plants. Here we see Fijian women using cues of age, success or knowledge, and prestige to figure out from whom to learn their taboos. (2016, 101)

Importantly, just like the abovementioned manioc case, the reason for the taboo is *casually opaque* to the Fijians. They don't abstain from eel, shark, and barracuda *because* of the risk of ciguatera poisoning. They merely abstain as a result of their cultural inheritance from the village elders, who, in turn, learned it from their village elders, etc. To drive this point home, consider this report on what Fijian women said when asked *why* they abstained from eating large predatory fish while pregnant or breastfeeding:

> We also looked for a shared underlying mental model of why one would not eat these marine species during pregnancy or breast-feeding—a causal model or set of reasoned principles. Unlike the highly consistent answers on what not to eat and when, women's responses to our why questions were all over the map. Many women . . . clearly thought it was an odd question. Others said it was "custom." Some did suggest that the consumption of at least some of the species might result in harmful effects to the fetus, but what precisely would happen to the fetus varied greatly, though a nontrivial segment of the women explained that babies would be born with rough skin if sharks were eaten and smelly joints if morays were eaten. . . . Unlike most of our interview questions on this topic, the answers here had the flavor of post-hoc rationalization: "Since I'm being asked

for a reason, there must be a reason, so I'll think one up now." This is extremely common in ethnographic fieldwork, and I've personally experienced it in the Peruvian Amazon with the Matsigenka and with the Mapuche in southern Chile. (Henrich 2016, 102)[9]

Amazingly, like Tukanoans regarding the processing of manioc, these indigenous Fijians seem to *know* not to eat eels, sharks, etc. when either pregnant or breastfeeding, even though the underlying causal reasons are wholly opaque to them.

Of course, one might respond by denying that the Tukanoans know a good/safe way to remove the toxin from manioc or deny that the Fijians know not to eat eels, sharks, and barracuda when pregnant or breastfeeding; however, such a response seems less than charitable. The anthropological literature certainly seems to talk as if the Tukanoans, Fijians, etc. have knowledge in these respective cases, and it's difficult to shake the worry that denying that they have knowledge can only be motivated by applying idiosyncratic Western conceptions of knowledge to non-Western contexts. Indeed, there is a real worry that to deny the Tukanoans knowledge of manioc or the Fijians knowledge that pregnant or breastfeeding women shouldn't eat large predatory fish would be to egregiously commit an act of epistemic injustice.

That said, if these are genuine instances of knowledge (as I think they surely are), then (as we've already noted), such examples of group knowledge are deeply challenging. For starters, if we grant that the Tukanoans *know* a good/safe way to process manioc and that the Fijians *know* not to eat eels, sharks, etc. while pregnant or breastfeeding, then it seems like some of the dominant accounts of group belief are lacking. Summativist accounts don't seem to work, since it's not at all clear that the relevant group members have the requisite beliefs. And non-summativists accounts like JAA don't seem to work since it's difficult to see how the Tukanoans or the Fijians are "intentionally and openly" expressing a desire to jointly accept *anything*, certainly nothing that would underwrite the knowledge in these respective cases.

Beyond that, it looks as if these cases from anthropology also pose a potential challenge for internalistic conceptions of warrant (which are meant to bridge the gap between true belief and knowledge). While the *externalism* versus *internalism* debate is notoriously murky, internalism is going to almost invariably require agents to have some sort of reflective access to the reasons for their belief or maybe reflective access "to evidence that the belief is true" (Conee and Feldman, "Evidentialism," *Philosophical Studies* (1985). It's difficult to imagine that such a condition would be satisfied in the abovementioned cases;

neither the Tukanoans nor the Fijians seem to have reflective access to the *why* of their belief. (And in some cases, asking for their evidence for their respective beliefs might be seen as deeply puzzling and foreign.)

These are, to be sure, serious ramifications, and we're simply not able to fully unpack them here. However, putting these broader challenges aside, if we grant that the Tukanoans *know* a good/safe way to process manioc and that the Fijians *know* not to eat eels, sharks, etc. while pregnant or breastfeeding, then I'd want to suggest that proper functionalist accounts of epistemic virtue are in a better position to account for that knowledge than either the agent-reliabilist accounts of Sosa, Greco, etc. or the agent-responsibilist accounts of Zagzebski.

For starters, given that Zagzebski's account of knowledge depends on an internalistic conception of warrant (where agents need some sort of reflective access for the reasons for their belief), it looks as if her approach to virtue epistemology is straightforwardly unable to accommodate the purported knowledge in the abovementioned cases. Again, it's difficult to imagine that the Tukanoans or the Fijians have reflective access to the *why* of their belief, to the evidence for the truth of the target belief. The anthropological literature seems to point to a broader and more universal conception of knowledge than Zagzebski's account would allow for.

Sosa, Greco, and related agent-reliabilist virtue epistemologists generally adopt *externalism*, which means they won't place a "reflective access" condition on their accounts of warrant; as such, the abovementioned cases won't be non-starters for their epistemologies like they were for Zagzebski's. That said, there are nevertheless puzzles in this direction that advocates of their brand of agent-responsibilism would need to address. While some scholars have tried to expand Sosa's virtue epistemology to apply to groups (e.g., Kallestrup 2016), it's not clear how that would work in the manioc case or the breastfeeding taboo case. For starters, scholars like Kallestrup typically propose to extend agent-reliabilist virtue epistemology to the group level by incorporating dominant accounts of group belief in the extant literature—like the abovementioned JAA. If we're right in thinking that such accounts of group belief are unable to capture the examples of group belief in the abovementioned cases from anthropology, then such "extensions" of virtue epistemology are going to be no more successful. But what is more, it's not at all clear that anything like a *true because competent* account of knowledge will be able to viably make sense of the manioc case or the breastfeeding taboos case. While we might plausibly think that the "competences of groups are nothing over and above the combined competences of their members," it's not at all clear that the competencies of the individual Tukanoans or the Fijians can add up to a competency that could explain or capture the truth of the target beliefs (at least not in how Sosa, Greco, and others typically explicate "competencies") (Kallestrup 2016, 5233). Indeed, in line with the broader claims of Joseph Henrich in *The Secret of Our Success* (2016), we might think the truth of the target beliefs transcend the competencies of individuals—that there are broader cultural forces at play here that underwrite the target examples of knowledge.

Proper functionalist conceptions of epistemic virtue, in contrast, seem flexible and able to adapt to the guidance of the anthropological literature. As we learn more about how cultural beliefs are generated and evolve, how they function, then we can have a better sense of when they are *aimed at truth* or when they are operating in the right environment. Insofar as there is knowledge in the abovementioned cases, clearly something is going right at the group level; however, there are presumably many cases where groups get things radically wrong (as anyone who's spent any time on social media can tell you!). But as we learn more about how group belief forms, develops, etc. from anthropologists, psychologists, sociologists, biologists, etc., there's no obvious reason to think that proper functionalist accounts won't be able to adapt to accommodate these emerging horizons of research.

Final Conclusion

In Plato's *Theaetetus*, we are asked to consider the difference between *knowledge* and *mere opinion*. Knowledge, we learn, must be about something that is true. While you might have a false *opinion*, you cannot be said to properly *know* something when it's false. And drawing from imagery in the *Meno*, we might add that knowledge is "tied down" in a way that a mere opinion is not—if you know that *p* then you have reason or justification for believing *p*. Mere opinions are fragile in a way that knowledge is not. Mere opinions might be swayed via rhetoric or persuasion. Knowledge, it's thought, is gained via education and is far less fragile. In sum, then, mere opinions are beliefs that are supported by little or at least insufficient justification and may or may not be true. And knowledge, in contrast, was thought to be a belief that is true and sufficiently justified. Belief, sufficient justification, and truth were considered, since time immemorial (or so the story goes), to be necessary and sufficient conditions for knowledge.

This was at least part of the reason why the Gettier Problem shook epistemology in the twentieth century; it seemed to call into question an intuitive account of knowledge that seemed to have a pedigree that extended all the way back to the very beginning of the Western philosophical tradition. To be sure, however, it's not at all obvious that Plato was trying to provide anything like a reductive analysis of knowledge in terms of necessarily and jointly sufficient conditions akin to how "bachelor" can be understood in terms of the necessary and jointly sufficient conditions of "unmarried" and "man." When Socrates argued that knowledge is human excellence, was he thinking about knowledge in terms of a reductive analysis? Seemingly not. When Plato, in Book V of the *Republic*, suggests that knowledge is an entirely different mental state from belief, was he thinking about knowledge in terms of necessary and jointly sufficient conditions? Again, seemingly not. Maybe, then, the Gettier Problem doesn't cut nearly as deep as we thought. Maybe the Gettier Problem doesn't undermine a fundamental idea of Western conceptions of knowledge; instead, maybe the Gettier Problem merely undermines a philosophical project that has its roots in the twentieth-century epistemology. Maybe *that's* a project we can more willingly give up. Indeed, as we saw in Chapters 1 and 2, that project—the project of defining knowledge in terms of a reductive analysis—is one we *must* be willing to give up.

Of course, the twentieth century also saw the birth (or rebirth) of virtue-theoretic accounts of knowledge, tracking our intuitions across a wide range of cases while giving intellectual agents and communities their due place (it seems to me) within epistemology. However, almost every single seminal account of virtue epistemology that was developed in the literature assumed that knowledge yielded a reductive analysis and tried to explicate that analysis in virtue-theoretic terms. As we saw in Chapters 3, 4, and 5, none of these virtue epistemologies are able to provide a viable reductive analysis—failing along the exact lines predicted in Chapter 1.

Returning to the very first sentence of this book, epistemology is indeed on the move. The central goal of this book has been to explore the possibility of and to endorse non-reductive virtue epistemology, to endorse the move away from the reductive analysis model while affirming the value of virtue-theoretic accounts of knowing. In Chapter 6, we outlined in broad stokes three general strategies for developing a non-reductive virtue epistemology: what I called, *knowledge plus virtue, knowledge as virtue*, and *knowledge within virtue* respectively. In Chapter 7, I tried to argue for (Sections 1 and 2) and develop (Section 3) my preferred account: a non-reductive proper functionalism in terms of the *knowledge as virtue* strategy. And in the final section of that chapter, we were able to get a sense of what such an account can ultimately give us. The answer: nothing less than a viable and intuitive response to the Gettier Problem (via avoiding the problem altogether), Fake Barn-styled cases, and the value problem. Not bad for a start! Finally, in *this* chapter, we explored two challenges on the epistemic horizon and how this new form of non-reductive proper functionalism might be positioned to face them; freed from the reductive analysis project, I suggest that the non-reductive proper functionalism on offer is particularly adept for meeting these immerging challenges.

There is, of course, always more work that needs to be done. Many questions linger around the issue of what counts as a cognitive faculty and how we delineate between cognitive faculties; here I think it would be natural for advocates of non-reductive proper functionalism to look to cognitive science for help—which could nicely bring epistemology into close dialogue with empirical research. And it would be worth exploring how the proposed non-reductive account avoids or provides new resources for responding to common objections to knowledge-first epistemology (though, of course, simply being non-reductive does not mean that my preferred view should be seen as a knowledge-first view). For example, how might proper functionalism help explicate Williamson's idea that knowledge is a mental state? To what extent (if at all) is the non-reductive proper functionalism sketched earlier committed to Williamson's E=K thesis? And to what extent (if at all) is non-reductive proper functionalism committed to the idea that knowledge isn't luminous? These are projects for another time; however, they point, one hopes, to new, fruitful lines of research.

Notes

Introduction

1. See "Is Justified True Belief Knowledge?" (1963).
2. Perceptively, John Greco's recent work, *Achieving Knowledge* (2010), shows signs of moving away from this trend. That said, however, Greco does not seem to endorse the whole-hog abandonment of the reductive analysis project in favor of alternative models that I will be advocating in this book. While Greco explicitly declines to provide a thoroughgoing reductive analysis, he does eventually seem to take himself as providing *enough* of an analysis (conditions on knowledge that are necessary and sufficient *enough*) to achieve viable, lasting progress against the Gettier Problem, a point that this book takes issue with (see 2010, 12–13, 73–80). Recent pushes in the direction of non-reductive virtue epistemology include Kelp 2017 and Miracchi 2015.
3. After all, to quote William G Lycan, "It is well to remind ourselves that no effort of analytic philosophy to provide strictly necessary and sufficient conditions for a philosophically interesting concept has ever succeeded" (2006, 150).
4. To be sure, it is not at all clear that Plato had anything like a reductive analysis in mind when he explicated knowledge in such terms in the *Meno*. See Plato 2002.
5. We need not concern ourselves with mechanics or scope of Gettier counterexamples at this point. A full diagnosis of the Gettier Problem will be provided in Chapter 1 of this book.
6. Consider the following diagnosis by Linda Zagzebski: "The moral drawn in the thirty years since Gettier published his famous paper is that either justified true belief (JTB) is not sufficient for knowledge, in which case knowledge must have an 'extra' component in addition to JTB, or else justification must be reconceived to make it sufficient for knowledge. I shall argue that given the common and reasonable assumption that the relation between justification and truth is close but not inviolable, it is not possible for either move to avoid Gettier counter examples. What is more, it makes no difference if the component of knowledge in addition to true belief is identified as something other than justification, e.g. warrant or well-foundedness. I conclude that Gettier problems are inescapable for virtually every analysis of knowledge which at least maintains that knowledge is true belief plus something else" (1994, 65).

7 Of course, virtue epistemology's philosophical roots go much deeper than the past thirty years. To quote John Greco and John Turri, "Practitioners [of virtue epistemology] draw inspiration from many important historical philosophers, including Plato (Zagzebski 1996, 139), Aristotle (Greco 2002, 311; Sosa 2009a, 2, 187; Zagzebski 1996, passim), Aquinas (Roberts and Wood 2007, 69–70; Zagzebski 1996, passim), Descartes (Sosa 2007, ch. 6), Kierkegaard (Roberts and Wood 2007, 29–30), and Peirce (Hookway 2000). Hints of [virtue epistemology] can also be found in Hume 1748, Reid 1785, Russell 1948 and Sellars 1956" (2011, sec. 2).

8 In accord with the surging popularity of virtue epistemology, a number of excellent edited collections have been produced. For example, see Axtell 2000; Brady and Pritchard 2003; DePaul and Zagzebski 2003; Fairweather and Zagzebski 2001; Greco 2004; Kvanvig 1996; Steup 2001.

9 See Quine 1969. Also see McDowell 1994, 133; Sosa 1991, 100–5; Zagzebski 1996, 334–8.

10 For more on virtue ethics and its distinctiveness, see Anscombe 1958.

11 See Pritchard 2005, 186; Greco 2010, 17–46. By this definition, then, deontic approaches to virtue epistemology wouldn't count as virtue epistemologies. Deontic approaches to epistemology wouldn't make the agent (or communities of agents) the primary object of epistemic assessment.

12 Chief proponents of agent-reliabilism include Alvin Plantinga 1993b, Ernest Sosa 2007, and John Greco 2010. Chief proponents of responsibilism or neo-Aristotelianism include Lorraine Code 1987, James Montmarquet 1993, and Linda Zagzebski 1996.

13 And because of its popularity, agent-reliabilism will get the lion's share of attention in this book (both Chapters 3 and 5 focus on different kinds of agent-reliabilism). Regarding the popularity of agent-reliabilism virtue epistemology over neo-Aristotelian virtue epistemology, see John Greco's "Two Kinds of Intellectual Virtue" (2000).

14 Also quoted in Pritchard 2005, 187.

15 Also quoted in Pritchard 2005, 188.

16 See Pritchard 2005, 188; Greco 2003a, 356–7.

17 See Dancy 1985, 134; Zagzebski 1999, 99–101; Pritchard 2005, 4–5; Steup 2006, §2.

18 While there are well over 100 different Gettier cases, they are united by a common theme: a warranted belief that is only luckily true. As L. Floridi notes, though there are all of these cases, nobody would expect them to be answered in a case-by-case basis (2004, 64).

19 Someone may occasionally elucidate safety as coming in degrees (see Smith 2009), but this is the closest, to my knowledge, philosophers have come to describing luck in terms of degrees aside from my own work on this subject.

20 Pursuing an infallibilist response to the Gettier Problem is, after all, very common. See Daniel Howard-Snyder, Frances Howard-Snyder, and Feit 2003 and Zagzebski 1994.
21 As I've noted previously, proper functionalism can be seen as a type of agent-reliabilism; however, it is markedly different from the agent-reliabilisms of Ernest Sosa and John Greco. As such, I continue to try to distinguish these views accordingly.

Chapter 1

1 While Zagzebski does uses the term "justification" instead of "warrant," I think this is the most charitable way to understand her diagnosis, since she's clearly referring to whatever bridges the gap between true belief and knowledge. (For other instances of "warrant" being used in this way, see Plantinga 1993a, 3; D Howard-Snyder, F Howard-Snyder, and Feit 2003, 1; Pritchard 2005, 5.) Additionally, given that warrant is something that comes in degrees, I take it that any *warranted true belief* analysis of knowledge assumes a sufficient degree of warrant.
2 See Zagzebski 1994, 69–70.
3 See Zagzebski 1994, 73.
4 See Zagzebski 1994, 72. While this is not a terribly popular view, it does have its advocates. See Stephen Hetherington (2001). We will consider Hetherington's account in Chapter 2.
5 Zagzebski's analysis, I think, rightly identifies the target of Gettier cases as conceptual necessity instead of metaphysical necessity as Timothy Williamson has argued in *The Philosophy of Philosophy* (2007). As Jonathan Schaffer pointed out in his presentation, "Modalities and Methodologies," viewing the target of Gettier cases as metaphysical is "too weak" such that "[even] if Gettier cases were metaphysically impossible, [Gettier's] counterexample to the proposed definition of knowledge would still stand" (Schaffer 2009). See Jackson 2009; Williamson 2009a.
6 See Dancy 1985, 134; Zagzebski 1999, 99–101; Pritchard 2005, 4–5; Steup 2006, §2. In Riggs 2007, Wayne Riggs explores some of the reasons it is so important that knowledge preclude (the relevant sort of) luck.
7 While there are well over 100 different Gettier cases, they are united by a common theme: to put it roughly, a warranted belief that is true for reasons not captured by the warrant. As L. Floridi notes, although there are many cases, nobody would expect them to be answered in a case-by-case basis (2004, 64).
8 Someone may occasionally elucidate safety as coming in degrees (see Smith 2009), but this is the closest, to my knowledge, philosophers have come to describing luck in terms of degrees.

9   See Nagel 1979, 25. Similar accounts can be found in Zimmerman 1993; Greco 1995.
10 Also see Statman 1991, 146; Latus 2000, 167.
11 To be sure, in more recent work, Pritchard has abandoned the significance condition, L2 (see Pritchard 2014). Given that our focus is centrally the modal condition, the question of whether or not the significance condition is necessary for luck is not relevant to our current discussion.
12 Also see Lackey 2008, 261–2.
13 Though the intuition that luck suits degrees can warrant an extension in and of itself, perhaps we can say a bit more in its favor. Say Jack is playing three lotteries—each of which has a jackpot prize of £1,000,000. Jack has 1 out of 1,000,000 chances of winning the jackpot of Lottery A. Jack has 1 out of 1 chances of winning the jackpot of Lottery B (Jack rigged it). Finally, Jack has 1 out of 2 chances of winning Lottery C (he bought half the tickets). As it happens, Jack wins all three lotteries. We can probably all agree that Jack's winning Lottery A is lucky. Additionally, we can probably all agree that Jack's winning Lottery B is not lucky. However, it is far from clear whether or not it was lucky that Jack won Lottery C. If we say that it was lucky, what would we say if Jack had 2 out of 3 chances of winning? Or 3 out of 4? If winning a lottery with 1 out of 1,000,000 odds is lucky and winning a lottery where you have 1 out of 1 is not, at what point does a lottery win stop being lucky? Whatever answer we pick, it will seem to be arbitrary. Instead of trying to decide when a lottery win becomes lucky, I think our intuition is simply that winning a lottery where you have 1 out of 2 chances is far less lucky than winning a lottery where you have 1 out of 1,000,000 chances. To account for this, perhaps we should extend L1 accordingly.
14 In light of this objection, someone may propose that luck varies according to how different the world would have to be in order for the given event not to occur. Though modeling degrees of luck in this way provides a way to make the distinction between Visitor's visits to Haven and Heaven, it runs into other problems. For example, say I am blindly drawing marbles out of a bag where there is a 10-to-1 ratio between black marbles and red marbles. Is the possible world in which I draw a black marble any farther away than the possible world in which I draw a red one? Seemingly not.
15 This case was inspired by the opening pages of David K. Lewis's *Counterfactuals* (2000).
16 See Zagzebski 1999, 102. To be sure, whether or not luck varies in accord with significance, a full account of degrees *must* incorporate something like a modal condition.
17 See Dancy 1985, 134; Zagzebski 1999, 99–101; Pritchard 2005, 4–5; Steup 2006, §2.
18 Also see Zagzebski 1994, 66. Duncan Pritchard notes that cases like Fake Barns are not Gettier case, because the protagonist does not make a "cognitive error," see Pritchard et al. 2010, 35–6.

19 For more on environmental luck, see Ben Jarvis's chapter in the *Routledge Handbook of the Philosophy and Psychology of Luck* (2019).
20 See Zagzebski1996, 295–9.
21 For worries regarding Pritchard's account of safety and its relationship to epistemic virtue, see Greco 2007b.
22 If I am right in thinking that even distant possible worlds can be of epistemic affect, the sufficiency of other safety theories *qua* safety theories may be called into question.
23 To be clear, given Pritchard's understanding of luck in general (MAL), it seems that cases like Dr. Jones and the Virus (once made suitably strong) would not officially exhibit luck, though clearly we still have a Gettier case.
24 In *The Nature and Value of Knowledge* (2010), Pritchard adds a virtue condition to his analysis of knowledge; as such, he might be able to employ such a condition to surmount Gettier counterexamples like the strengthened Dr. Jones and the Virus case (see Pritchard, Millar, and Haddock 2010, chapter 3). We will not concern ourselves here with the details regarding whether or not such a proposal would in fact work. Nevertheless, given the pervasiveness of luck and the shortcomings of eminent virtue epistemologies in Chapters 3, 4, and 5, I think we have a prima facie reason to be pessimistic.
25 To be sure, Pritchard could alternatively take warrant to be completely divorced from truth—effectively denying that luck is of any epistemic consequence—but surely that is a move Pritchard would not be willing to make.
26 This point is also highlighted in Chisholm 1982; Dretske 1978; Goldman 1986; Howard-Snyder et al. 2003; Nozick 1981; Sturgeon 1993. To be sure, Howard-Synder et al. (2003) highlight this agreement in the literature and try to suggest that it's misplaced; we'll consider Howard-Synder et al.'s objection later in this chapter.
27 Now, to be sure, this all assumes that warrant bears some close, if not infallible, relationship to the truth. Some epistemologists (e.g., Hetherington 2001 and Hetherington in this volume) have denied this—denied that warrant needs to bear any relationship to the truth. While such views have been powerfully argued for, they are nevertheless outliers in the literature; unfortunately, we will not have time to address them in this chapter.
28 This is a point I made in "Getting 'Lucky' with Gettier" (2013a).

Chapter 2

1 To be sure, *fallibilism* and *infallibilism* are used here as positions within *the standard analysis of knowledge*. That said, what is important for the proposed diagnosis of the Gettier Problem is that fallibilism, within the standard analysis, cannot surmount

Gettier counterexamples, which says nothing about the viability of fallibilism simpliciter. Fallibilism within a Williamsonian model, say, may very well be a viable position, but that is not of concern given the current thesis.

2 This premise is asserting that the Gettier Problem can be solved *within the standard analysis*. One way to, in effect, "solve" the Gettier Problem would be to abandon the analysis of knowledge enterprise altogether, but that solution is not what Howard-Snyder et al. had in mind. Premise 2, then, is something the current thesis is pessimistic about.
3 See Sturgeon 1993, 160.
4 See Goldman 1967, 357.
5 See Goldman 1967, 370.
6 See Goldman 1986, 46–55.
7 See Nozick 1981, 173.
8 See Dretske 1978, 42, 57.
9 See Chisholm 1982, 45–7.
10 For Howard-Snyder et al.'s response to this worry, see Daniel Howard-Snyder, Frances Howard-Snyder, and Feit 2003, 311–12.
11 For Howard-Snyder et al.'s response to these worries, see Daniel Howard-Snyder, Frances Howard-Snyder, and Feit 2003, 314–16.
12 See Zagzebski 1996, 65.
13 This is not, to be sure, of central importance for my subsequent argument; my worry for Howard-Snyder et al.'s account can run regardless of whether they are truly conflating luck with accidents. I make this point because (1) it seems like a fair one to make and (2) it offers continuity with the previous chapter.
14 I start with *Good Knowledge, Bad Knowledge* (2001) instead of his paper "Actually Knowing" (1998), because while the latter indeed advocates the relevant view, the former is more complete and is, I think, better able to stand under recent criticisms (cf. Madison 2011). Also see Hetherington 2005, 2007, 2013, 2018.
15 I have replaced "justification" with "warrant" in the abovementioned quote, because, given the general way Hetherington is understanding "justification" (cf. Hetherington 2001, 88) and the running definition of "warrant" in this book, such terms are synonymous; indeed, Hetherington expressly admits as much in Hetherington 2001, 109.
16 As Hetherington points out, it would be a fallacy to confuse *almost* failing to achieve knowledge with *genuinely* failing to achieve knowledge (Hetherington 1998, 456–9).
17 For a full account of what Hetherington means by "failable knowledge," see Hetherington 2001, 40–7.
18 See Hetherington 2001, chap. 4; Hetherington 2007; Hetherington 2010. In "Is This a World Where Knowledge Has to Include Justification?" (2007), for example, Hetherington posits that in a random and shifty world, a world where warrant is

simply not possible, having beliefs that are luckily true can stand as knowledge—the luck, according to Hetherington, now bearing the value typically attributed to warrant (Hetherington 2007, 43–6). But this sounds crazy. A world where warrant is simply not possible strikes us, whether we are committed to the analysis of knowledge or not, as a world where knowledge is not possible. Good luck is in no way a substitute for warrant, and to suggest that mere true belief can be knowledge seems to suggest that Hetherington has changed the subject; what he means by "knowledge" simply cannot be what the rest of us seem to mean by "knowledge." Perhaps his alternative "epistemology" is not a relevant alternative after all.

19 See Madison 2011.
20 After all, such a weak response is fitting because I do not think either meta-objection under consideration is meant to be offering a "conclusive argument" (Weinberg, Nichols, and Stich 2001, 429).
21 "Intuition-Driven Romanticism" is a rhetorically charged term, and, regardless of Weinberg et al.'s intentions, it is something of a guise. If what we are doing in contemporary epistemology only has roots that go back to nineteenth-century romanticism, then an "uprooting" proposal (so to speak) like Weinberg et al.'s will not seem that implausible. However, if what we are doing in contemporary epistemology has roots that go far deeper (e.g., arguable back to Plato), as Weinberg et al. seem to concede, then we should expect an uprooting proposal to be far more cataclysmic and, as such, far less plausible.
22 Weinberg et al. respond to an objection along these lines, where it is suggested that those surveyed were thinking of "know" more informally, as a term expressing a high degree of subjective certainty (see Weinberg, Nichols, and Stich 2001, 449–50). But this is not quite what I mean here; my worry is not that the survey subjects were using "know" informally; my worry is that the East Asians, for example, understand "know" in a fundamentally different way than Westerners do.
23 But even here we'd want to be careful. But even if Weinberg et al.'s findings did suggest that epistemic intuitions will vary according to various demographics, this does not mean we should embrace a wholesale rejection of epistemological intuitions. Weinberg et al.'s argument will presumably generalize to intuitions across philosophy and in other fields.
24 See, for example, Church, Warcol, and Barrett 2021; Church, forthcoming.; Stich and Machery 2021.)
25 It's worth noting that other scholars have argued in defense of the method of cases on other grounds. See Nagel (2013, 2012). Others have pushed back and further questioned the stability of Gettier intuitions. See Machery et al. (2017). This debate is certainly ongoing.
26 Even as the Gettier intuition seems stable, conceptions of knowledge might nevertheless be diverse. See Machery et al. 2015, 2017.
27 See Cummins 1998.

28 See Sosa 1998.
29 This raises a point that Weatherson seems to overlook: that we are not stuck with the intuitions we have; our intuitions can be corrected and changed—often thanks to other intuitions. In "What Good Are Counterexamples?" Weatherson makes much of the fact that people have at various points in history had intuitions that led to wildly false beliefs—such as whales are fish, the sun is not a star, and that the earth is flat. But what Weatherson does not seem to appreciate is that our intuitions regarding such beliefs seem to have been corrected, thanks to our intuitions in other domains.

Chapter 3

1 See Sosa 1991.
2 To be sure, Sosa goes on to add a "triple S" (involving notions of seat, shape, and situation) analysis of knowledge on top of this "triple A" analysis (apt, adroit, and accurate). See, for example, Sosa's work in *Knowing Full Well* (2011) and *Judgment and Agency* (2015). As innovative and important as these additions are, our primary focus will be on Sosa's basic account of knowledge elucidated in his 2007 and 2009 work, since the later work simply further elucidating/adding to the earlier framework.
3 For a big picture of how Sosa sees his account in light of the Gettier Problem, see Sosa 2009a, 2:185–9.
4 For Sosa, (i) and (ii) are seemingly necessary and jointly sufficient conditions on knowledge. What is more, Sosa presumably takes *belief* and *aptness* to be conceptually prior to *knowledge*—*knowledge*, after all, is understood in terms of *belief* and *aptness* and not vice versa. While Sosa's simple analysis looks substantially different from more classic and more complex reductive analyses like Plantinga's, Sosa's virtue epistemology is a reductive analysis, nevertheless. See Sosa 2009b; Williamson 2009b. To see Williamson's critique of Sosa's earlier work, see Williamson 2004 in Greco's edition *Sosa and His Critics* (2004); unfortunately, Sosa's "Replies" (2004) contains no response.
5 That's not to say that Sosa's approach to the Kaleidoscope case hasn't faced challenges. See Cohen 2009.
6 We should note that it is confusing at this point what exactly aptness requires. On the one hand, Sosa seems to say that the protagonist's higher-order belief fails to be apt because its truth is somehow not appropriately contingent on the relevant epistemic competence. On the other hand, Sosa seems to be saying that the higher-order belief fails to be apt because the relevant competence could have very easily led to a false conclusion.

7. While Sosa explicitly wants aptness to be distinct from safety (Sosa 2007, 1:29), it is at points like this where it looks like a safety principle is somehow built into Sosa's understanding of aptness. For example, it seems like Sosa is saying that the protagonist in the Kaleidoscope case does not have reflective knowledge because the relevant competence could have led to a false belief in close possible worlds—because the truth of the belief, given the relevant competence, is not safe. Contrast Sosa's definition of safety (Sosa 2007, 1:25) with his explanation why the Kaleidoscope perceiver fails to have reflective knowledge (Sosa 2007, 1:33).
8. See Sosa 1996, 33–5.
9. See Austin 1962, 48–9 and the last paragraph of Descartes' *Meditations* in 1955.
10. Similar accounts of knowledge of a similar form can be found in Greco 2003, 2007, 2009; Riggs 2002; Sosa 1991, 277; Zagzebski 1996, 1999.
11. This is, of course, assuming that warrant should bear *some* relationship to the truth.
12. These cases can originally be found in Greco 2010, 82–3.
13. And this is in keeping with a body of literature that suggests that virtue-theoretic proposals (like Greco's) are ultimately going to be unable to surmount the Gettier Problem viably—see Pritchard 2003, 2005, chap. 7; Pritchard 2007; Pritchard, Millar, and Haddock 2010, chap. 3; Kallestrup and Pritchard 2012. But what is more, it is keeping with the growing pessimism regarding the possibility of *any* reductive account of knowledge (virtue-theoretic or otherwise) viably surmounting the Gettier Problem—see Williamson 2000; Floridi 2004; Church 2013a.
14. These cases can originally be found in Greco 2010, 82–3.
15. To be sure, it is worth stressing that Ernest Sosa's distinction between "animal knowledge" and higher-order "reflective knowledge" is not going to come into play here (see Sosa 2007, 23–4). Sosa employs such a distinction to defuse certain Gettier-*like* cases (e.g., Fake Barn scenarios); but insofar as he wants to honor the standard intuition that genuine Gettier cases (like Expert Ichthyologist) genuinely preclude knowledge (both animal and reflective), such a distinction will be of no consequence.
16. It is worth stressing that Expert Ichthyologist exhibits all the features of a regular, run-of-the-mill Gettier case. As Turri explains, "Gettier cases follow a recipe. Start with a belief sufficiently justified (or warranted) to meet the justification requirement for knowledge. Then add an element of bad luck that would normally prevent the justified belief from being true. Lastly, add a dose of good luck that 'cancels out the bad,' so the belief ends up true anyhow" (2011, 1). The case of Expert Ichthyologist exhibits this "double-luck" structure hallmark of Gettier counterexamples, and insofar as we are willing to assume that this double-luck structure precludes knowledge, I think we are safe in assuming that Jim genuinely lacks knowledge.

17 If we were tempted to think that knowledge suits degrees, then we might suppose that degrees of knowledge correspond to degrees of manifestation. If this were the case, could Turri argue that Gettier counterexamples (in this case, those counterexamples that exhibit manifestation) are merely instances of weak, low-grade knowledge? Seemingly not. What cases like Expert Ichthyologist show is that Gettier counterexamples can be created that exhibit a very high degree of manifestation, and as such even scenarios which would presumably exhibit a very high degree of knowledge can be Gettiered.

Chapter 4

1 Interestingly, where I am wanting to point to the Gettier Problem to highlight a trend to abandon the standard analysis of knowledge, Levin begins his paper "Virtue Epistemology: No New Cures" by pointing to the Gettier Problem to highlight a trend to abandon the notion of justification—where I would see virtue epistemology as bucking trends Levin sees virtue epistemology as a trend-setter. In this paper Levin argues that, despite being a *response* to the Gettier Problem, virtue epistemology's solution to it is inadequate. He does this by focusing on the work of Linda Zagzebski, who, according to Levin, was the only virtue epistemologist to tackle the Gettier Problem—arguing that if Zagzebski's solution is found inadequate we have prima facie reason to think "other, weaker, versions" of virtue epistemology will be so too (Levin 2004, 397).

2 In accord with what I have said in Chapter 1, Levin describes Zagzebski's diagnosis of Gettier problems as turning "on bad luck canceled by good"—any viable (i.e., Gettier-proof) account of warrant *must entail truth* because otherwise it would "be liable to such double accidents" (Levin 2004, 398; emphasis mine). Strangely, however, immediately after providing some quick examples that lend credence to such a diagnosis, Levin concludes that "[a]ccording to Zagzebski . . . a Gettier-proof condition for knowledge must (*not only entail* but) be responsible for truth" (Levin 2004, 399; emphasis mine). On the face of it, Levin seems to be saying conflicting things about Zagzebski's diagnosis; to avoid Gettier counterexamples is it enough for warrant to entail truth or must it also "be responsible for truth"? To be sure, while Zagzebski's virtue epistemology may be one such account where warrant not only entails truth but is also responsible for it (Zagzebski 1996, 270; 1999, 108–9), I do not take Zagzebski as saying that as much is the threshold for avoiding Gettier counterexamples. For example, consider Fake Barn-type cases. Regarding such a case Zagzebski notes, "Gettier cases are based on situations in which the belief is true, but it might just as well have been false," but if warrant entails truth, then the possibility that Henry

picks a barn façade is "excluded from the class of justified (warranted) beliefs." According to Zagzebski one could simply assume that warrant entails truth to avoid cases like Fake Barns because in so doing one would be concluding that the barn facsimiles are epistemically ineffectual just so long as the protagonist in question is looking at a real barn. More generally, it looks like someone *could indeed* avoid any Gettier counterexample by (just) assuming that warrant entails truth because it is simply impossible for a belief to be so warranted and false. To be sure, such a move would seemingly be very ill-advised—surely the barn facsimiles *are* epistemically effectual—but one seemingly could, nevertheless, avoid Gettier problems in such a way, unpalatable though it may be. Regardless, this is presumably why Zagzebski, in her own account of warrant, wishes to do something more than simply entail truth—she wants warrant to "be responsible for truth." This is precisely the feature of Zagzebski's account that Levin wishes to criticize. Regardless, this is presumably why Zagzebski, in her own account of warrant, wishes to do something more than simply entail truth; she wants warrant to "be responsible for truth." This is precisely the feature of Zagzebski's account that Levin wishes to criticize.

3 To see additional worries for *true "because" virtue*-type accounts of knowledge, see Shope 2008.
4 See Pritchard 2005, 194–9. To be sure, Zagzebski, unlike Sosa, does not seem to have the conceptual resources for defusing (or purportedly defusing) Fake Barn-type cases—that is, the animal knowledge/reflective knowledge distinction.
5 Also quoted in Pritchard 2005, 196–7.
6 It is worth noting that even if we are skeptical as to whether this is the definition of knowledge that Zagzebski intends, it is nevertheless very similar to Sosa's definition—apt belief, that is belief whose attainment of truth is because of or due to a cognitive competence. As such, even if Levin is wrong about how we should read Zagzebski, his reading nevertheless will inform our understanding of Sosa.
7 As Levin points out in a footnote, the exception would be when "p asserts, self-referentially, that $B(p)$ was produced by that very motive" (Levin 2004, 403).
8 As Levin points out, some people may find it "implausible that Zagzebski could have gone wrong in the fundamental way suggested" (Levin 2004, 408). This is, it seems to me, a very legitimate worry to have; nevertheless, in response, Levin highlights a way Zagzebski (and perhaps other, like-minded virtue epistemologists) could have easily been so confused:
"Let C be a condition reasonably thought to be by definition necessary (and with truth sufficient) for knowledge. Some traditional epistemologists allegedly confused analyses of the form

(E) $\Box(p \text{ is known} \equiv p \text{ is true \& } C)$

with

(F) p is known $\equiv \Box(p$ is true & $C)$,

and inferred from that what is known is necessarily true, or, worse, that there is a necessary connection between the truth of p and C. On its face Zagzebski's definition,

(G) $\Box$(knowledge = truth via motives from which truth arises),

gives $\Box$ properly wide scope, hence requires nothing from which truth arises necessarily. But 'arises' as Zagzebski understands it carries necessity already built in. Recall her central argument that motive (or any other factor) merely contingently connected to truth is Gettierable, *hence insufficient for knowledge*. It is natural to conclude (and the suggestion is that Zagzebski has concluded) that knowledge calls for something close enough to truth to exclude the possibility of error and accident, in effect pushing the $\Box$ in (F) right next to 'arises,' or, more accurately, turning 'arises' into 'necessarily issues.' . . . The idea that the knowledge-creating condition is motivational plus the ideal that it be necessary would explain the quest for a motivational state capable by itself of attaining truth" (Levin 2004, 408–9).

9 See footnote 2.
10 One way to try to understand such a "because" relationship is reliabilistically; however, such an interpretation is not open to Zagzebski agent-responsibilism virtue epistemology. But even if we were to abandon agent-responsibilism in order to pursue such a reading, such an account would seemingly befall the same criticisms leveled against agent-responsibilism virtue epistemologies in Chapter 3.
11 To be sure, it is worth stressing that Ernest Sosa's distinction between "animal knowledge" and higher-order "reflective knowledge" is not going to come into play here (see Sosa 2007, 23–4). Sosa employs such a distinction to defuse certain Gettier-*like* cases (e.g., Fake Barn scenarios); but insofar as he wants to honor the standard intuition that genuine Gettier cases (like Expert Ichthyologist) genuinely preclude knowledge (both animal and reflective), such a distinction will be of no consequence.
12 Many of the other agent-responsibilist virtue epistemologies have actually given up on the project of defining knowledge in light of character virtues and become anti-theorists—spending most of their time on the nature of intellectual virtues with very little connection to the concept to knowledge.

Chapter 5

1 Or more accurately, *sufficiently* warranted true belief.
2 See Plantinga 1993b, 19.
3 For other tabulations of Plantinga's 1993 account of warrant (what later iterations refer to as the "nutshell" or "central core" of warrant), see Chignell 2003, 445; Plantinga 2000, 156.

4 The same would be true if, say, the radiation from the elephant didn't produce the belief that "a trumpet is playing nearby," but instead that "a big grey object is nearby" (Plantinga 1993b, 7).

5 So in order for a given belief to have warrant, it needs to be produced by cognitive faculties that are functioning properly within a congenial environment, but just how congenial? What if I am knowingly in an uncongenial environment and know how I might be misled—would relevant beliefs still be barred from warrant? Such issues, Plantinga admits, highlight a vagueness in the theory. There may not be an answer to such questions. See Plantinga 1993b, 11.

6 There is, to be sure, an ongoing debate whether or not "proper function" can be viably understood in a non-theistic way. We're not going to be concerned with that debate here.

7 See Plantinga's description of what he meant by environment in 1993b, 6–7. Also see Plantinga 2000, 156–8.

8 Also see Hume 1948, part 5.

9 How high must the statistical objective probability of the beliefs being true be? Here again, Plantinga concedes that there is vagueness. For Plantinga, the amount of warrant a given belief enjoys is relative to how firmly it is believed by the given agent. However high the statistical objective probability of the belief's truth needs to be, Plantinga presumes that "the degree of reliability varies as a function of degrees of belief" (Plantinga 1993b, 18).

10 Quoted in Klein 1996, 106. Notice that Plantinga seems to express one of the guiding intuitions of this book: that infallibilism about warrant is ultimately unfeasible. Plantinga also seems to expressly allow for warranted false beliefs in 1993b, 40–1. To be sure, in later iterations of his epistemology, Plantinga denies the possibility of warranted false beliefs in an attempt to surmount Gettier counterexamples (see Plantinga 1996, 311–12, 329). We will consider the success of such a venture in the next section.

11 For more on Plantinga's objections to internalism, see Feldman 1996, 199–209.

12 Quoted in Feldman 1996, 211.

13 Also see Feldman 1996, 211.

14 Quoted in Feldman 1996, 211.

15 Referenced in Feldman 1996, 213.

16 Quoted in Feldman 1996, 213–14.

17 See Plantinga 1993b, 31–2, 37, 39.

18 Also see Feldman 1996, 214.

19 Feldman expressly argues for the implausibility and not the refutation of such a strategy because "there are so few constraints on what one might say about the 'direct aims' of various segments of our design plan . . . there is so little to restrict what one says about the aims of the segments of the design plan that govern the production of our beliefs, it is possible for a defender of Plantinga's theory to say

what's necessary to defend the theory from potential counterexamples. However, what one has to say becomes increasingly implausible" (1996, 215).

20 See Feldman 1996, 216.
21 Feldman goes on to muse over Plantinga's theistic commitments and how that might explain aspects of his theory; such considerations, however, do nothing to stave off Feldman's "wildly ad hoc" indictment. That is to say, the claim that "the segments of our design plan that get us knowledge are 'directly' aimed at truth while the segments responsible for the beliefs in Gettier cases have other aims" is going to lead to ad hoc conclusions whether or not you are a theist.
22 See Klein 1996, 106; Clark 1963; Shope 1983, 21–6.
23 See Klein 1996, 106–7.
24 See Plantinga 1996, 308–29.
25 For other tabulations of Plantinga's 1993 account of warrant (what later iterations refer to as the "nutshell" or "central core" of warrant), see Chignell 2003, 445; Plantinga 2000, 156.
26 See Plantinga 1993b, 19.
27 Also see Plantinga 1997, 144n.
28 Plantinga goes on to reference some other points where the standard counterfactual semantics are inadequate. Quantum effects: "perhaps in fact the photon went through the right slit rather than the left; that is not enough to entail that if it had gone through either slit, it would have gone through the right" (1996, 328–9). Die tossing: "I toss the die; it comes up 5. That is not sufficient to entail that if I had tossed the die, it would have come up 5" (1996, 329).
29 Though Crisp's paper is not explicitly mentioned, Plantinga credits Crisp with prompting his later 2000 modification. See Plantinga 2000, 159n. Presumably if Crisp's paper did not explicitly prompt the change in Plantinga's account, we can assume that informal ancillary conversations between Crisp and Plantinga on account of said paper did.
30 For another worry on the 1996/1997 conception of "favorability" concerning mini-environments, see Chignell 2003, 448.
31 Other aspects of Plantinga's 1996/1997 account were critiqued as well, though failing to motivate a change in the 2000 account. For example, in "Gettier and Plantinga's Revised Account of Warrant" (2000), Thomas Crisp argued that no state of affairs fulfills Plantinga's definition of mini-environments. In sum, Crisp's worry is that "for any exercise E of one's cognitive power in maximally specific circumstances C, there will be . . . reasons for doubting that there is a *closest* state of affairs to C that neither includes nor precludes the proposition that E yields true belief" (2000, 45). The "reasons for doubting" that Crisp mentions are that for any given state of affairs that is taken to be closest to C, we can think of one that is closer. In other words, there may be an infinite series of states of affairs that get closer and closer to C indeterminate in regard to the truth of the given belief such

that one never arrives at a "closest" point. Though I have not fully elucidated Crisp's argument by any means, let me just note that by my lights Plantinga is not putting nearly the same amount of weight on there being a "closest state of affairs" as Crisp assumes. After all, Plantinga invites us to make a given mini-environment as full and as detailed *as we please* (1996, 314)—seemingly implying that getting to the absolute "closest state of affairs" is not centrally important to Plantinga's account.

32 One may worry that Mini-Favorability 2000 sneaks knowledge into the definition of warrant, since, as Thad Botham notes, having a proposition *p* be detectable to S could perhaps be seen as simply akin to having S know *p* (2003, 434). If this were the case, then Plantinga's account of knowledge would appear to be viciously circular. However, according to Botham, Plantinga presumably has a viable response to this worry. He says: "A merchant's scale detects its being the case that the goods weigh 400 pounds, but the scale cannot detect its being the case that a handful of chocolates weighs three ounces. A thermostat detects its being the case that the room's ambient temperature is eighty degrees Fahrenheit but cannot detect the temperature to four significant digits. A speedometer detects the automobile's moving 50 miles per hour but cannot detect the precise rate of 50.2 miles per hour. Even though the scale, thermostat, and speedometer detect various states of affairs only when they function properly, they do not have knowledge. Neither do they have anything close to justified or warranted beliefs. Thus it's not clear that detection entails anything as strong as knowledge or justified belief" (Botham 2003, 434).

33 See Plantinga 2000, 161.

34 See Plantinga 1996, 311–12, 329.

35 Plantinga is not clear in such passages as to how a given belief can have any degree of warrant without meeting all of the conditions of warrant. It is reasonable to assume that this relates to the other woes afflicting Plantinga's understanding of degrees of warrant. See Markie 1996.

36 This understanding of Plantinga's 2000 account of warrant was affirmed during my personal correspondence with Plantinga while presenting at the University of Notre Dame in 2009.

37 See Botham 2003; Chignell 2003.

38 This state of affairs would presumably apply even if I was completely orthodox in my use of such terms. In other words, there may be lots of people who misuse such terms; but as far as the state of affairs as stated earlier is concerned, I would not know if I was one of them.

39 Within such literature there were a number of diverse proposals trying to salvage Plantinga's reductive virtue epistemology. See, for example, Botham 2003; Chignell 2003; Crisp 2000. Unfortunately, because of our limited goals and space, we are not able to consider such proposals here; however, given the proposed diagnosis of Gettier problems and the light of experience, I think we have excellent prima facie reason to suspect that such proposals are ultimately no more successful.

Chapter 6

1. Though that's not to say that all non-reductive approaches to knowledge need to be Williamsonian.
2. As Williamson notes, "[t]he programme of analysis had its origin in great philosophical visions [e.g., logical positivism].... Now the philosophical visions which gave it a point are no longer serious options. Yet philosophers continue to pursue the programme long after the original motivation has gone. Correct deep analyses would doubtless still be interesting if they existed; what has gone is the reason to believe that they do exist" (2000, 32).
3. To be sure, the merit of a Williamsonian model of knowledge is not strictly contingent upon every analysis somehow failing. While we may have very good reason to doubt the viability of the reductive analysis project, Williamson's epistemology can still get off the ground even if a successful analysis of knowledge in terms of necessary and jointly sufficient conditions *is* found. While "[t]he present account does not strictly entail that no analysis of the traditional kind provides correct necessary and sufficient conditions for knowing," it does call into question the reasoning for pursing such an analysis in the first place (Williamson 2000, 30). To quote Williamson, "[e]ven if some sufficiently complex analysis never succumbed to [Gettier] counterexamples, that would not entail the identity of the analyzing concept with the concept *knows*. Indeed, the equation of the concepts might well lead to more puzzlement rather than less. For knowing matters; the difference between knowing and not knowing is very important to us. Even unsophisticated curiosity is a desire to *know*. This importance would be hard to understand if the concept knows were the more or less ad hoc sprawl that analyses have had to become; why should we care so much about *that*?" (2000, 30–1).
4. For example, "[a]ttempts to analyse the concepts of *means* and *causes* . . . have been no more successful than attempts to analyse the concept *knows*, succumbing to the same pattern of counterexamples and epicycles. The analysing concept does not merely fail to be the same as the concept to be analysed; it fails even to provide a necessary and sufficient condition for the latter" (Williamson 2000, 31). "The pursuit of analyses," it seems, "is a degenerating research programme" (Williamson 2000, 31).
5. To be sure, Williamson does not give us any reason for thinking that knowledge is not simply equi-primitive with related concepts like belief and justification, for thinking that knowledge is not on conceptually equal footing with belief and justification. Indeed, most of Williamson's arguments in favor of his primitive-knows hypothesis would apply equally well to an equi-primitive-knows hypothesis.
6. A similar reading of Williamson can be found in Cassim 2009, 13.
7. Of course, as is typical in philosophy, there is not universal agreement here. While the thought that *knowledge requires truth* is very nearly a ubiquitous platitude, there

8 To be sure, someone might respond to this strangeness by trying to find some liberal sense in which *believing truly* might be construed as a mental state; however, as Williamson points out, even if there is some such liberal understanding of "mental state" "there is also a more restrictive but still reasonable sense in which believing truly is not a mental state but the combination of a mental state with a non-mental condition" (Williamson 2000, 28). When Williamson defines knowledge as a state of mind, he means that "knowing is a mental state in *every* reasonable sense of that term: there is no more restrictive but still reasonable sense of 'mental' in which knowing can be factored, like believing truly, into a combination of mental states with non-mental conditions" (Williamson 2000, 28).

9 See Williamson 2000, 34, 29.

10 Given that our goal here is to explore how virtue might be incorporated into a non-reductive model, how virtue might relate to a non-reductive account of knowledge, we will satisfy ourselves with merely exploring the various ways knowledge might entail (and/or be entailed by) virtue, ways virtue might be a necessary condition for knowledge (and vice versa), and the conceptual ordering of the two. The complexities that arise from considering other possible epistemic concepts and facets (i.e., safety, belief, etc.) will be put aside.

11 For any given entailment there is always a question regarding the order of determination, of conceptual priority (this is clearest in the case of biconditionals). So when we consider whether knowledge entails virtue and vice versa, we will be interested in who is taking the conceptual lead, so to speak. Is knowledge conceptually more primitive than virtue (column 1)? Is virtue conceptually more primitive than knowledge (column 3)? Or are they conceptually co-primitive (column 2)? There does not seem to be the space for a fourth option.

12 What is more, C3 designates the possibility of a reductive analysis of knowledge *solely in terms of sufficiency conditions* and will presumably be no more viable (and probably less so) than regular reductive analysis.

13 This is not to say, of course, that Williamson himself would approve of any of these strategies, just that there is nothing inherent to his epistemology that precludes them.

14 To be sure, someone like Williamson may wonder if necessary conditions like virtue can really be understood apart from our concept of knowledge. After all, this seems to be Williamson's take on other necessary conditions like belief. Belief for Williamson is sometimes seen as nothing but a failed attempt at knowledge. See Williamson 2000, 44–8.

15 See Williamson 2000, chap. 5–7

16 To be clear, the goal here is manifestly *not* to provide a reductive analysis of "epistemic virtue" in terms of necessary and jointly sufficient conditions. If

knowledge is a mental state and if mental states are understood roughly as what I am calling a virtuous state, then to pursue a reductive analysis of "virtuous state" would place us well on our way to a reductive analysis of knowledge, a project we are currently avoiding.

17 This is, to be sure, Wright's conclusion as well. See 2010, 8.
18 Insofar as Williamson wants to explicate *believing something is so* as a failed attempt to *knowing something is so* (2000, 41–8), applying the knowledge as virtue proposal to mental states is both helpful and elucidating. Within a virtue-theoretic framework, perhaps *believing something is so* can be described as an example of an epistemic act that is sufficiently (virtuously) motivated while falling short of its virtuous telos (in this case, truth).
19 Though if we *can* explicate quintessential mental states (e.g., love, hate, imagining that something is so, believing that something is so, etc.) within a virtue-theoretic framework, all the better.
20 The exceptions being virtuous states where the given telos includes a truth that is internal to the relevant agent.
21 To put it one way, virtuous states are not in people, people are in virtuous states.
22 This only gestures toward an outline, without filling in much detail. Williamson's epistemology is revolutionary, with far-reaching ramifications that touch on many subjects in contemporary epistemology. A full account would carefully track the overall effect this virtue-theoretic adaptation has on Williamson's broader epistemic project—making amendments and modifications as need be.
23 And of course, none of these recapitulations of Sosa's epistemology does anything to prohibit his innovative approaches to topics like the internalism/externalism debate; a similar two-tiered account of knowledge can still be provided along first-order versus second-order lines, which will allow for just the sort of arguments Sosa is wanting to make.
24 See Levin 2004, 399.
25 Again, while this strategy does indeed preserve many of the merits of virtue-theoretic epistemology, the lover of robust virtue epistemology may not find it ultimately satisfying. For example, the heart and soul of Sosa's virtue epistemology is the veritic exercise of cognitive competencies, so reducing such a concept to a mere addendum significantly changes the account.

Chapter 7

1 As I've noted previously, proper functionalism can be seen as a type of agent-reliabilism; however, it is markedly different from the agent-reliabilisms of Ernest Sosa and John Greco. As such, I continue to try to distinguish these views accordingly.

2 For more on this problem, see Pritchard 2005, 197.
3 Though, again, I'd like to suggest that the motivation for doing this is significantly undercut once the inability of such agent-reliabilist accounts to address the Gettier Problem (as was argued in Chapter 3) becomes clear.
4 See, for example, Church 2021.
5 See, for example, Klein 1996.
6 See, for example, Markie 1996.
7 The "swampman" objection seems particularly relevant here. See, Sosa 1996.
8 See, for example, Chapter 5 in this book and Feldman 1996.
9 For Plantinga's own response to these issues, see his "Respondeo" (1996).
10 Linda Zagzebski's account of epistemic virtue makes a similar qualification. See, for example, Zagzebski 1996, 248.
11 To be sure, an account of epistemic virtue like PF, in contrast, might indeed be ideally situated for the knowledge plus virtue strategy.
12 See, for example, Reed (2005).
13 This might even help further elucidate Williamson's externalistic conception of the mental.
14 To be sure, there are also places where Williamson's knowledge-first epistemology could potentially come apart from our target species of non-reductive proper functionalism. For one thing, it's not obvious that our brand of proper functionalism would be committed to Williamson's *knowledge as evidence* thesis; however, given that such a thesis is widely taken to be very controversial, such a disconnect might not be entirely welcome. Indeed, the abovementioned brand of non-reductive proper functionalism might even give us conceptual resources for avoiding such a conclusion—perhaps by explicating degrees of knowledge in terms of proper function (like Plantinga does with warrant).
15 For an eliminativist view, see Kvanvig's *The Intellectual Virtues and the Life of the Mind* (1992). For some examples of *expansionist* views, see Fricker's *Epistemic Injustice* (2007) or Hookway's "How to be a Virtue Epistemologist" (2003).
16 Though, of course, it would have to entail that whatever counts as virtue has to entail knowledge in some sense—perhaps even a knowledge-how and not just a knowledge-that. This feature, to be sure, might put some eliminativists off.
17 For example, consider Wittgenstein's famously quote, from the *Tractatus Logico-Philosophicus*, "Philosophy is not a body of doctrine but an activity" (2001, 29).
18 Though perhaps the degree to which a cognitive faculty needs to be properly functioning in order to manifest knowledge or epistemic virtue can be further elucidated by drawing from Williamson's externalistic conception of mental states.
19 Also see Plantinga 1997, 144n.
20 Plantinga goes on to reference some other points where the standard counterfactual semantics are inadequate. Quantum effects: "perhaps in fact the photon went through the right slit rather than the left; that is not enough to entail that if it had

gone through either slit, it would have gone through the right" (1996, 328–9). Die tossing: "I toss the die; it comes up 5. That is not sufficient to entail that if I had tossed the die, it would have come up 5" (1996, 329).

21 It's worth noting how safety seems to be built into this understanding of mini-environment favorability. As we discussed in Section 2.1 of this chapter, this allows us to appeal to our account of epistemic virtue as the *only* necessary condition on knowledge without needing to appeal to separate, plausible necessary conditions like safety.

22 Also see Hume 1948, part 5.

23 And this simply wasn't the case for the approaches to virtue epistemology we considered in Chapters 3, 4, and 5. They all were aiming at viable reductive analyses of knowledge, which was why Gettier counterexamples were such a serious threat for those accounts.

24 To be sure, some epistemologists have been so motivated to avoid the Gettier Problem that they have chosen to avoid talking about knowledge altogether, instead focusing on other epistemic goods (like understanding or justification).

25 To be sure, there are other interesting applications that could be explored; however, for the sake of space I omitted them here. One interesting application would be how going non-reductive might impact Plantinga's religious epistemology. See Church 2015 and Barrett and Church 2013.

26 Examples of the sort of virtue epistemology that analysis knowledge in this way include Sosa 1988, 1991, 2007; Zagzebski 1996, 1999; Greco 2003, 2007, 2009b.

27 To be sure, while Pritchard seems to think that virtue epistemology, so understood, can viably solve the value problem *if* the thesis that knowledge is a success produced by a cognitive achievement is defensible, he fails to appreciate the fact that success from achievements come in degrees—something that virtue epistemologists like Ernest Sosa freely admit (Sosa 2007, 1:23n). Once this is clear, it is not at all obvious how reductive virtue epistemology is meant to solve either the secondary or tertiary value problems, since it is no longer clear what makes knowledge more valuable than that which falls short of knowledge nor how such value could be a difference in kind. However, since the details surrounding virtue-theoretic answers to the value problem are outside the purview of this chapter, I will not be addressing this point further here.

28 See Lackey 2009; Pritchard, Millar, and Haddock 2010, chap. 2; Vaesen 2011.

29 It is worth noting that Pritchard is not quite this optimistic. While he's not pessimistic either, Pritchard remains uncertain about whether or not a knowledge-first epistemology like Williamson's has the tools to handle the tertiary value problem. After all, as Pritchard points out, even if knowledge has fundamental value, this doesn't mean that it has *final* value simpliciter. For example, the fundamental value of knowledge could still be an "instrumental value relative to some further non-epistemic good (e.g. practical goods)" (2010, 12). And while that

is, no doubt, a good point, the motivation driving such a worry seems never the less greatly diminished once knowledge is no longer placed on a continuum. It is no longer clear why one would think that knowledge doesn't have finally valuable, and I suggest that the onus lies with the defender of the value problem to rekindle our concern.

Chapter 8

1. Also quoted in De Cruz (2015, 4).
2. It's worth noting that consensus on a particular intuition is not necessarily an indicator of reliability or truth. De Cruz (2015) points us to Nagel (2012) who cites Koriat (2008) on this score. As De Cruz summarizes, "empirical evidence by Koriat (2008) . . . indicates that the strength of an intuition correlates with the consensus that people have about it, not necessarily with its correctness" (2).
3. This is presumably part of the reason why so many philosophers are skeptical of the work that's done within philosophy of religion, for example. For example, Draper and Nichols (2013) suggest that the contemporary philosophy of religion literature is permeated by scholars who "suffer from cognitive biases and group influences" (2013, 420). There are significant worries that many scholars working within philosophy of religion (myself included!) are simply constructing arguments for conclusions they're already committed to accepting. The psychological mechanisms behind our beliefs surely do indeed matter.
4. For a critique of Plantinga's proper functionalism along these lines, see Peter Klein's "Warrant, Proper Function, Reliablism, and Defeasibility" (1996).
5. This openness to the guidance of psychology and cognitive science also nicely positions proper functionalism to respond to extensions of the situationist challenge into virtue epistemology. (See Mark Alfano's article, "Expanding the Situationist Challenge to Responsibilist Virtue Epistemology," 2012.) In other words, where other accounts of epistemic virtue might rely on a conception of the human intellect that is not substantiated in the empirical literature, proper functionalism seems specially situated to directly respond to insights from empirical literature.
6. Also quoted in Lackey 2020, 189.
7. Also quoted in Lackey 2020, 189-90.
8. Unfortunately, the world history has demonstrated as much. Quoting Henrich:

   At the beginning of the seventeenth century, the Portuguese trans- ported manioc from South America to West Africa for the first time. They did not, however, transport the age-old indigenous processing protocols or the underlying commitment to using those techniques. Because it is easy to plant and provides high yields in infertile or drought-prone areas, manioc spread rapidly across Africa and became a staple food for many populations. The processing techniques, however, were not readily or consistently regenerated. Even after hundreds of years, chronic cyanide poisoning remains a serious health problem in Africa. (2016, 99)

9   And it's worth noting that Westerners frequently do the same sort of thing. As Henrich explains:

Of course, it's not particularly difficult to get similar responses from educated Westerners, but there remains a striking difference: educated Westerners are trained their entire lives to think that behaviors must be underpinned by explicable and declarable reasons, so we are more likely to have them at the ready and feel more obligated to supply "good" reasons upon request. Saying "it's our custom" is not considered a good reason. The pressure for an acceptable, clear, and explicit reason for doing things is merely a social norm common in Western populations, which creates the illusion (among Westerners) that humans generally do things based on explicit causal models and clear reasons. They often do not. (2016, 102)

Bibliography

Alfano, Mark. 2012. "Expanding the Situationist Challenge to Responsibilist Virtue Epistemology." *Philosophical Quarterly* 62 (247): 223–49.

Anscombe, Gertrude Elizabeth Margaret. 1958. "Modern Moral Philosophy." *Philosophy* 33 (124): 1–19.

Atran, Scott. 2002. *In Gods We Trust: The Evolutionary Landscape of Religion*. Oxford: Oxford University Press.

Austin, John Langshaw. 1962. *Sense and Sensibilia*. Oxford: Oxford University Press.

Axtell, Guy, ed. 2000. *Knowledge, Belief, and Character: Readings in Contemporary Virtue Epistemology*. London: Rowman & Littlefield Publishers.

Baron, Reed. 2005. "Accidentally Factive Mental States." *Philosophy and Phenomenological Research* 71 (1): 134.

Barrett, Justin L. 2004. *Why Would Anyone Believe in God?* Lanham, MD: AltaMira Press.

Barrett, Justin L. 2011. *Cognitive Science, Religion, and Theology: From Human Minds to Divine Minds*. West Conshohocken, PA: Templeton Press.

Barrett, Justin L., and Ian M. Church. 2013. "Should CSR Give Atheists Epistemic Assurance? On Beer-Goggles, BFFs, and Skepticism Regarding Religious Beliefs." *The Monist* 96 (3): 311–24.

Battaly, Heather. 2008. "Virtue Epistemology." *Philosophy Compass* 3 (4): 639–63. https://doi.org/10.1111/j.1747-9991.2008.00146.x.

Battaly, Heather. 2009. "A Virtue Epistemology: Apt Belief and Reflective Knowledge, Volume I—by Ernest Sosa." *Analysis* 69 (2): 382–5.

Bering, Jesse M. 2011. *The Belief Instinct: The Psychology of Souls, Destiny, and the Meaning of Life*. New York: W. W. Norton and Company.

Bloom, Paul. 2007. "Religion is Natural." *Developmental Science* 10: 147–51.

Botham, Thad M. 2003. "Plantinga and Favorable Mini-Environments." *Synthese* 135 (3): 431–41.

Boyd, Kenneth, and Jennifer Nagel. 2014. "The Reliability of Epistemic Intuitions." In Edouard Machery and O'Neill Elizabeth (eds.), *Current Controversies in Experimental Philosophy*, 109–27. New York, NY: Routledge.

Boyer, Pascal. 2001. *Religion Explained: The Evolutionary Origins of Religious Thought*. New York: Basic Books.

Brady, Michael, and Duncan Pritchard, eds. 2003. *Moral and Epistemic Virtues*. Oxford: Blackwell Publishing.

Cassim, Quassim. 2009. "Can the Concept of Knowledge be Analysed?" In Patrick Greenough and Duncan Pritchard (eds.), *Williamson on Knowledge*, 12–30. Oxford, UK: Oxford University Press.

Chignell, Andrew. 2003. "Accidentally True Belief and Warrant." *Synthese* 137 (3): 445–58.
Chisholm, Roderick M. 1977. *Theory of Knowledge*. 2nd ed. Englewood Cliffs, NJ: Prentice-Hall.
Chisholm, Roderick M. 1982. *The Foundations of Knowing*. Brighton: The Harvester Press.
Church, Ian M. 2009. "'Entitlement of Cognitive Project' and the Possibility of Gettier-Proof Basic Beliefs." Presented at the University of Notre Dame.
Church, Ian M. 2011. "Accidentally Apt Belief and Skepticism." Presented at the Edinburgh Epistemology Graduate Conference, The University of Edinburgh.
Church, Ian M. 2013a. "Getting 'Lucky' with Gettier." *European Journal of Philosophy*. doi:10.1111/j.1468-0378.2010.00433.x.
Church, Ian M. 2013b. "Manifest Failure Failure: The Gettier Problem Revived." *Philosophia* 41 (1): 171–7.
Church, Ian M. 2015. "50 Years of Gettier: A New Direction in Religious Epistemology." *Journal of Analytic Theology* 3: 147–71.
Church, Ian M. 2021. "Virtue Epistemology and the Gettier Dilemma." *Metaphilosophy* 52 (5): 681–95. https://doi.org/10.1111/meta.12518.
Church, Ian M. Forthcoming. "Experimental Philosophy of Religion." In A. M. Bauer and S. Kornmesser (eds.), *Compact Compendium of Experimental Philosophy*. Walter de Gruyter.
Church, Ian M, Isaac Warcol, and Justin L. Barrett. 2021. "The Context of Suffering: Empirical Insights into the Problem of Evil." *TheoLogica: An International Journal for Philosophy of Religion and Philosophical Theology* 6 (1): 4–19.
Clark, Kelly James. 2019. *God and the Brain: The Rationality of Belief*. Grand Rapids, MI: Eerdmans.
Clark, Michael. 1963. "Knowledge and Grounds: A Comment on Mr. Gettier's Paper." *Analysis* 24 (2): 46–8.
Code, Lorraine. 1987. *Epistemic Responsibility*. Hanover, NH: Published for Brown University Press by University Press of New England.
Cohen, Stewart. 2009. "Knowledge as Aptness." *Philosophical Studies* 144 (1): 121–5.
Crisp, Thomas M. 2000. "Gettier and Plantinga's Revised Account of Warrant." *Analysis* 60 (265): 42–50.
Cummins, Robert E. 1998. "Reflections on Reflective Equilibrium." In Michael DePaul and William Ramsey (eds.), *Rethinking Intuition*, 113–28. London: Rowman & Littlefield Publishers.
Dancy, Jonathan. 1985. *An Introduction to Contemporary Epistemology*. Oxford: Blackwell Publishing.
De Cruz, Helen. 2015. "Where Philosophical Intuitions Come From." *Australasian Journal of Philosophy* 93 (2): 233–49.
De Cruz, Helen. 2017. "Religious Disagreement: An Empirical Study Among Academic Philosophers." *Episteme* 14 (1): 71–87.

DePaul, Michael, and Linda Zagzebski, eds. 2003. *Intellectual Virtue: Perspectives from Ethics and Epistemology*. Oxford: Oxford University Press.

Descartes, René. 1955. *The Philosophical Works of Descartes*. Elizabeth S. Haldane and G. R. T. Ross (trans.). Vol. 1. 2 vols. New York, NY: Dover Publications.

Draper, Paul, and Ryan Nichols. 2013. "Diagnosing Bias in Philosophy of Religion." *The Monist* 96 (3): 420–46.

Dretske, Fred I. 1978. "Conclusive Reasons." In George Sotiros Pappas and Marshall Swain (eds.), *Essays on Knowledge and Justification*, 41–60. Ithaca, NY: Cornell University Press.

Einav, Shiri, and Elizabeth J. Robinson. 2011. "When Being Right Is Not Enough: Four-Year-Olds Distinguish Knowledgeable Informants from Merely Accurate Informants." *Psychological Science* 22 (10): 1250–3. https://doi.org/10.1177/0956797611416998.

Fairweather, Abrol, and Linda Trinkaus Zagzebski, eds. 2001. *Virtue Epistemology: Essays on Epistemic Virtue and Responsibility*. Oxford: Oxford University Press.

Feldman, Richard. 1996. "Plantinga, Gettier, and Warrant." In Jonathan L. Kvanvig (ed.), *Warrant in Contemporary Epistemology: Essays in Honor of Plantinga's Theory of Knowledge*, 199–220. London: Rowman & Littlefield Publishers.

Feldman, Richard, and Earl Conee. 1985. "Evidentialism." *Philosophical Studies* 48 (1): 15–34. https://doi.org/10.1007/bf00372404.

Floridi, Luciano. 2004. "On the Logical Unsolvability of the Gettier Problem." *Synthese* 142 (1): 61–79.

Freud, Sigmund. 1953. *The Standard Edition of the Complete Psychological Works of Sigmund Freud*. James Strachey (trans.). 24 vols. London: Hogarth Press.

Fricker, Miranda. 2007. *Epistemic Injustice: Power and the Ethics of Knowing*. 1st ed. Oxford; New York: OUP Oxford.

Gettier, Edmund. 1963. "Is Justified True Belief Knowledge?" *Analysis* 23 (6): 121–3.

Gilbert, Margaret. 1989. *On Social Facts*. London and New York: Routledge.

Goldman, Alvin I. 1967. "A Causal Theory of Knowing." *Journal of Philosophy* 64 (12): 357–72.

Goldman, Alvin I. 1976. "Discrimination and Perceptual Knowledge." *The Journal of Philosophy* 73 (20): 771–91.

Goldman, Alvin I. 1986. *Epistemology and Cognition*. Cambridge, MA: Harvard University Press.

Goldman, Alvin I. 2020. "The What, Why, and How of Social Epistemology." In Miranda Fricker, Peter J. Graham, David Henderson, and Nikolaj J. L. L. Pedersen (eds.), *The Routledge Handbook of Social Epistemology*, 10–19. New York, NY: Routledge.

Greco, John. 1993. "Virtues and Vices of Virtue Epistemology." *Canadian Journal of Philosophy* 23 (3): 413–32.

Greco, John. 1995. "A Second Paradox Concerning Responsibility and Luck." *Metaphilosophy* 26 (1–2): 81–96.

Greco, John. 1999. "Agent Reliabilism." *Philosophical Perspectives* 13: 273–96.

Greco, John. 2000. "Two Kinds of Intellectual Virtue." *Philosophy and Phenomenological Research* 60 (1): 179–84.

Greco, John. 2002. "Virtues in Epistemology." In Paul K. Moser (ed.), *The Oxford Handbook of Epistemology*, 287–315. New York, NY: Oxford University Press.

Greco, John. 2003a. "Virtue and Luck, Epistemic and Otherwise." *Metaphilosophy* 34 (3): 353–66.

Greco, John. 2003b. "Knowledge as Credit for True Belief." In Michael DePaul and Linda Zagzebski (eds.), *Intellectual Virtue: Perspectives From Ethics and Epistemology*, 111–34. Oxford: Oxford University Press.

Greco, John, ed. 2004. Ernest Sosa and His Critics. Philosophers and their Critics 12. Oxford: Blackwell Publishing.

Greco, John. 2007a. "The Nature of Ability and the Purpose of Knowledge." *Philosophical Issues* 17 (1): 57–69.

Greco, John. 2007b. "Worries about Pritchard's Safety." *Synthese* 158 (3): 299–302.

Greco, John. 2009a. "Knowledge and Success from Ability." *Philosophical Studies* 142 (1): 17–26.

Greco, John. 2009b. "The Value Problem." In Adrian Haddock, Alan Millar, and Duncan Pritchard (eds.), *Epistemic Value*, 313–22. Oxford: Oxford University Press.

Greco, John. 2010. *Achieving Knowledge: A Virtue-Theoretic Account of Epistemic Normativity*. Cambridge: Cambridge University Press.

Greco, John. 2012. "A (Different) Virtue Epistemology." *Philosophy and Phenomenological Research* 85 (1): 1–26.

Greco, John, and John Turri. 2011. "Virtue Epistemology." http://plato.stanford.edu/entries/epistemology-virtue/.

Greenough, Patrick, and Duncan Pritchard, eds. 2009. *Williamson on Knowledge*. Oxford: Oxford University Press.

Henrich, Joseph. 2016. *The Secret of Our Success: How Culture Is Driving Human Evolution, Domesticating Our Species, and Making Us Smarter*. Princeton; Oxford: Princeton University Press.

Hetherington, Stephen. 1998. "Actually Knowing." *Philosophical Quarterly* 48 (193): 453–69.

Hetherington, Stephen. 2001. *Good Knowledge, Bad Knowledge: On Two Dogmas of Epistemology*. Oxford: Oxford University Press.

Hetherington, Stephen. 2005. "Gettier Problems." http://www.iep.utm.edu/gettier/.

Hetherington, Stephen. 2007. "Is This a World Where Knowledge has to Include Justification?" *Philosophy and Phenomenological Research* 75 (1): 41–69.

Hetherington, Stephen. 2010. "Elusive Epistemological Justification." *Synthese* 174 (3): 315–30.

Hetherington, Stephen. 2013. "Knowledge Can Be Lucky." In Matthias Steup and John Turri (eds.), *Contemporary Debates in Epistemology*, 164–76. Oxford: Blackwell.

Hetherington, Stephen. 2018. *The Gettier Problem*. Cambridge: Cambridge University Press.

Hintikka, Jaakko. 1999. "The Emperor's New Intuitions." *Journal of Philosophy* 96 (3): 127–47. https://doi.org/10.5840/jphil199996331.

Hookway, Christopher. 2000. *Truth, Rationality, and Pragmatism: Themes From Peirce*. Oxford: Oxford University Press.

Hookway, Christopher. 2003. "How to Be a Virtue Epistemologist." In Linda Zagzebski and Michael DePaul (eds.), *Intellectual Virtue: Perspectives From Ethics and Epistemology*, 183–202. New York: Oxford University Press.

Howard-Snyder, Daniel, Frances Howard-Snyder, and Neil Feit. 2003. "Infallibilism and Gettier's Legacy." *Philosophy and Phenomenological Research* 66 (2): 304–27.

Hume, David. 1748. *An Enquiry Concerning Human Understanding*. Oxford: Clarendon Press.

Hume, David. 1948. Dialogues Concerning Natural Religion. The Hafner Library of Classics. Henry D. Aiken (ed.). London: Hafner Press.

Hume, David. 1975. *Enquiries Concerning Human Understanding and Concerning the Principles of Morals*. 3rd ed. Oxford: Clarendon Press.

Jackson, Frank. 2009. "Thought Experiments and Possibilities." *Analysis* 69 (1): 100–9.

Jaswal, Vikram K., A. Carrington Croft, Alison R. Setia, and Caitlin A. Cole. 2010. "Young Children Have a Specific, Highly Robust Bias to Trust Testimony." *Psychological Science* 21 (10): 1541–7. https://doi.org/10.1177/0956797610383438.

Javis, B. 2019. "The Problem of Environmental Luck." In Ian Church and Robert Hartman (ed.), *The Routledge Handbook of the Philosophy and Psychology of Luck*. New York, NY.

Kant, Immanuel. 1998. "Critique of Pure Reason." In Roger Ariew and Eric Watkins (eds.), *Modern Philosophy: An Anthology of Primary Sources*, 634–749. Cambridge: Hackett Publishing Company.

Kallestrup, Jesper. 2016. "Group Virtue Epistemology." *Synthese* 197 (12): 5233–51.

Kallestrup, Jesper, and Duncan Pritchard. 2012. "Robust Virtue Epistemology and Epistemic Anti-Individualism." *Pacific Philosophical Quarterly* 93 (1): 84–103. https://doi.org/10.1111/j.1468-0114.2011.01417.x.

Kelp, Christoph. 2017. "Knowledge First Virtue Epistemology." In Adam Carter, Emma Gordon, and Benjamin Jarvis (eds.), *Knowledge First: Approaches in Epistemology and Mind*, 223–45. Oxford: Oxford University Press.

Kim, Minsun, and Yuan Yuan. 2015. "No Cross-Cultural Differences in the Gettier Car Case Intuition: A Replication Study of Weinberg Et Al. 2001." *Episteme* 12 (3): 355–61. https://doi.org/10.1017/epi.2015.17.

Klein, Peter. 1996. "Warrant, Proper Function, Reliabilism, and Defeasibility." In Jonathan L. Kvanvig (ed.), *Warrant in Contemporary Epistemology: Essays in Honor of Plantinga's Theory of Knowledge*, 97–130. London: Rowman & Littlefield Publishers.

Knobe, Joshua. 2019. "Philosophical Intuitions Are Surprisingly Robust Across Demographic Differences." *Epistemology and Philosophy of Science* 56 (2): 29–36. https://doi.org/10.5840/eps201956225.

Knobe, Joshua. 2021. "Philosophical Intuitions Are Surprisingly Stable Across Both Demographic Groups and Situations." *Filozofia Nauki* 29 (2): 11–76. https://doi.org/10.14394/filnau.2021.0007.

Knobe, Joshua, and Shaun Nichols. 2007. "An Experimental Philosophy Manifesto." In Joshua Knobe and Shaun Nichols (eds.), *Experimental Philosophy*, 3–14. Oxford: Oxford University Press.

Koriat, Asher. 2008. "Subjective Confidence in One's Answers: The Consensuality Principle." *Journal of Experimental Psychology. Learning, Memory, and Cognition* 34 (4): 945–59. https://doi.org/10.1037/0278-7393.34.4.945.

Kvanvig, Jonathan L. 1992. *The Intellectual Virtues and the Life of the Mind: On the Place of the Virtues in Epistemology*. Savage, MD: Rowman & Littlefield Publishers.

Kvanvig, Jonathan L. ed. 1996. *Warrant in Contemporary Epistemology: Essays in Honor of Plantinga's Epistemology*. London: Rowman & Littlefield Publishers.

Lackey, Jennifer. 2006. "Pritchard's Epistemic Luck." *Philosophical Quarterly* 56 (223): 284–9.

Lackey, Jennifer. 2008. "What Luck is Not." *Australasian Journal of Philosophy* 86 (2): 255–67.

Lackey, Jennifer. 2009. "Knowledge and Credit." *Philosophical Studies* 142 (1): 27–42.

Lackey, Jennifer. 2020. "Group Belief: Lessons From Lies and Bullshit." *Aristotelian Society Supplementary Volume* 94 (1): 185–208. https://doi.org/10.1093/arisup/akaa007.

Latus, Andrew. 2000. "Moral and Epistemic Luck." *Journal of Philosophical Research* 25: 149–72.

Levin, Michael. 2004. "Virtue Epistemology: No New Cures." *Philosophy and Phenomenological Research* 69 (2): 397–410.

Lewis, David K. 2000. *Counterfactuals*. 2nd ed. Oxford: Blackwell Publishing.

List, Christian. 2005. "Group Knowledge and Group Rationality: A Judgment Aggregation Perspective." *Episteme* 2 (1): 25–38.

Lycan, William G. 2006. "On the Gettier Problem Problem." In Stephen Hetherington (ed.), *Epistemology Futures*, 148–68. Oxford: Oxford University Press.

Machery, Edouard, Stephen Stich, David Rose, Mario Alai, Adriano Angelucci, Renatas Berniūnas, Emma E. Buchtel, et al. 2017. "The Gettier Intuition from South America to Asia." *Journal of Indian Council of Philosophical Research* 34 (3): 517–41. https://doi.org/10.1007/s40961-017-0113-y.

Machery, Edouard, Stephen Stich, David Rose, Amita Chatterjee, Kaori Karasawa, Noel Struchiner, Smita Sirker, Naoki Usui, and Takaaki Hashimoto. 2015. "Gettier Across Cultures." *Noûs* 51 (3): 645–64.

Madison, B. J. C. 2011. "Combating Anti Anti-Luck Epistemology." *Australasian Journal of Philosophy* 89 (1): 47–58.

Markie, Peter. 1996. "Degrees of Warrant." In Jonathan L. Kvanvig (ed.), *Warrant in Contemporary Epistemology: Essays in Honor of Plantinga's Theory of Knowledge*, 221–38. London: Rowman & Littlefield Publishers.

McCauley, Robert N. 2011. *Why Religion Is Natural and Science Is Not*. New York: Oxford University Press.

McDowell, John Henry. 1988. "Criteria, Defeasibility, and Knowledge." In Jonathan Dancy (ed.), *Perceptual Knowledge, Oxford Readings in Philosophy*, 209–19. Oxford: Oxford University Press.

McDowell, John Henry. 1994. *Mind and World*. Cambridge, MA: Harvard University Press.

Millar, Alan. 2008. "Perceptual-Recognitional Abilities and Perceptual Knowledge." In Adrian Haddock and Fiona Macpherson (eds.), *Disjunctivism: Perception, Action, Knowledge*, 330–47. Oxford: Oxford University Press.

Millar, Alan. 2009. "What Is It that Cognitive Abilities are Abilities To Do?" *Acta Analytica* 24 (4): 223–36.

Miracchi, Lisa. 2015. "Competence to Know." *Philosophical Studies* 172 (1): 1–28.

Mizrahi, Moti. 2020. "If Analytic Philosophy of Religion Is Sick, Can It Be Cured?" *Religious Studies* 56 (4): 558–77.

Montmarquet, James A. 1993. *Epistemic Virtue and Doxastic Responsibility*. Lanham, MD: Rowman & Littlefield Publishers.

Nagel, Jennifer. 2012. "Intuitions and Experiments: A Defense of the Case Method in Epistemology." *Philosophy and Phenomenological Research* 85 (3): 495–527. https://doi.org/10.1111/j.1933-1592.2012.00634.x.

Nagel, Jennifer. 2013. "Defending the Evidential Value of Epistemic Intuitions: A Reply to Stich." *Philosophy and Phenomenological Research* 86 (1): 179–99.

Nagel, Jennifer, Valerie San Juan, and Raymond A. Mar. 2013. "Lay Denial of Knowledge for Justified True Beliefs." *Cognition* 129 (3): 652–61. https://doi.org/10.1016/j.cognition.2013.02.008.

Nagel, Thomas. 1979. *Mortal Questions*. Cambridge: Cambridge University Press.

Nozick, Robert. 1981. *Philosophical Explanations*. Oxford: Oxford University Press.

Pettit, Philip. 2003. "Groups with Minds of Their Own." In Frederick F. Schmitt (ed.), *Socializing Metaphysics: The Nature of Social Reality*, 167–93. New York: Rowman and Littlefield.

Plantinga, Alvin. 1993a. *Warrant: The Current Debate*. New York, NY: Oxford University Press.

Plantinga, Alvin. 1993b. *Warrant and Proper Function*. New York, NY: Oxford University Press.

Plantinga, Alvin. 1996. "Respondeo." In Jonathan L. Kvanvig (ed.), *Warrant in Contemporary Epistemology: Essays in Honor of Plantinga's Theory of Knowledge*, 307–78. New York, NY: Rowman & Littlefield Publishers.

Plantinga, Alvin. 1997. "Warrant and Accidentally True Belief." *Analysis* 57 (2): 140–5.

Plantinga, Alvin. 2000. *Warranted Christian Belief*. New York, NY: Oxford University Press.

Plantinga, Alvin. 2011. *Where the Conflict Really Lies: Science, Religion, and Naturalism*. Oxford: Oxford University Press.

Plantinga, Alvin, and Michael Tooley. 2008. *Knowledge of God*. Great Debates in Philosophy. Malden, MA: Blackwell Publishing.

Plato. 2002. *Five Dialogues*. George M. A. Grube (trans.). 2nd ed. Cambridge: Hackett Publishing Company.

Polanyi, Michael. 1974. *Personal Knowledge: Towards a Post-Critical Philosophy*. London: Routledge & Kegan Paul.

Pritchard, Duncan. 2005. *Epistemic Luck*. Oxford: Oxford University Press.

Pritchard, Duncan. 2007. "Anti-Luck Epistemology." *Synthese* 158 (3): 277–97.

Pritchard, Duncan. 2009. "The Value of Knowledge." *The Harvard Review of Philosophy* 16 (1): 86–103. https://doi.org/10.5840/harvardreview20091616.

Pritchard, Duncan. 2014. "The Modal Account of Luck." *Metaphilosophy* 45 (4–5): 594–619. https://doi.org/10.1111/meta.12103.

Pritchard, Duncan, Alan Millar, and Adrian Haddock. 2010. *The Nature and Value of Knowledge: Three Investigations*. Oxford: Oxford University Press.

Pyysiäinen, Ilkka. 2009. *Supernatural Agents: Why We Believe in Souls, Gods, and Buddhas*. New York: Oxford University Press.

Quine, W. V. 1969. "Epistemology Naturalized." In *Ontological Relativity and other Essays*, 69–90. 6th ed. New York, NY: Columbia University Press.

Reid, Thomas. 1785. *Essays on the Intellectual Powers of Man*. London: Printed for John Bell, and G. G. J. & J. Robinson.

Riggs, Wayne. 2002. "Reliability and the Value of Knowledge." *Philosophy and Phenomenological Research* 64 (1): 79–96.

Riggs, Wayne. 2007. "Why Epistemologists Are So Down on Their Luck." *Synthese* 158 (3): 329–44.

Rosch, Eleanor, and Carolyn B. Mervis. 1975. "Family Resemblances: Studies in the Internal Structure of Categories." *Cognitive Psychology* 7 (4): 573–605.

Rosenberg, Jay F. 2003. *Thinking about Knowing*. Oxford: Oxford University Press.

Russell, Bertrand. 1948. *Human Knowledge: Its Scope and Limits*. London: Routledge.

Russell, Bertrand. 1972. *A History of Western Philosophy*. New York, NY: Simon & Schuster/Touchstone.

Schaffer, Jonathan. 2009. "Modalities and Methodologies." Presented at the Arché Methodology Workshop, The University of St Andrews.

Schjødt, Uffe, Andreas Roepstorff, Hans Stødkilde-Jørgensen, and Armin W. Geertz. 2009. "Highly Religious Participants Recruit Areas of Social Cognition in Personal Prayer." *Social Cognitive and Affective Neuroscience* 2: 199–207.

Schloss, Jeffrey, and Michael Murray, eds. 2009. *The Believing Primate: Scientific, Philosophical, and Theological Reflections on the Origin of Religion*. Oxford: Oxford University Press.

Sellars, Wilfrid. 1956. "Empiricism and the Philosophy of Mind." *Minnesota Studies in the Philosophy of Science* 1: 253–329.

Shope, Robert K. 1983. *The Analysis of Knowing: A Decade of Research*. Princeton, NJ: Princeton University Press.

Shope, Robert K. 2008. "Abnormality, Cognitive Virtues, and Knowledge." *Synthese* 163 (1): 99–118.

Smith, Martin. 2009. "Transmission Failure Explained." *Philosophy and Phenomenological Research* 79 (1) : 164–89.

Sosa, Ernest. 1980. "The Raft and the Pyramid: Coherence versus Foundations in the Theory of Knowledge." *Midwest Studies in Philosophy* 5 (1): 3–26.

Sosa, Ernest. 1988. "Beyond Scepticism, to the Best of Our Knowledge." *Mind* 97 (386): 153–88.

Sosa, Ernest. 1991. *Knowledge in Perspective: Selected Essays in Epistemology*. Cambridge: Cambridge University Press.

Sosa, Ernest. 1996. Proper Functionalism and Virtue Epistemology. In Jonathan L. Kvanvig (ed.), *Warrant in Contemporary Epistemology: Essays in Honor of Plantinga's Theory of Knowledge*, 253–70. London: Rowman & Littlefield Publishers.

Sosa, Ernest. 1998. "Minimal Intuition." In Michael DePaul and William Ramsey (eds.), *Rethinking Intuition*, 257–70. London: Rowman & Littlefield Publishers.

Sosa, Ernest. 2004. "Replies." In John Greco (ed.), *Ernest Sosa and His Critics*, 275–326. Oxford: Blackwell Publishing.

Sosa, Ernest. 2007. *A Virtue Epistemology: Apt Belief and Reflective Knowledge*. Vol. 1. Oxford: Oxford University Press.

Sosa, Ernest. 2009a. *Reflective Knowledge: Apt Belief and Reflective Knowledge*. Vol. 2. Oxford: Oxford University Press.

Sosa, Ernest. 2009b. "Timothy Williamson's Knowledge and its Limits." In Patrick Greenough and Duncan Pritchard (eds.), *Williamson on Knowledge*, 203–16. Oxford: Oxford University Press.

Sosa, Ernest. 2009c. "Replies to Commentators on a Virtue Epistemology." *Philosophical Studies* 144 (1): 137–47.

Statman, Daniel. 1991. "Moral and Epistemic Luck." *Ratio* 4 (2): 146–56.

Steup, Matthias, ed. 2001. *Knowledge, Truth, and Duty: Essays on Epistemic Justification, Responsibility, and Virtue*. Oxford: Oxford University Press.

Steup, Matthias. 2006. "The Analysis of Knowledge." http://plato.stanford.edu/entries/knowledge-analysis/.

Stich, Stephen. 1988. "Reflective Equilibrium, Analytic Epistemology and the Problem of Cognitive Diversity." *Synthese* 74 (3): 391–413.

Stich, Stephen. 1993. *The Fragmentation of Reason: Preface to a Pragmatic Theory of Cognitive Evaluation*. Cambridge, MA: MIT Press.

Stich, Stephen P., and Edouard Machery. 2022. "Demographic Differences in Philosophical Intuition: A Reply to Joshua Knobe." *Review of Philosophy and Psychology*, 1–34. https://doi.org/10.1007/s13164-021-00609-7.

Sturgeon, Scott. 1993. "The Gettier Problem." *Analysis* 53 (3): 156–64.

Tuomela, Raimo. 1992. "Group Beliefs." *Synthese* 91 (3): 285–318.

Turri, John. 2011. "Manifest Failure: The Gettier Problem Solved." *Philosophers' Imprint* 11 (8): 171–7.

Unger, Peter. 1968. "An Analysis of Factual Knowledge." *The Journal of Philosophy* 65 (6): 157–70.
Vaesen, Krist. 2011. "Knowledge without Credit, Exhibit 4: Extended Cognition." *Synthese* 181 (515): 515–29.
Weatherson, Brian. 2003. "What Good are Counterexamples?" *Philosophical Studies* 115 (1): 1–31.
Weinberg, Jonathan M., Shaun Nichols, and Stephen Stich. 2001. "Normativity and Epistemic Intuitions." *Philosophical Topics*, 29 (1–2): 429–60.
Williamson, Timothy. 2000. *Knowledge and Its Limits*. Oxford: Oxford University Press.
Williamson, Timothy. 2004. "Sosa on Abilities, Concepts, and Externalism." In John Greco (ed.), *Ernest Sosa and His Critics*, 263–72. Oxford: Blackwell Publishing.
Williamson, Timothy. 2007. *The Philosophy of Philosophy*. Oxford: Blackwell Publishing.
Williamson, Timothy. 2009a. "Replies to Kornblith, Jackson and Moore." *Analysis* 69 (1): 125–35.
Williamson, Timothy. 2009b. "Replies to Critics." In Patrick Greenough and Duncan Pritchard (eds.), *Williamson on Knowledge*, 279–384. Oxford: Oxford University Press.
Wittgenstein, Ludwig. 1980. *Culture and Value*. Amended 2nd ed. with English translation. Oxford: Blackwell Publishing.
Wittgenstein, Ludwig. 2001. *Tractatus Logico-Philosophicus*. 2 ed. London : New York: Routledge.
Wolterstorff, Nicholas. 2011. "How Philosophical Theology Became Possible within the Analytic Tradition of Philosophy." In Oliver Crisp and Michael Rea (eds.), *Analytic Theology: New Essays in the Philosophy of Theology*, 155–69. Oxford: Oxford University Press.
Wood, W. Jay, and Robert C. Roberts. 2007. *Intellectual Virtues : An Essay in Regulative Epistemology*. Oxford: Oxford University Press.
Wright, Tom. 2010. *Virtue Reborn*. London: SPCK Publishing.
Zagzebski, Linda. 1994. "The Inescapability of Gettier Problems." *The Philosophical Quarterly* 44 (174): 65–73.
Zagzebski, Linda. 1996. *Virtues of the Mind: An Inquiry into the Nature of Virtue and the Ethical Foundations of Knowledge*. Cambridge: Cambridge University Press.
Zagzebski, Linda. 1999. "What is Knowledge?" In Ernest Sosa and John Greco (eds.), *The Blackwell Guide to Epistemology*, 92–116. Oxford: Blackwell Publishing.
Zimmerman, Michael J. 1993. "Luck and Moral Responsibility." In Daniel Statman (ed.), *Moral Luck*, 217–34. Albany, NY: State University of New York Press.

Index

ad hoc   47–8, 50, 125, 128, 154, 164–5, 222, 224
agency   6–8, 21–2, 30, 198, 210
agent-reliabilism   6–8, 11–14, 73–98, 173
agent-responsibilism   12, 99–114, 220
analysis of knowledge, the   1–5, 10–13, 20, 30, 100, 115, 155, 166
analytic philosophy   209
Anscombe, Gertrude Elizabeth Margaret   210
anthropology   15, 198, 201, 204–5
apt belief   75–6, 78–80, 164
"arising out of" relation. *See* "because of" relation
Aristotle   193–4, 210

barn facade cases   31, 33, 77, 140, 177, 186, 219
Battaly, Heather   181
"because of" relation   100–5, 108–12, 173
belief   3, 30–9, 45–6, 48–9, 54, 56, 75, 79–86, 88, 91–7, 102–13, 116–43, 148–50, 171–2, 198–201, 204–6, 216–17, 221

casually opaque   203–4
character   6, 165–6
Chisholm, Roderick M.   44, 213–14
Code, Lorraine   210
cognitive abilities   83–5, 87–93, 112, 172
cognitive character   101–2, 104, 106
cognitive faculties   6, 116–33, 167, 179–80, 184–9, 196–7
cognitive science   15, 197, 208, 229
Cohen, Stewart   216
conceptually primitive   8, 14, 66, 155–6, 158, 169, 178
conceptual priority   150, 154–5, 160, 225
credit   74–7, 80, 88, 90
culture   203, 206

De Cruz, Helen   194–7, 229
defeasibility   4, 44, 177
Descartes, Rene   7, 80, 210
design plan   116, 119–20, 122–8, 130–2, 166, 173–5, 179–80, 184, 187–8, 221–2
disagreement   15
dogmatism   193
doxastic involuntarism   21
Dretske, Fred   44, 213–14
"due to" relation. *See* "because of" relation

environmental luck   31, 77, 189, 213
environment favorability   136–7, 139, 228
epistemic
   absolutism   51–2, 54–6
   injustice   204
   justification (*see* justification)
   luck   21, 30–6, 56, 85–7
   value (*see* value problem, the)
   virtue (*see* intellectual virtues)
epistemic virtue or knowledge   179–80, 184
evidence   49–50, 67, 150, 197, 204–5, 227
evidentialism   204
experimental philosophy   15, 58–62, 192–7
expertise   91, 93, 97, 112
extended cognition   83–9, 98, 172–3
externalism. *See under* justification

factive states   150–4, 163–7, 180, 187
faculties. *See* cognitive faculties
faith   202
fake barn cases   14, 31–2, 77, 101, 136, 162, 170, 177, 186–9, 195, 208, 217–20
fallibilism   39, 42–50, 213–14
Feldman, Richard   124–8, 204, 221–2, 227

Frege, Gottlob   63–4, 117
Fricker, Miranda   227

Gettier, Edmund   1, 3, 44, 66, 122, 188
Gettier cases   9, 19, 23, 29–36, 39, 41,
    44–8, 51, 53–4, 56–7, 62, 64–6,
    81–2, 87–9, 91–2, 95–6, 98, 101,
    110–12, 121–3, 127–9, 133–4, 196,
    210–11, 217–18, 220, 222
  classic cases   3, 31–2, 122–33, 138
  diagnosis of   1, 8–14, 19–51, 69–70,
    135–44, 218
  dilemma   12, 35–6, 38–40, 83–91, 93,
    96, 99, 107, 111
Gettier counterexamples. *See* Gettier cases
Goldman, Alvin   15, 31, 33, 44, 198, 213–14
Greco, John   5, 7, 12–14, 70, 73–4, 81–2,
    86–94, 96, 98, 115, 169–73, 181,
    196, 198, 205–6, 209–13, 216–17,
    226, 228
grounding problem   15, 192, 194–5
group belief   15, 198–201, 204–6
  non-summativism   200
  summativism   199

Hetherington, Stephen   4, 11, 42, 51–7,
    69, 211, 213–15
Howard-Snyder, Daniel   11, 42–50, 69,
    211, 213–14
Hume, David   119, 188, 193–4, 210, 221, 228

infallibilism   11, 39, 42–5, 48–51, 69–70,
    135, 142, 213, 221
intellectual courage   6, 101, 109, 166
intellectual perseverance   6
intellectual vices   102
intellectual virtues   102, 106–7, 112–13,
    165–6, 171, 181, 220
internalism. *See under* justification
intuitions   55–68, 194–6

joint acceptance account   200
justification   3–4, 34, 150, 181, 189, 191,
    206, 209, 211, 214, 217–18, 224, 228
  externalism   164, 204–5, 226
  internalism   120–1, 164, 204, 221, 226
Kallestrup, Jesper   15, 199, 201, 205–6, 217
Kant, Immanuel   147
Kelp, Christoph   170, 172, 219

Klein, Peter   122, 129, 221–2, 227, 229
Knobe, Joshua   62, 193
knowledge
  analysis of   1–2, 4–5, 8–13, 20, 30,
    39–40, 64, 115, 144, 148, 155, 183
  first   147, 150, 178, 190–1, 208, 227
  necessary conditions for   2, 156–7,
    175–80, 184, 225, 228
  perceptual   21, 117, 124, 126, 184–5
  plus virtue   155–9, 162–5, 167, 169,
    175–6, 178, 183, 207, 227
  sufficient conditions for   1–3, 8–9, 19,
    62, 66, 131–2, 136–7, 139, 155–6,
    158, 164–6, 173, 175–6, 178–81,
    183–4, 206–7, 209, 216, 224, 225
  testimonial (*see* testimony)
  as virtue   14, 155, 157–9, 162–4, 166–
    9, 175–6, 178–84, 191, 207, 226
  within virtue   155, 159–67, 169,
    175–6, 181–3, 207
  virtue-theoretic accounts of (*see*
    virtue(s), epistemology)
Kvanvig, Jonathan   121, 174, 210, 227

Lackey, Jennifer   22–5, 82–3, 85–90, 93,
    98, 172, 199–200, 212, 228–9
Levin, Michael   12–13, 99–108, 171–2,
    218–20, 226
Lewis, David   134, 185, 187, 212
luck
  as accident   21–2, 48, 214
  as chance   21–2
  content   56
  degrees of   10, 20–9, 36, 49, 107–13, 212
  doxastic   56
  evidential   56
  intervening   31–2, 39–40
  as lack of control   21–2
  modal account of   10, 20–5, 29–33,
    36, 213
  veritic   30–6, 56

Machery, Edouard   62, 215
maxi-environment   133, 142, 166
mental states   150–4, 161–3, 180, 187,
    196, 225–7
Millar, Alan   190, 213, 217–18
mini-environment   133–43, 166, 186–7,
    222–3

Miracchi, Lisa   170, 172, 219
Montmarquet, James   210
motive reliabilism   103

Nagel, Jennifer   195
Nagel, Thomas   21
naturalized epistemology   5
Neo-Aristotelian virtue epistemology. *See* agent-responsibilism
non-reductive
  epistemology   14, 157
  model(s)   14, 147, 154–7, 161–3, 170, 175, 183, 190–1, 225
  proper functionalism   1, 14–15, 168–70, 175, 180, 183–4, 188–90, 192, 196, 198, 207–8, 227
  virtue epistemology   1, 5, 8–9, 13–14, 70, 115, 147–70, 172, 174–5, 181–3, 188, 190–1, 207, 209
Nozick, Robert   44, 213–14

object of epistemic assessment   6, 210
open-mindedness   6, 166
opinion   76, 125, 193, 206

philosophy   5, 13, 15, 60–1, 115, 182, 193–4, 199, 215, 224, 229
Plantinga, Alvin   7–8, 13–14, 44, 70, 114–44, 147, 166–9, 173–8, 181–8, 197, 210–11, 216, 220–3, 227–9
Plato   3, 66, 194, 206–7, 209–10, 215
Pritchard, Duncan   7, 10, 20–5, 29–36, 70, 103, 189–90, 210–13, 217, 219, 227, 228
process reliabilism   6–8, 44
proper function   1, 8, 13–15, 22, 70, 114–24, 130–7, 144, 147, 162–3, 166–70, 173–80, 182–90, 192, 196–8, 201, 205–8, 211, 221, 223, 226–7, 229
psychology   5, 15, 193, 195, 197, 213, 229

Quine, W. V.   5, 210

reductive analysis of knowledge. *See* analysis of knowledge
Reid, Thomas   210
reliabilism. *See* process reliabilism; agent-reliabilism
religion   13, 115, 229

religious epistemology   162, 228
resolution condition   133–7
Riggs, Wayne   211, 217
robust virtue epistemology   157, 176–7, 226
Russell, Bertrand   125, 131–3, 138, 210

safety condition   4, 10, 20, 29–30, 32–5, 100, 156–7, 161–2, 175–7, 210–11, 213, 217, 225, 228
sensitivity condition   4, 44, 177
Shope, Robert K.   219, 222
skepticism   4, 10–12, 37–42, 47–51, 63, 67–70, 79–81, 85–6, 89, 92–4, 96, 98–100, 106, 108–9, 111, 113, 130–1, 139, 141–2, 164–6
social epistemology   15, 198
Sosa, Ernest   11–14, 44, 67–8, 70, 73–81, 98–100, 115, 164–5, 169–73, 181, 196, 198, 205–6, 210–11, 216–17, 219–20, 226–8
Spinoza, Baruch   179
standard analysis of knowledge. *See* analysis of knowledge, the
stative   153–4, 180
Steup, Matthias   2, 210–12
Stich, Stephen   11, 42, 57–63, 215
success from ability   11–12, 73–4, 81–93, 171

taboo   203, 205
Testimonial injustice. *See* epistemic injustice
testimony   15, 33–4, 52, 82–3, 85–9, 98, 127–8, 173, 196, 198
theology   13, 115
traditional analysis of knowledge. *See* analysis of knowledge, the
truth   2–4, 9–11, 19–20, 30, 35–51, 53–7, 64, 66–7, 69–70, 75, 85, 87–8, 91–113, 118–139, 142–4, 148, 151–2, 154, 156, 158, 163–7, 171–84, 187–8, 197, 206, 213, 217–22, 226
Turri, John   5, 12–13, 70, 73–4, 81, 93–9, 115, 170, 172–3, 196, 210, 217–18

understanding   193–4

value problem, the   188–91, 208, 228–9
veritic luck. *See* luck

virtue(s)
- character 6, 101–7, 165–6, 169, 173–4, 177, 220
- epistemology 1–6, 8–15, 19–20, 73–4, 82–93, 98–9, 109–16, 129, 131, 138, 144, 147, 154–8, 161–2, 164–77, 181–3, 188, 190–2, 205, 207, 210, 216, 218, 220, 223, 226, 228–9
- faculty (*see* cognitive faculties)
- intellectual (*see* virtue(s), epistemology)
- moral 6

warrant 3–13, 19–20, 32, 36–57, 64, 66–70, 100, 102, 107–44, 174, 189, 197, 205, 211–23

Williamson, Timothy 4, 14, 36, 57, 65, 67, 146–68, 176–83, 187, 190–1, 208, 211, 214, 224–8

wisdom 182

Wittgenstein, Ludwig 227

Zagzebski, Linda 9–14, 19–20, 29, 34, 36, 40–1, 47, 57, 70, 99–113, 121, 130, 165–6, 169–73, 181, 196, 198, 205, 209–14, 217–20, 227–8

www.ingramcontent.com/pod-product-compliance
Lightning Source LLC
Chambersburg PA
CBHW062137300426
44115CB00012BA/1954